BUSH-OBAMA
SCHOOL REFORM

THE EDUCATIONAL INNOVATIONS SERIES

The Educational Innovations series explores a wide range of current school reform efforts. Individual volumes examine entrepreneurial efforts and unorthodox approaches, highlighting reforms that have met with success and strategies that have attracted widespread attention. The series aims to disrupt the status quo and inject new ideas into contemporary education debates.

BUSH-OBAMA SCHOOL REFORM

Lessons Learned

FREDERICK M. HESS
MICHAEL Q. MCSHANE

Editors

Harvard Education Press
Cambridge, Massachusetts

Paperback ISBN 978-1-68253-217-1
Library Edition ISBN 978-1-68253-218-8

Library of Congress Cataloging-in-Publication Data

Names: Hess, Frederick M., editor. | McShane, Michael Q., editor.
Title: Bush-Obama school reform : lessons learned / Frederick M. Hess, Michael Q.. McShane, editors.
Other titles: Educational innovations.
Description: Cambridge, Massachusetts : Harvard Education Press, 2018. | Series: Educational Innovations series. | Includes bibliographical references and index.
Identifiers: LCCN 2018023305| ISBN 9781682532171 (pbk.) | ISBN 9781682532188 (library edition)
Subjects: LCSH: Education and state--United States. | Education--Standards--United States. | Educational accountability--United States. | Educational change--United States. | Education--Aims and objectives--United States. | Public schools--United States. | United States. No Child Left Behind Act of 2001.
Classification: LCC LC89 .B875 2018 | DDC 379.73--dc23 LC record available at https://lccn.loc.gov/2018023305

Published by Harvard Education Press,
an imprint of the Harvard Education Publishing Group

Harvard Education Press
8 Story Street
Cambridge, MA 02138

Cover Design: Wilcox Design
Cover Image: Evgeniy Rodionov/Imagezoo/Getty Images
The typefaces used in this book are Minion Pro and Myriad Pro

Contents

Introduction

Frederick M. Hess and Michael Q. McShane

On December 10, 2015, as he signed the Every Student Succeeds Act (ESSA) into law, President Barack Obama hailed the rewrite of federal law governing K–12 education as a "Christmas miracle." ESSA had sailed through the US Senate, 85–12, and the US House, 359–64, supported by a broad bipartisan coalition that thought Washington's efforts on schooling during the Bush-Obama years had gone too far and needed to be reined in. The new law pruned the federal government's authority, especially on hot-button questions like accountability, school improvement, and teacher quality. Two years later, the dawn of the Trump presidency was accompanied by the ardent insistence that the Bush-Obama reforms had failed, and that expanding school choice and reducing the federal footprint was the more promising path.

Even a few years earlier, the reversal embodied by ESSA and embraced by Trump would have been hard to imagine. In 2009, Obama's election had ignited a burst of federal educational activism. Jumping off from the Bush administration's earlier, ambitious efforts to expand Washington's role in K–12 schooling, Obama's efforts enjoyed lots of early success. Obama's nominee for secretary of education, Arne Duncan, was feted with bipartisan hurrahs. Senator Lamar Alexander, a former Republican US secretary of education, told Duncan, "President-elect Obama has made several distinguished Cabinet appointments. From my view of it all, I think you're best."[1]

In 2009, as part of that year's massive economic stimulus bill, Congress authorized new programs that would capture the imagination of the educational world. The $4.35 billion Race to the Top program, in particular, would be celebrated as a signature Obama policy. Former Republican Florida governor Jeb Bush, the brother of Obama's predecessor, opined, "I think Secretary Duncan and President Obama deserve credit for putting pressure on states to change, particularly the states that haven't changed at all."[2]

Notably, the burst of enthusiasm for Race to the Top reprised the similarly upbeat early days of the George W. Bush administration that preceded it. In 2001, taking office after a hard-fought campaign and a contested recount, Bush confronted Democratic anger and skepticism. Against that backdrop, his education efforts became a celebrated bipartisan bright spot. Bush's campaign pledge to "leave no child behind" resonated across party lines, and Bush made it a point to cultivate influential Democratic partners like Senator Ted Kennedy and Representative George Miller. Together they negotiated the No Child Left Behind Act, which passed in late 2001—with overwhelming bipartisan majorities in Congress—to a host of cheers.

However, No Child Left Behind (NCLB) proved far more popular in Washington and with editorial writers than in schools and communities. NCLB required states to administer regular tests in reading and math, use those results to develop accountability systems for schools, intervene in schools deemed to be "in need of improvement," and set the goal that 100 percent of students would test "proficient" in reading and math by 2014. While the elements were all easy to like in principle, they would prove vastly more problematic and controversial in practice. The workings of NCLB and the backlash against it would, in time, come to fundamentally alter the nation's educational landscape. Indeed, by 2008, public opinion on NCLB had turned broadly negative and NCLB itself had become something of a poisoned brand—in fact, by that point, polling showed that simply mentioning "No Child Left Behind" served to sharply reduce support for school accountability.[3]

Given what had transpired with NCLB, the dawn of the Obama presidency served as something of a post-Bush reset on school reform. It brought new energy to the cause, replaced a divisive and unpopular president with a charismatic young icon, and gave Democrats a chance to lead the parade. Building on the upsized federal role pioneered under Bush, the Obama team moved to extend the education agenda far beyond accountability—to things like teacher evaluation, academic standards, and school discipline. Initially, these efforts seemed to soften the edges of reform and rekindle support.

Within a few years, though, those Obama efforts would themselves turn controversial, breeding backlash that rivaled the dissatisfaction with No

Child Left Behind. Obama's reforms would also get mired in bitter debates about their emphasis on test scores and whether they constituted federal overreach. What happened? Why did each of these initially promising, seemingly popular efforts at federal leadership ultimately lose its luster?

While we can offer no simple answers to these questions, exploring them can be extraordinarily useful. Indeed, this book was inspired by extended conversations and lively disagreements about how to best make sense of high-profile initiatives from the Bush-Obama years. Were these ambitious efforts a much-needed kick start that forced America to get serious about school improvement, or a recipe for slipshod policy making and rushed implementation that ultimately undermined reform? Did these major reforms reflect a gutsy commitment to putting students first, or political gamesmanship that yielded a counterproductive series of distracting mandates? Though the answers to these questions are complex and perhaps unsatisfying, they just may help us inform and improve our efforts in the years to come.

After all, the twenty-first century has been a remarkable time in American schooling. The universalization of testing and accountability has come to shape our visions of and beliefs about schooling. Charter schooling and other choice-based reforms moved from the margins to the middle of the education discourse. Federal efforts to promote teacher quality, standards, and school turnarounds were tried on a scale that would have been unimaginable a few years earlier. The creation of the Institute of Education Sciences launched a new and ambitious chapter in federally supported education research, while the Obama-era efforts at the Office of Civil Rights thrust that agency into a newly combative and assertive role. Many have opined about what reformers got right and wrong. But a more useful path may be to begin by asking what actually happened and what we've learned along the way.

HOW WE GOT HERE

Before we dive into the particulars of the Bush-Obama years, it's worth taking a moment to recall the history of the federal government's role in K–12 education. While there are isolated, earlier instances of federal activity regarding schools, a sensible starting point is with the US response to the Soviet Union's 1957 launch of its *Sputnik* satellite. In 1958, alarmed that the United States was losing the Space Race to its Cold War rival, Congress enacted the National Defense Education Act (NDEA), with the goal of improving math and science instruction. The NDEA represented the first substantial federal foray into education funding and policy.

Less than a decade later, President Lyndon Johnson made expanding the federal role in education a key part of his War on Poverty. In 1965, Johnson signed the Elementary and Secondary Education Act (ESEA) into law, providing federal funding for low-income students, the professional development of teachers, and instructional materials in schools and libraries. ESEA's Title I remains, a half-century later, the single largest federal outlay for K–12 education. Almost immediately after the passage of ESEA, Washington began to wrestle with just how it should ensure that federal dollars for schooling were being spent wisely and well.

In practice, Washington had no real means to guarantee that dollars were making a difference for students, even as concerns about school performance increasingly became a national concern. The result was a growing chorus of critics insisting that more should be done to ensure that funds were being spent effectively and were enhancing equity. Meanwhile, the rules and regulations written to govern the use of federal funds were denounced as a frustrating, bureaucratic morass. Those concerns—about accountability, equity, and ineffective regulation—would become themes of the Bush-Obama years.

During the 1970s, 1980s, and 1990s, a number of other major federal education laws were enacted. Special education funding evolved from the Education for All Handicapped Children Act, first passed in 1975, to the Individuals with Disabilities Education Act (IDEA), passed in 1990. IDEA put terms like *individualized education plan* and *free and appropriate public education* into the educational lexicon. Concerns from parents about their children's privacy were addressed in the Family Educational Rights and Privacy Act of 1974. That same year, the Equal Educational Opportunities Act was enacted to address discrimination against minority faculty members and racial segregation in school districts.

Presidents emphatically used the bully pulpit to advance education reform. In 1983, President Reagan's administration released *A Nation at Risk*, the report that famously argued that "a rising tide of mediocrity" was swallowing the nation's schools and that "if an unfriendly foreign power had attempted to impose on America the mediocre educational performance that exists today, we might well have viewed it as an act of war." In 1989, President George H. W. Bush, after having pledged to be the "education president," convened the nation's governors for an extraordinary meeting in Charlottesville, Virginia, where they sketched a set of goals for America's schools to achieve by the year 2000.

In 1994 President Bill Clinton incorporated "Goals 2000" into statute, codifying the remarkably ambitious goals that he and other then-governors had settled upon with then-President Bush a few years earlier. By the year 2000, the goals called for every school in America to be drug free; every adult to be literate; every child in grades 4, 8, and 12 to demonstrate competency in subjects ranging from English to math to world languages to civics; and the high school graduation rate to hit 90 percent.

As 2000 approached, the nation remained dishearteningly far away from those targets. Meanwhile, the end of the Cold War had given Washington policy makers more room to focus intensely on domestic policy. In that environment, calls for dramatic education reform gathered momentum. When George W. Bush narrowly won the 2000 presidential contest while emphasizing education, denouncing the "soft bigotry of low expectations," and pledging to "leave no child behind," the scene was set for the passage of No Child Left Behind and the grand educational experiments of the Bush-Obama years.

A BRIEF RECAP OF TWENTY-FIRST-CENTURY EDUCATION REFORM

For those who did not follow education during the Bush-Obama years, or who may be young enough that much of the period is a bit hazy, it may be useful to talk a bit more fully about the developments that got us from NCLB to where we are today. In 2001, as noted earlier, Congress enacted NCLB. This upsizing of the Elementary and Secondary Education Act dramatically expanded the federal role in K–12 schooling. In order to receive their Title I funding, states would henceforth have to regularly test students in reading and math, use those results to design accountability systems, and intervene in schools that failed to make "Adequate Yearly Progress" toward the goal of 100 percent student proficiency in reading and math by the year 2014.

While it was perhaps the signature domestic policy of the Republican Bush administration, NCLB also enjoyed crucial support from many influential Democrats. These political leaders and advocates saw NCLB as a landmark victory for educational equity and regarded NCLB as the education bill they wished the Clinton administration could have passed in the 1990s.

In 2007, a handful of those "reform Democrats" came together to launch a new organization called Democrats for Education Reform (DFER). Mounting a direct challenge to the teacher unions, a core Democratic constituency, DFER would prove instrumental in helping to shape the Obama administration's educational efforts.

In 2008, as Illinois Democrat Barack Obama was battling Republican senator John McCain for the presidency, the global economy was wracked by a financial crisis. Triggered by financial shenanigans that fueled a speculative bubble, the housing market suffered an unprecedented, devastating collapse. The resulting financial crisis led to a stock market crash, put major banks on the verge of failing, and plunged the global economy into the "Great Recession." In Washington, the crisis spurred calls for bold action.

The Great Recession profoundly affected the nation's schools and colleges. At the local level, cratering housing prices meant declines in property taxes, a key revenue source for school districts. At the state level, the tightening of household purse strings meant less sales tax revenue flowing into state coffers, affecting another key revenue source for education funding. But the Great Recession ultimately created big opportunities for federal policy makers.

When Obama won the 2008 election, with coattails that gave Democrats firm control of the US Congress, he rapidly moved to address the crisis. With unemployment climbing and states starved for funds, in early 2009, Congress enacted a $787 billion stimulus bill (formally known as the American Reinvestment and Recovery Act). The financial crunch would provide the backdrop for Obama's first term, a period during which state governments and school systems were struggling with revenue shortfalls and painful budget cuts. That environment amplified the impact of federal spending on schools and colleges, which was turbocharged (to the tune of more than $100 billion) as part of the stimulus.

The most celebrated and influential component of that education funding was the $4.35 billion allocated to a new competitive grant program known as Race to the Top. The stimulus bill itself offered only a vague sketch of how the program should run, requiring simply that Race to the Top funds be directed to states that were taking steps to improve teaching and school leadership, data systems, struggling schools, and academic standards and assessments. Because the stimulus was intended to spur economic recovery and mitigate budget cuts, the Department of Education committed to awarding the full $4.35 billion in less than two years.

The Department of Education then developed a program that laid out nineteen priorities that states would need to address. Those priorities were refined into a five-hundred-point grading rubric, against which applications were judged by panels of Education Department–selected judges. The exercise's grand ambitions, catchy title, and rapid pace served to capture the education world's imagination and became Obama's education signature. Over time, however, Race to the Top's tight timelines and political coloration would complicate some of the very reform efforts that it had sought to boost—especially those relating to teacher evaluation and the Common Core State Standards.

After Republicans claimed control of the US House in 2010 and the final Race to the Top winners were named in 2011, the Obama administration's K–12 agenda was increasingly framed by the Department of Education's ability to issue "waivers" from NCLB and provide "guidance" to school districts through the Office of Civil Rights. In issuing the waivers, the administration promised to release states from some of the most headache-inducing provisions of NCLB so long as the US secretary of education decided they were complying with the spirit of the law. In practice, waivers were issued conditional on states agreeing to adopt the same general policies—like "rigorous" standards and revamped teacher evaluation—that the administration had cited as priorities in Race to the Top.

Concerns about overtesting, federal overreach, the use of waivers, and the substance of the Obama reform agenda slowly stirred opposition—among the teacher unions on the left and the Tea Party movement on the right. That backlash ultimately came to a boil in a clash over Common Core State Standards. Initially launched under the auspices of the National Governors Association and the Council of Chief State School Officers, the Common Core sketched uniform K–12 standards for math and English language arts. In its early stages, the Common Core drew support from an impressively broad coalition—spanning from the major teacher unions to the US Chamber of Commerce. It was championed by Democratic and Republican governors and enjoyed deep-pocketed support from major foundations.

States pursuing Race to the Top funds were strongly encouraged to embrace Common Core and the new Common Core–aligned tests. As a result, within months of its release, the Common Core had been adopted in more than forty states. The speed of that early success elicited skepticism among Tea Partiers distrustful of Obama and intent on shrinking federal influence. Conservative opponents took to calling Common Core

"ObamaCore" (linking it to Obama's massive health care law, which was hugely unpopular on the right). The Common Core got caught up in debates about excessive testing and turned into a partisan football that merited routine campaign trail denunciations from Donald Trump, the Republican who would follow Obama into the presidency.

By 2015, the pushback on testing and on Washington's efforts in K–12 schooling yielded the Every Student Succeeds Act, softening or even erasing much of NCLB's accountability framework. ESSA also put an end to the Obama administration's waivers and made it very clear that the federal government could no longer encourage states to adopt particular academic standards (like the Common Core). By the end of Obama's term, and the beginning of the Trump presidency, a sea change was evident in the federal role. Meanwhile, the ranks of foundations, advocacy groups, and reformers focused on K–12 seemed intent on moving on from much of their agenda during the Bush-Obama years in favor of a newfound emphasis on social and emotional learning, early childhood education, and career and technical education.

THE BOOK AHEAD

In tackling this volume, we parceled the key reform strategies of the Bush-Obama years into nine topics, and then enlisted an array of talented scholars to take on the various parts. In doing so, we asked that they make a particular effort to highlight specific lessons and practical advice for policy makers, practitioners, and reformers. As you will see, the contributors more than delivered on their end of the deal.

In chapter 1, the University of Oklahoma's Deven Carlson tackles perhaps the signature education policy of the Bush and Obama years: testing and accountability. Carlson reviews the evolution of testing and accountability policy and how small-scale experiments in a handful of states ultimately fueled a seismic shift in federal policy. He outlines the progression of federal efforts and explores what we have learned about the effects of accountability on achievement, as well as its unintended consequences. Carlson closes by reflecting on whether or not we can ever get testing and accountability "right," and just what the answer means for policy and practice.

In chapter 2, Ashley Jochim of the University of Washington examines what we've learned about school "turnarounds." Interventions designed to turn around struggling schools gained new urgency and visibility during the

Bush and Obama years due to NCLB-style accountability and the Obama-era School Improvement Grant program. These initiatives were designed to transform "persistently low-performing" schools. Yet, concluding that these efforts led to little obvious improvement, Jochim considers just how difficult it is to translate federal mandates into street-level change.

In chapter 3, Drew University's Patrick McGuinn examines how Bush and Obama used incentives and sanctions to shape education policy. More specifically, he explores the seeming contradiction that while federal carrots and sticks can spur policy changes, circumventing local decision making and debate can ultimately undermine their viability. McGuinn surveys federal mandates, programs, and waivers to examine what happened and what those efforts teach us about the potential of these approaches—and their potential limits.

In chapter 4, Brown University's Matthew A. Kraft takes up the array of efforts intended to improve teacher quality. He notes that improving teacher quality moved into the center of policy debates in the Bush and Obama years and was a central goal of both Bush's NCLB and Obama's Race to the Top competition. While these efforts were highly visible and had real effects on state and district data systems and practices, they failed to produce the significant impacts that many had hoped for. Kraft explores what to make of that mixed legacy and offers insights to guide those who will tackle teacher quality in years to come.

In chapter 5, Robert Pianta and Tara Hofkens of the University of Virginia assess the attempts by the Bush and Obama administrations to enhance educational research and fuel educational innovation. In particular, the Bush-era creation of the Institute of Education Sciences transformed the infrastructure of federal education research, with the What Works Clearinghouse designed to serve as a portal to implementation and practice. But did those changes help us better understand the most important issues regarding educational improvement? Did methodological biases cause researchers to ignore important questions? The story is complicated, and Pianta and Hofkens consider what all this has taught us about how to improve educational research and how that research can be used to improve schools.

In chapter 6, the Brookings Institution's Tom Loveless takes a look at the Bush- and Obama-era emphasis on standards-based reform and the impact it had on schooling. Academic standards, first required of every state by NCLB and then made into a quasi-national campaign by the Common Core, define what students will learn and when they will learn it. After nearly two decades of bipartisan political support, the advent of the Common Core frayed this bipartisan comity. Loveless sketches the practical and the political missteps of the Common Core movement and offers a deeply skeptical look at the role that "raising standards" plays in educational improvement.

In chapter 7, Anna J. Egalite of North Carolina State University explores what we learned about school choice during the Bush and Obama years. While both presidents offered clear rhetorical support for charter schooling, in particular, their support never became as definitive or programmatic as it did in areas like standards, turnarounds, or accountability. Almost all federal action took place at arm's length. Egalite explores whether this was an unexpected boon, how it shaped reaction at the state and local levels, and whether it can or should provide a roadmap for future federal forays into state policy.

Ultimately, of course, the American system dictates that the responsibility for making system reform work inevitably falls heavily on the states. Under both Bush and Obama, Washington pushed state education agencies to play a much larger role in shaping and implementing reform. In chapter 8, Sara E. Dahill-Brown of Wake Forest University considers how states were equipped to handle the challenges posed by the Bush-Obama era, how states responded, and what it teaches us about the dynamics of federalism and the capacities of states.

In chapter 9, Joshua Dunn of the University of Colorado Colorado Springs looks at the expansive Bush-Obama efforts to approach school reform as a civil rights issue and the Obama administration's efforts to markedly extend the reach of civil rights enforcement to reshape policies governing school discipline, school finance, and the rights of transgender students. Dunn considers the political and practical consequences of Washington wielding its newly asserted authority in this way.

Finally, in the volume's conclusion, we will try to distill some larger themes and insights from all of the foregoing. We approached this project with a simple question in mind: What do we know now about school improvement that we didn't know in 2000? By summarizing key lessons from the preceding chapters, we will try to offer some answers to that question.

CLOSING THOUGHTS

We see the Bush-Obama era of school reform as remarkable, if only because so much was going on. The role played by Washington was unprecedented. No Child Left Behind massively ratcheted up Washington's involvement in every public school in America, while both Race to the Top and the Department of Education's waivers to NCLB expanded the elements of schooling under federal purview.

In contemplating the chapters that follow, we have been struck time and again by the lesson that initial success and rapid adoption of a reform may actually complicate long-term success in unexpected ways. Why that may be and what it means is one of the big questions we hope readers will better understand when they set this volume down.

Ultimately, we do not try here to provide a thumbs-up or thumbs-down verdict on the Bush-Obama reform efforts or to make the case for the efforts of one administration or the other. Rather, we have sought to tease out some of the lessons we might draw from the ambitious experiment that dominated American education in the first decades of the twenty-first century. With that goal in mind, we hope readers will find this project as illuminating and useful as we do.

Testing and Accountability

What Have We Learned and Where Do We Go?

Deven Carlson

P resident Bush's 2001 signing of No Child Left Behind (NCLB) produced an immediate and dramatic change in the federal government's relationship with states, districts, and schools across the country. Gone were the days when the federal government doled out dollars to states and districts with relatively few strings attached. Instead, NCLB ushered in an era where—under the threat of withheld Title I dollars—states were required to adopt challenging standards, administer annual reading and math assessments aligned with those standards, and hold schools accountable on the basis of the assessment results. Almost overnight, the notion that standards, testing, and accountability could be combined in an effort to drive school improvement morphed from a diverse set of initiatives in place in about half the states to a federal policy affecting every public school and district across the country.

The fact that NCLB broke so sharply with past federal education policy effectively guaranteed that there would be growing pains as states and districts worked to meet the new federal mandates. The hope was that these pains would ultimately be justified by significant improvements in educational outcomes for students across the United States. Whether the law fulfilled this justification has been—and remains—a hotly debated topic in the education policy community. Regardless of one's view of the ultimate wisdom of NCLB, there is broad consensus that we learned a wide range of important lessons about standards, testing, and accountability policy throughout the Bush-Obama educational era.

This chapter explores these lessons. It delves into those we have learned about the ability of standards, testing, and accountability to drive academic improvement, which is the primary goal of these policies. Just as importantly, though, it examines those we have learned about the unintended consequences of these policies, such as the nature of states' responses to federal mandates and schools' reactions to accountability pressures. This chapter also explores what we know today about the politics of testing and accountability policy that we did not yet know in 2001. Finally, the chapter concludes by discussing whether it is reasonable to think we can ever get testing and accountability policy "right," and by predicting the direction these policies will take in future years. Prior to delving into those topics, however, the chapter sets the stage by briefly describing the evolution of federal policy on standards, testing, and accountability.

HOW DID WE GET HERE? TESTING AND ACCOUNTABILITY AT THE FEDERAL LEVEL

Education fell almost exclusively under the purview of the states for the first 150-plus years of the United States' existence. States' control of this issue is attributable to the fact that the US Constitution does not specify a fundamental right to education—an interpretation cemented by the Supreme Court's 1973 decision in *San Antonio Independent School District v. Rodriguez*—combined with the Tenth Amendment, which reserves powers not explicitly delegated to the federal government for the states. Thus, through the mid-twentieth century there had been no meaningful federal involvement in education in the United States. Passage of the Elementary and Secondary Education Act (ESEA) of 1965 changed that. Part of the Johnson administration's broader War on Poverty, ESEA was driven by concerns over educational inequity across the country. This initial federal foray into education was designed to alleviate these inequities by providing federal dollars to states, which would then distribute this money to districts in an effort to improve the quality of education available to disadvantaged students. The law contained nominal reporting requirements for states and districts, but no formal testing or accountability mandates.

Throughout the 1970s, ESEA's strict focus on promoting educational equity reflected the prevailing view of the proper federal role in education. Beginning in the 1980s, though, there was a growing sense that the federal government should promote educational excellence, in addition to equity. Initially, federal efforts to promote educational excellence took place outside of the legislative arena. For example, the 1983 report *A Nation at Risk* recommended that states adopt challenging standards and raise graduation requirements. Although the report caused quite a stir, its recommendations were nothing more than mere suggestions that states were free to take or leave. Similarly, at the 1989 National Education Summit, President George H. W. Bush and the nation's governors agreed to develop a set of national education goals—one of which involved adopting challenging standards and administering assessments aligned to those standards—and hold themselves accountable for achieving those goals. States were again at liberty to ignore the recommendations of the National Education Summit, but the event is notable for its insertion of testing and accountability into the federal policy conversation.

It was not long before these events began to shape congressional priorities. In 1994 Congress passed the Goals 2000 legislation, which codified the goals that had emerged from the National Education Summit, including the objective that students demonstrate mastery—via assessments—of challenging curricular content. Although the legislation was careful to note that participation in Goals 2000 was voluntary, it offered states financial assistance for developing and implementing plans for achieving the goals, so states that opted out effectively declined the possibility of millions of federal dollars. Despite the voluntary nature of Goals 2000, the legislation officially put the federal government on record in support of testing and accountability.

The feds reiterated their endorsement of testing and accountability through the 1994 ESEA reauthorization—titled the Improving America's Schools Act (IASA)—that followed close on the heels of Goals 2000. Whereas Goals 2000 provided financial incentives for states to adopt challenging standards and administer assessments aligned to those standards, IASA mandated it. In particular, IASA required states to adopt standards by the 1997–1998 school year and implement assessment systems by the 2000–2001 school year. The law mandated that states assess students in reading and math once each in grades 3–5, 6–9, and 10–12. The bill, however, contained no provisions specifying sanctions or rewards on the basis of the assessment results—there was no accountability. Implementation and enforcement of IASA was haphazard, with the US Department of Education routinely issuing waivers to states that were lagging in development of their assessment systems. Unsurprisingly, by the time the 2000–2001 school year rolled around, a significant number of states had not developed any sort of meaningful assessment system.

The No Child Left Behind Era

The 2000 election changed the politics of education reform at the federal level. President Bush brought with him several years of experience with testing and accountability in Texas, a strong conviction that such was the optimal approach to school improvement, and a secretary of education— Rod Paige—who had significant experience with these policies in Houston. With education as one of its top domestic priorities, the Bush administration worked throughout 2001 with leaders of both parties in Congress to reauthorize ESEA. The bill they negotiated, which garnered substantial bipartisan support, pulled hard on the levers of testing and accountability in an effort to reach aspirational learning goals.

The legislation mandated that by the 2005–2006 school year states adopt challenging standards in reading and math, and annually test students in grades 3–8 and once in high school using an assessment aligned to those standards. The law also required states to identify grade-specific scores on those tests—*cut scores*—that corresponded to proficiency. Students scoring above the relevant cut score would be deemed proficient, while students scoring below it would not. NCLB compelled states to annually report the percent of proficient students not only for each school, but also for each of several subgroups within the school. Specifically, similar to IASA, the law called for separate subgroup reporting on the basis of race/ethnicity, eligibility for free or reduced-price lunch, disability status, and English language learner (ELL) status.

Unlike IASA, NCLB did not end with subgroup reporting requirements. The law also set a goal of all students in each school reaching proficiency by the 2013–2014 school year. Further, it required states to specify a trajectory that schools must maintain in order to reach the universal proficiency goal. Schools lagging behind that state-specified trajectory were classified as failing to make Adequate Yearly Progress (AYP). This requirement was stringent—a school was classified as failing to make AYP if just a single subgroup fell off the trajectory toward universal proficiency in either reading or math. Schools that received Title I funding and failed to make AYP were subject to a series of sanctions, the severity of which increased with the number of consecutive years that a school failed to make AYP. The sanctions

TABLE 1.1   Sanctions for missing AYP

Consecutive year missing AYP	Sanction
1	None
2	Transfer option
3	Transfer option; supplemental educational services
4	Transfer option; supplemental educational services; corrective action
5	Restructuring plan
6	Transfer option; supplemental educational services; corrective action; restructuring

included offering students the ability to transfer to a school in the district that had made AYP, providing supplemental educational services (i.e., tutoring), and taking "corrective action" or "restructuring" with regard to some aspect of school personnel, management, or structure.[1] Table 1.1 summarizes the sanctions that schools faced for each consecutive year they failed to make AYP.

The US Department of Education (ED) was serious about implementation and enforcement of NCLB, and took a hard line with states, which were accustomed to the lax enforcement of IASA and thus prone to drag their feet in implementing NCLB. This hard-nosed approach likely contributed to states successfully implementing the testing and accountability provisions of NCLB on the specified timeline. This is not to say that the implementation process was all peaches and cream—there were plenty of hurdles and difficulties—but by the time the 2005–2006 school year rolled around, states were largely in compliance with the testing and accountability provisions.

NCLB was scheduled for reauthorization in 2007, but it quickly became clear that the law would not be addressed on that timeline, and implementation of NCLB continued apace. In 2008, just a few years after the testing and accountability requirements took effect, the United States was rocked by the financial crisis and ensuing Great Recession. The severe economic downturn decimated state and school district revenues, and officials began to look for dollars wherever they could. They found a potential funding source in the American Recovery and Reinvestment Act (ARRA), which Congress passed in 2009 as its primary legislative response to the Great Recession.

Contained in ARRA were a few lines of statute that provided the secretary of education with $4.35 billion to operate a competitive grant program among states based on criteria the secretary "determines appropriate" that would issue grants to "consortia of states to develop academic assessments that are aligned with academic standards."

Secretary Arne Duncan took advantage of this authority to design the Race to the Top (RTTT) grant competition, which based award decisions—each worth up to hundreds of millions of dollars—on states' plans to advance reforms on each of several priorities identified by ED. The priority most relevant here is the adoption of "college- and career-ready" standards, and implementation of common, high-quality assessments aligned to those standards. This was a barely disguised euphemism for adopting the newly developed Common Core State Standards and participating in one of two consortia awarded RTTT funding to develop assessments aligned to the Common Core. Unsurprisingly, as states began to put together their RTTT applications—forty-six states and the District of Columbia submitted applications in at least one of the phases—the vast majority pledged to adopt the Common Core standards and one of the two assessments intended to complement the standards. Moreover, to demonstrate their commitment to "high standards," several states pledged to increase the cut scores students would need to achieve to be classified as proficient. In doing so, however, these states were also making it more difficult for their schools to meet AYP under NCLB, which continued to be the law of the land.

As the legislative stalemate over ESEA reauthorization continued into 2011, NCLB began to lose legitimacy in the eyes of both policy makers and the public. Among the public, results from the annual PDK/Gallup poll on education revealed that the percentage of the public viewing NCLB unfavorably grew from 27 percent in 2005 to 46 percent in 2010. The growth in public dissatisfaction over this time is partially attributable to the fact that, each year, more and more schools were failing to meet AYP and thus subject to NCLB's sanctions. Testifying before Congress in the spring of 2011, Secretary Duncan stated that, according to estimates produced by the department he led, 82 percent of schools across the country could fail to make AYP in 2011. Although these comments generated considerable press and attention, they did not spur Congress to reauthorize ESEA. In September 2011 President Obama announced that, due to congressional inaction, his administration would offer states flexibility with respect to several provisions of

NCLB, including the provisions governing AYP status and the corresponding sanctions. As with RTTT, though, it quickly became clear that this flexibility would come with strings attached. In particular, the administration made clear that states would be granted waivers from NCLB only if they promised to work to implement a series of administration priorities, notably adoption of "college- and career-ready standards," high-quality assessments aligned to those standards, and accountability systems that provided differentiated levels of recognition and support.

In effect, the administration used NCLB waivers as a method for driving their preferred approach on standards, testing, and accountability. The requirements surrounding standards and testing echoed those emphasized under RTTT, but the accountability provisions were newly developed for the NCLB waiver process. These provisions required states to design accountability systems with the following features: first, states had to set "ambitious but achievable" performance objectives in reading and math and, mirroring NCLB, design accountability systems that incorporated reading and math test scores for all students, as well as for student subgroups. Unlike NCLB, though, these systems had to incorporate measures of student test score growth—not just performance levels—into accountability calculations. Second, states were required to group schools into at least four categories on the basis of accountability calculations. This requirement was designed to encourage states to adopt A–F school report cards, or at least a variant thereof. Finally, states had to identify "priority" and "focus" schools, which are defined, respectively, as the lowest-performing 5 percent of schools in the state and the 10 percent of schools in the state with the largest achievement gaps.

Considered together, the waivers offered by the Obama administration certainly provided flexibility from NCLB, but did not provide states with much flexibility around testing and accountability generally. The waivers effectively replaced the testing and accountability requirements in NCLB with requirements better aligned to the Obama administration's preferences on the issues. Brushing aside potential concerns about the legality of the waiver process, most states reasoned that continued operation under the outdated requirements of NCLB was so onerous that they would seek a waiver from the law. Indeed, over the next few years, forty-five states submitted waiver applications, and ED ultimately approved forty-three of these requests.

For the forty-three states granted NCLB waivers, the promises they made in their applications served as the status quo testing and accountability policy for the next several years; the handful of states not granted waivers continued to operate under NCLB. Conventional wisdom held that this status quo would persist until after the 2016 general election, when a newly elected president and a Congress facing no imminent electoral pressures might work together on a bipartisan basis to reauthorize ESEA. This conventional wisdom proved wrong, however. It seems that pundits underestimated the breadth of dissatisfaction across the political spectrum with NCLB and the ensuing waiver process. The left was displeased with how the process played out, while the right was unhappy that the process had happened at all.

This broad dissatisfaction provided the common ground necessary for strong bipartisan consensus on the latest ESEA reauthorization. Although reaching this consensus involved several fits and starts, on December 10, 2015, President Obama signed the Every Student Succeeds Act (ESSA) into law. In doing so, he brought to an end a fifteen-year era where testing and accountability policy were largely determined in Washington, DC. Although ESSA maintained annual testing and reporting requirements, it provided states with significant autonomy to determine the design of their accountability systems. On this score, ESSA delivered the flexibility that waivers had been portrayed as providing. In a very real sense, ESSA is closer in spirit to IASA than to NCLB. The end of the NCLB era provides a natural point for reflecting on the lessons the past fifteen years have taught us.

LESSONS LEARNED

Lesson 1: Test-Based Accountability Increases Test Scores in Reading and Math

Research into the effects of accountability systems followed close on the heels of their implementation. Initially, this research focused primarily on the effects of test-based accountability on students' reading and math test scores—increasing achievement in these subjects was seen as the main goal of NCLB, and of test-based accountability more generally. The vast majority of this research focuses on estimating the effect of a single provision of NCLB or a particular aspect of accountability policy design on students' test scores. A couple of rigorous studies, though, attempt to estimate the effects of NCLB writ large on students' reading and math achievement. These studies use state-level reading and math scores on the National Assessment of Educational Progress (NAEP) from both pre-NCLB and post-NCLB years.[2] Using this data, the studies compare the change in test scores from pre-NCLB years to post-NCLB years for two groups: 1) states that first implemented accountability systems in response to the NCLB mandates, and 2) states and private schools for whom NCLB did not require a meaningful change in accountability requirements. Together, the preponderance of evidence from these studies suggests that NCLB increased math achievement at both the fourth- and eighth-grade levels, but had little effect on reading scores, at least as measured by NAEP.

Along with these studies on NCLB writ large, a large body of work examines the achievement effects of accountability in a manner more modest in scope. This work typically evaluates a single aspect of accountability system design, or a particular provision of NCLB. For example, several studies estimate the effect of a school receiving an F rating, relative to a D, on an A–F school rating system. Results from New York City and Florida provide consistent evidence that an F rating has a positive effect on students' test scores in subsequent years, compared to students in D-rated schools that scored just above the threshold for receiving an F.[3]

Finally, a series of studies analyze the achievement effects of accountability using data from states that implemented these policies on their own accord in the years prior to NCLB, comparing their outcomes to those of states that had not implemented accountability systems. These cross-state analyses typically use NAEP scores as their achievement measure and generally find that the adoption of high-stakes testing led to increases in both reading and math scores.[4] Other studies take a similar approach, but limit themselves to studying accountability in a single state or district. Studies of this sort from Chicago and Texas conclude that accountability increased reading and math scores, although work from Charlotte finds no evidence that accountability improved student test performance.[5]

Considered together, the bulk of the evidence emerging from research on test-based accountability points toward these policies increasing test scores in the subjects for which schools are held accountable, typically reading and math. On their face, these achievement increases are a good thing. However, the last fifteen years have taught us that the interpretation is not that simple, which brings us to lesson 2.

Lesson 2: It Is Not Clear These Achievement Increases Always Correspond to Actual Learning Gains

There are several reasons that student reading and math scores might increase in response to accountability pressures. First, increased test scores could reflect student learning gains, either generally or in the specific subject(s) being tested. Regardless, these sorts of achievement increases are generally desirable. Second, test score improvements could reflect greater familiarity with the testing process, and this acclimation process produces higher scores, even if the underlying degree of student learning remains unchanged. Third, test score increases could be generated by schools and teachers placing greater emphasis on test preparation. Finally, increased test scores could be a product of manipulation, which could take the form of outright cheating, but also less nefarious forms such as the timing of test administration. The second, third, and fourth reasons for test score gains are unequivocally less desirable than the first one. Unfortunately, most analyses finding that test-based accountability produces achievement gains cannot distinguish between these and other potential reasons for the observed test score gains.

A few studies do shed light on this important issue, though. For two primary reasons, we can be reasonably confident that the set of studies showing that accountability increases NAEP scores reflects true student learning gains. First, the low-stakes nature of NAEP—there are no sanctions or rewards tied to NAEP performance—means that schools typically do not prepare their students for the assessment. The lack of preparation incentives is further reinforced by NAEP's biannual administration to students in a relatively small number of schools within a state. Second, NAEP has long been regarded as a high-quality assessment effective at gauging a broad range of student knowledge in a given subject. NAEP's quality further contributes to an interpretation of increased NAEP scores representing true student learning gains, particularly when considered alongside the low stakes of the assessment and its administration protocol.

The interpretation of studies showing that accountability increases student scores on high-stakes tests is much murkier. In these cases, score gains attributable to intense test preparation activities, increased familiarity with the assessment process, or even manipulation are very real possibilities. A couple of studies—conducted in Chicago and Florida—provide direct evidence on this issue.[6] Both studies show that accountability-induced test score gains were much larger on the high-stakes assessment than they were on the low-stakes one. Taken as a whole, the evidence suggests that accountability led to true increases in students' math and reading ability, but that the size of these gains is somewhat smaller than what analysis of high-stakes exams would indicate.

Lesson 3: Reading and Math Gains Often Come at the Expense of Instruction in Other Subjects

NCLB was explicit that states must hold schools accountable on the basis of reading and math scores, but was largely silent on other subjects—it required grade-span testing in science, but attached no rewards or sanctions to test performance in that subject. Thus, schools faced immense pressure to maximize test scores in reading and math, but had few formal incentives to focus on instruction in other subjects.

Almost from the beginning of NCLB implementation, a collection of parents, teachers, and other stakeholders began to express concerns that the emphasis on increasing reading and math scores was crowding out instruction in subjects like art, music, social studies, and even science. Studies of this phenomenon provided evidence that these concerns were well founded. One particularly well-done study drew a representative sample of districts across three states—California, Pennsylvania, and Georgia—and surveyed superintendents, principals, and teachers in those districts from 2003 to 2005.[7] Across each of the three states, about half of principals reported requiring their teachers to increase the time they spent on tested subjects, with corresponding reductions in nontested areas. And 40 percent of district superintendents reported that they eliminated one or more programs, such as art or music, in order to increase instruction in tested subjects. Other studies conducted in different contexts echo these conclusions, finding that schools would focus time, effort, and resources on maximizing math and reading instruction at the expense of instruction in other subject areas.[8]

Even within math and reading, many schools focused instruction primarily on the concepts and content that would appear on the tests. And, to put it generously, many of the tests that states adopted were not of the highest quality, particularly in the early years of NCLB—these assessments were typically multiple choice and assessed relatively superficial knowledge and skills. So even the extensive math and reading instruction that schools provided was often one particular type of math and reading instruction, a type that was often criticized for failing to promote creative thinking, a deep understanding of the content, and a true love of learning.

There is no denying that developing math and reading skills is an important endeavor; these skills underlie just about every aspect of life to one degree or another. There are valid questions, though, over the ideal balance between developing math and reading skills and meaningfully exposing students to a broad range of subjects. There is certainly an argument to be made that schools focused on math and reading to an insufficient degree in the pre-NCLB era. There is also an argument to be made, however, that NCLB swung the pendulum too far in the other direction, and placed far too much focus on these subjects. Indeed, the near single-minded pursuit of math and reading achievement over the past fifteen years has been disconcerting to those who value a balanced and well-rounded education.

Lesson 4: States, Districts, and Schools Respond to Accountability Pressures in Unintended Ways

By design, NCLB provided states with substantial autonomy in developing standards, adopting assessments, and defining the student performance level on those assessments that corresponded to proficiency or mastery of the standards. The hope was that states would adopt rigorous standards that, when mastered upon high school graduation, would set students up for success in postsecondary education or the workforce. Moreover, policy makers envisioned states adopting high-quality assessments and carefully calibrating the level of student performance on these tests that denoted mastery of the standards. It quickly became clear, however, that the reality of states' decisions on these issues would not match the original visions.

Out of the gate, some states did adopt reading and math standards that were judged to be rigorous and "world class." At least as many states, though, did not. It became something of a parlor game among education policy organizations to assess the quality of the standards that states adopted in response to NCLB. For example, the Thomas B. Fordham Institute issued a series of reports titled *The State of State Standards* where it graded states' reading and math standards on an A–F scale. The 2005 version of this report assigned only five states an A grade for their reading standards, but gave eight states a D or an F. In math, just three states earned an A from Fordham's evaluators, and a majority of states received a D or an F. It wasn't until the Obama administration incentivized adoption of the Common Core State Standards through RTTT and NCLB waivers that most states adopted the sort of standards that policy makers initially envisioned.

In addition to going their own way on the adoption of standards, a number of states also defined proficiency in a manner contrary to policy makers' visions. Instead of ratcheting up the level of test performance required for a student to be deemed proficient—that is, to have demonstrated true mastery of the standards—some states actually lowered the proficiency bar in an effort to put their schools in a better position to meet the universal proficiency requirement of NCLB. For example, between 2005 and 2009 South Carolina substantially lowered the proficiency bar across all grades in both reading and math.[9] These decisions flew directly in the face of policy makers' intentions on these issues. In response, the Obama administration again used the RTTT and NCLB waiver application process to incentivize states to raise proficiency thresholds. They wanted states to define proficiency as originally intended by policy makers, which would convey the "hard truths" that most kids in the United States were not on track to succeed in postsecondary education or the workforce.

States were not the only entity that responded to accountability mandates in unintended ways. Districts and schools also exhibited their share of undesirable responses to the pressures created by implementation of high-stakes accountability, including the intense focus on math and reading outlined previously. Initially, the school accountability systems required by NCLB were based almost entirely on the percent of students deemed proficient. Even today, proficiency levels are the primary component of most states' accountability systems. Along with their undesirable property of rewarding or sanctioning schools primarily on the basis of the characteristics of the students they serve, these systems also provide an incentive for schools to focus on students they believe have a reasonable shot of scoring above the proficiency bar. From an accountability perspective, there is little reason to attend to students who will surely score well on the test, or those who will not approach the proficiency threshold under any circumstances. And indeed, multiple studies provide evidence that accountability leads to a focus on "bubble kids," those who are thought to be just above or just below the proficiency cutoff.[10]

Perhaps the most problematic response of districts and schools to accountability pressures has been outright cheating. Over the past fifteen years, audits and analyses have uncovered cheating scandals in several districts, including

Columbus, Washington, DC, and Atlanta, among others. In Atlanta, schools were facing significant pressure from Superintendent Beverly Hall—who had a reputation as a no-nonsense, hard-driving leader—to improve their test performance. A number of schools in the district did improve their test scores, oftentimes substantially. The massive achievement increases gained these schools accolades, but also aroused suspicion: How were these schools able to produce achievement increases of a magnitude almost never seen? This issue caught the attention of the *Atlanta Journal-Constitution*, which commissioned an analysis of the test score improvements, concluding that the observed score increases were highly improbable. This spurred an investigation by Atlanta Public Schools and—when its investigation proved lackluster—by the Georgia Bureau of Investigation, which uncovered evidence of widespread cheating across the district. This led to the indictment of thirty-five educators, nearly all of whom either pled guilty or were convicted for their role in the conspiracy. Situations like the one in Atlanta illustrate the potential dark side of accountability policy.

Lesson 5: Unrealistic Expectations and Goals Are Counterproductive

At the time NCLB passed in 2001, its goal of universal student proficiency in math and reading was more than a decade away. Policy makers, who are notoriously short-sighted, relished the immediate sound bite the law provided them—the legislation was going to ensure that each and every student was ready for college or the workforce—and gave relatively little thought to future implications. Surely, they thought, NCLB would be reauthorized before this blatantly unrealistic goal caused any real problems.

Problems started to appear on this score sooner than anticipated, however. Schools could be labeled as failing to make AYP if just one subgroup fell off the state-specified trajectory toward universal proficiency by 2014. Consequently, just a year or two into NCLB's testing and accountability regime, schools started to face the sanctions laid out in table 1.1. Predictably, these failure labels did not always go over well with educators or parents. Educators resented their school being labeled a "failure" for not achieving something that, by any reasonable standard, was simply not possible to achieve, no matter how much blood, sweat, and tears they poured into the cause. What kind of law, from their point of view, penalizes schools and teachers for not doing the undoable? These feelings quickly turned many educators, a hugely important constituency for the long-term viability of any education policy, against both NCLB and testing and accountability policy more generally.

Many parents also reacted negatively to the "failure" label being slapped on their school. Indeed, the past fifteen years have taught us that people are fine with a law that tells them that other people's schools are failing, but are less receptive when the law tells them that *their* school is a failure. This is particularly true if they paid hundreds of thousands—or even millions—of dollars for a house that provided entry to that school, or if they walk into that school multiple times per week and see all the positive things that are happening and sense the teachers' and principal's commitment to it. In cases like that, whose judgment are people going to believe? The judgment of a formula designed by congressional staffers and bureaucrats in Washington, DC, or their own eyes and experiences?

Lesson 6: Accountability Policy Has a Politics Problem

The blowback from parents and educators just described highlights a broader political lesson that we have learned about testing and accountability policy over the past fifteen years: these policies—particularly accountability—do not have any sort of natural or sizable political constituency. Political science teaches us that in order for a policy to have any meaningful staying power, it needs to develop a vocal grassroots constituency who will advocate for it in times of turmoil. As the testing and accountability era has progressed, though, it has become increasingly clear that testing and, particularly, accountability have not developed such a constituency.

When you dig down into the issue, it is not difficult to see why such a constituency has failed to form. Who sees direct and tangible benefits from accountability? Certainly not teachers or principals. Similarly, it is hard to see any direct benefits of accountability accruing to parents or kids. At least testing provides families with information on the academic performance of their children. More broadly, the annual testing and subgroup reporting requirements shined a light on potential differential performance across demographic subgroups, a tangible benefit that commanded the support of civil rights groups for annual testing. Accountability, on the other hand, does not provide these sorts of perceptible benefits to any particular group. Accountability supporters often claim that these policies offer clear benefits to taxpayers by ensuring that schools and districts are spending their money well. This may well be true, but any such benefits are relatively intangible and so imperceptible that it is difficult to imagine that they motivate or mobilize anyone on their behalf.

The failure of accountability to generate any sort of meaningful grassroots constituency is primarily attributable to its structural flaws. However, the economic and political contexts that evolved during the mid- to late-2000s generated additional headwinds for the policy. Economically, the Great Recession hit just as NCLB sanctions began to affect schools and districts. This economic downturn decimated education budgets at both the state and district levels, which prevented policy makers from providing schools and districts with any additional money to ease the bite of NCLB sanctions.

Politically, education has long been considered an issue with wide bipartisan support at the elite level, as evidenced by NCLB's passage with broad bipartisan majorities. Recently, though, there are indications that education is becoming more partisan in nature, particularly at the federal level, with one party's support of a given policy position almost certainly corresponding to opposition by the other. Thus, the Obama administration's wholesale embrace of accountability policy, particularly federal accountability, corresponded to diminished support for the policy among Republican elites. And the fact that this embrace occurred before accountability policy had fully matured and entrenched itself in the federal education landscape left it susceptible to the vagaries of partisan politics. Together, the lack of broad support for accountability at either the grassroots or elite level left the policy in a politically precarious situation.

Lesson 7: We Would Not Have Learned Many of These Lessons Without the Testing and Reporting Requirements of NCLB

The defining legacy of the testing and accountability policy of the last fifteen years seems likely to be twofold: 1) a shift from measuring inputs to focusing primarily on outcomes, and 2) increased transparency surrounding those outcomes, particularly student achievement. Throughout much of the 1980s and even into the 1990s, most folks in education focused primarily on the resources that were going into schools, and less on the outcomes those resources were generating. If *A Nation at Risk* is generally recognized as the starting point in moving from an input- to outcome-oriented view of education, then it is reasonable to consider NCLB as the capstone of that movement.

Prior versions of the law had certainly addressed the issues of testing and accountability, but had done so in a manner where enforcement was lax and states were given wide discretion in determining how far they wanted to go down those roads. NCLB changed that through its testing mandates and strict reporting requirements—states, districts, and schools had to report attendance rates, teacher qualifications, student performance by subgroup, and numerous other topics. Recognizing that some of these reporting requirements were unduly burdensome, it is also true that this information has been instrumental in allowing us to learn the aforementioned lessons. It has allowed us to learn about the achievement effects of accountability, institutional and individual responses to accountability pressures, and even about the politics of these issues.

Although there is general agreement that many of the accountability requirements of NCLB were quite ham-handed, there is also broad consensus that the transparency provisions of the law were one thing policy makers got right. It has illuminated schools that achieved excellence and equity, as well as those that fell short on either, or both, of those dimensions. It has allowed for discussions of what different numbers on different topics mean, whether they are important, and what we should do about them. These sorts of discussions have proved valuable and contribute to a broad desire to maintain requirements to collect and publish this information. To the degree that constituencies continue to see a benefit of this information—and it seems likely that they will—transparency surrounding educational processes and outcomes will probably be the defining legacy of the testing and accountability era.

CONCLUSION

Can We Get Testing and Accountability Policy "Right"?

In the wake of all the lessons we have learned about testing and accountability over the past decade and a half, it is reasonable to question whether we can ever design and implement these policies in a manner that commands broad support over the long haul. The experiences over the past fifteen years suggest that such a reality seems unlikely, particularly with respect to accountability, for perhaps the most important lesson we have learned over the NCLB era is that we, as a society, do not agree on the purpose or intent of K–12 schooling in the United States. Or, at least, we do not agree on the ideal balance of the various things we want schools to do. Some folks think schools should primarily focus on developing skills—particularly reading and math—that will set students up for success in postsecondary education or the workforce. Others want schools to expose students to a broad curriculum, focusing less on standardized assessment of student knowledge and skills, and more on developing curiosity and instilling a love of learning. These tensions have always existed, but NCLB brought them to the surface by effectively privileging one conceptualization of the purpose of schools over others. Thus, debates that purportedly began over accountability generally mutated, at least to some degree, to a debate over the appropriate purpose and design of schooling.

If we cannot reach consensus on the purpose and design of schooling, then it is silly to think that we could design an accountability policy that commands broad support. As has been the case over the past fifteen years, there would likely be a constant stream of arguments and complaints over this provision being too strong or that requirement being irrelevant. More generally, as long as there are substantial differences across society in what we want schools to do—and it is tough to imagine those differences disappearing anytime soon—it is difficult to imagine an accountability system that adequately balances all stakeholders' priorities and addresses their concerns.

Even on the off chance that we can reach some sort of consensus on the purpose of schooling, accountability policy would still have a tough row to hoe. The lessons discussed in this chapter demonstrate the difficulty of designing an accountability policy that induces all relevant entities—states, schools, and districts—to act in intended ways. It is a near-guarantee that the policy will leave open some loopholes or will create perverse incentives, and these institutions and organizations will exploit these loopholes or respond to the perverse incentive structure.

So where does that leave us? What does the future of testing and accountability policy in the United States look like? Of course, it is difficult to make detailed predictions on this score, but the lessons we have learned in recent years do support two general forecasts. First, broad support for shifting the focus from inputs to outcomes, coupled with the recognition that information on those outcomes can be quite valuable, renders it likely that the testing and reporting requirements mandated in NCLB—and reiterated in ESSA—will remain in place for the foreseeable future. Indeed, there is widespread recognition that the increased information on student and school performance was not the problem; it was what we did with that information that proved most problematic. This leads to the second prediction: that test-based accountability seems likely to continue the retreat that started with ESSA. In the near term, this retreat could manifest itself by states deciding to throw in the towel on accountability under ESSA; they will follow the letter of the law, but will design systems with fairly meaningless rewards or sanctions. Further down the line, perhaps in the next ESEA reauthorization, this retreat may become codified in statute. In the long term, it seems likely we will get to a point where Congress mandates that states produce information on student achievement—and student outcomes more generally—but leaves it entirely to states, districts, and parents to decide how to use that information.

2

The Limits of Policy for School Turnaround

Ashley Jochim

Improving schools that serve large numbers of disadvantaged students has long been a focus of federal education policy. These efforts gained increased urgency during the Bush and Obama years, as the federal government deepened its commitment to school turnaround through an expansive set of programs that sought to enhance local leaders' commitment and capacity to transform persistently low performing schools. Almost two decades after these efforts were first initiated, success remains isolated.

This chapter considers why Bush's and Obama's signature school improvement initiatives ended with so little to show for the effort. While the two administrations pursued distinctive approaches to school improvement, they shared the optimistic assumption that federal policy could push and prod low performing schools to improve, and districts and states to offer their support. The challenges that emerged along the way suggest that while scalable school improvement strategies remain elusive, more constructive federal roles are possible. These include recognizing the limits of policy as a tool for school improvement; maximizing opportunities for leaders at the school, district, and state level to support innovative school improvement programs; offering targeted support to culture change initiatives; and diversifying the types of improvement strategies that federal policy makers are willing to support.

THERE AND BACK AGAIN: A SHORT HISTORY OF FEDERAL SCHOOL IMPROVEMENT PROGRAMS

School improvement has been the guiding focus of federal education policy for half a century. Inspired by broader movements, including equal opportunity for black and Latino children and international pressures to improve the nation's economic competitiveness, federal policy makers have invested billions of dollars and pressed numerous reform strategies to improve schools.

And while the scope of the school improvement challenge is large, America's ambitions have always been grand. When President Lyndon Johnson signed the Elementary and Secondary Education Act (ESEA) into law, as he sat before the one-room schoolhouse he attended as a child, he declared that the new law would "bridge a gap between helplessness and hope for more than five million educationally deprived children."[1]

Federal efforts to support school improvement have confronted a series of tensions—between the value of local control versus state and federal oversight, between respecting the professional autonomy of educators versus empowering administrators and experts, and between the need for capacity building versus accountability to spur school improvement. If history offers any insight, none of these approaches has provided a full resolution to the challenges schools face, though each may have represented a rational response to the challenges of the day.

Setting the Stage: Comprehensive School Reform Demonstration Program

Since the passage of ESEA, federal policy makers have experimented with using federal funds as a lever to support improvement in low performing schools. Title I, the law's signature program, provided local school systems with additional resources to support targeted programs for disadvantaged students. This approach was based on the optimistic assumption that local school systems would use the additional resources to improve educational outcomes for such students.[2] Studies of Title I found the impact of ESEA on disadvantaged students was mostly "piecemeal," resulting in remedial instruction in core subjects.[3]

These problems helped to shift the focus of school improvement programs toward more integrative efforts. Mirroring similar reform strategies in England, New Zealand, and Australia, President George H. W. Bush called for "a new generation of schools" that would offer a more comprehensive approach to school reform. Business leaders supplied the money required to finance the new school designs in establishing the New American Schools Development Corporation (later renamed New American Schools, or NAS), a privately funded, nonprofit organization. NAS founders believed that previous federal reform efforts were too fragmented and that improvement could best be supported through the creation of integrative, research-based, whole-school reform strategies.[4]

But NAS faced an immediate problem; districts lacked the resources to support the intensive technical assistance that the new school designs required.[5] That changed in 1997, when Congress passed the Comprehensive School Reform Demonstration Program (CSRDP), which awarded $150 million in competitive grants to support district implementation of the new reform models. The program provided three years of seed funding to Title I schools to support adoption and implementation of one of the school designs. By the end of the program, more than 10 percent of all Title I schools (about seven thousand in total) had participated, and between 10 and 20 percent of *all* public schools in the United States had adopted a comprehensive school reform model.[6]

The CSRDP offered a seemingly perfect reform strategy. It married privately funded research and development and publicly funded scale-up support. It directly targeted the perceived failures of previous reform efforts by providing integrative whole-school designs, intensive technical assistance support, and evidence-based reform models. And it sought to preserve local autonomy and reform "fit" by enabling schools to select among competing reform models. All told, more than 1.6 billion federal dollars were distributed to schools through the CSRDP.

Yet in 1999, the American Institutes for Research examined twenty-four comprehensive school reform programs and found "only a few approaches have documented their positive effects on student achievement" and in a number of cases, "the school systems . . . never got around to conducting a systematic evaluation."[7] A US Department of Education–funded evaluation of federally funded comprehensive-school-reform schools found less than one-third of schools used an evidence-based reform model, implementation remained mixed after three years, and receipt of a grant was not associated with any achievement gains in either math or reading.[8]

Moving from Inputs to Outputs: School Improvement Under No Child Left Behind

The lack of evidence around CSRDP did not extinguish federal policy makers' attention to school improvement, and later reauthorizations of ESEA sought to put "teeth" behind these efforts. Couched in the language of the civil rights mandate that came before, the No Child Left Behind Act of

2001 (NCLB) required all states to establish standards for student learning in core subjects, track students' progress toward those standards, and sanction schools that failed to improve.

Policy makers in the United States were not alone in their shifting focus to enhancing accountability for results. In England, Australia, and New Zealand, national policy makers, who had long been frustrated by the limits on their ability to shape local education systems, worked to enhance scalability and control using incentives aligned to student outcomes. This included the rise of the "inspectorate" model in England as well as other efforts to set standards, monitor progress, and improve student achievement in low performing schools.

Under NCLB, schools that failed to make Adequate Yearly Progress (AYP), a measure meant to capture the annual improvement necessary in order to bring all students up to proficiency by 2013–2014, were required to offer students supplementary education services (SES) and public school choice. These programs aimed to put pressure on "failing" schools to improve by offering families educational alternatives. Schools that did not improve after four years faced escalating sanctions. This included handing over the school to the state education agency, making changes in leadership and staff, converting the school to a charter school, or embracing another "comprehensive school reform," a reference to the long-running CSRDP, which eventually was discontinued in 2006.

NCLB also sought to bolster state and district capacity to support school improvement. The law established the School Improvement Fund (SIF), the precursor to a later Obama administration program, to help schools adopt and implement effective improvement strategies, and provided states nearly $500 million to support local improvement efforts.[9] The fund gave schools that failed to reach accountability targets three-year grants to support necessary investments, such as a new curriculum or professional development.[10] State education agencies were required to help schools design and implement their improvement plans.

Like CSRDP, NCLB embraced an evidence-based agenda for school improvement. The law itself referenced "scientifically based research" more than one hundred times (making it among the most quoted phrases) and required all programs funded under Title I, including SIF, to be based on research that met rigorous scientific standards.[11] Schools deemed in need of improvement were encouraged to embrace a "what works" approach, using data to identify problems, put in place proven curriculum and professional development, and reallocate funds to more effective programs.

While evaluations of NCLB's accountability provisions suggest the law had small but positive effects on student achievement, especially for low-income children and children of color, the results fell far short of what its designers had sought. As Brenda Cassellius, an assistant principal turned Minnesota state chief, put it, "[NLCB] turned out to be kind of a false promise that we were going to get additional funding, additional resources, support for school improvement . . . It just kind of turned into, 'Oh, we're just going to test kids and put out these failing lists of schools.'"[12]

While the law required districts to offer students supplementary education services, just 17 percent of eligible students ever took advantage of the program.[13] Rural students, in particular, struggled to gain access, citing transportation problems, lack of Internet availability, and geographic barriers stemming from their remote locations.[14] In Dallas, officials called the program a federally mandated "racket," with providers "recruiting students with promises of iPods and other gifts" to get a share of the $200 million the district dedicated to the program over five years.[15] Allegations of fraud in the program led to an Office of Inspector General investigation, which turned up findings of falsified records, corruption by public officials, and use of improper financial incentives to enroll students.[16] A 2007 brief evaluating the program found that state and local administrators lacked the expertise to provide effective oversight and that results for participating students were uneven.[17]

Participation in public school choice, which allowed students in failing schools to transfer to higher-quality alternatives, was even lower, reaching just 1 percent of eligible students. Districts often did not adequately notify families of their rights to transfer and sometimes actively dissuaded them from participating.[18] One notification letter that went home to eligible families in Clark County, Nevada, warned, "Will your child miss friends he/she made? Will there be a loss of continuity of instruction and/or of the extra programs your home school has as a result of receiving Title I funds? How early will your child have to get up to catch the bus?"[19] And even without such warnings, some families opted to keep their children at the neighborhood school rather than send them to an unfamiliar environment.

NCLB required states and districts to offer struggling schools assistance and supported them in doing so via Title I set-asides targeted toward capacity building. All states established systems of support and provided some form of assistance to schools identified for improvement.[20] But very often, these supports did not meet the needs of struggling schools, offering little more than a "school support team" who lacked authority to make changes to school budgets, staffing, or curriculum.[21]

Unsurprisingly, many schools advanced disjointed school improvement plans and failed to address systemic issues around staffing and resource allocation.[22] The most radical restructuring options, such as closure, staff replacement, or chartering, were rarely pursued. States and districts, which were charged with offering oversight and assistance, more often than not lacked the capacity to provide effective support.[23] By 2009, over thirteen thousand American schools were under some form of improvement status.[24] Of those in restructuring between 2006 and 2009, just 12 percent (503 schools) improved enough to exit.

These challenges substantially undermined political support and sparked a noteworthy political rebellion among states, which usually lack incentives to act collectively to resist federal mandates.[25] Thirty-eight states considered or passed legislation critical of specific provisions, and at least one state sued the administration in opposition (*Connecticut v. Spellings*).[26] By the mid-2000s, President George W. Bush's Secretary of Education Margaret Spellings declared the law a "toxic brand."[27]

Engineering Dramatic Action: School Improvement Under Obama

The shortcomings of previous federal efforts to support school improvement invited a new approach. Secretary of Education Arne Duncan, a reform firebrand who came to the Obama administration via Chicago, where he was formerly CEO of Chicago Public Schools under Mayor Richard Daly, was eager to use his post to engineer dramatic actions in persistently low performing schools. The Great Recession provided the perfect backdrop to induce states, districts, and schools to act in accordance with federal priorities as a condition to receive an infusion of federal funds. Duncan left his mark on school improvement through three ambitious programs: Race to the Top, the School Improvement Grant (SIG) program, and ESEA flexibility waivers (see table 2.1).

Together, these programs represented the nation's largest investment in school improvement ever. The SIG program alone expanded the federal government's previous investment in turnaround more than sevenfold, at a

TABLE 2.1   Obama administration shifts federal approach to turnaround

Initiative (year)	What it did	Impact on school turnaround
Race to the Top (2009) $4.3 billion	Winning states received hundreds of millions of dollars in exchange for putting forth bold reform plans on standards, assessments, teacher evaluation, and turnaround.	States were required to use one of four federally sanctioned turnaround strategies.
School Improvement Grant program (2009) $3.5 billion	Low performing schools were provided ~$2 million over three years to support improvement.	
ESEA flexibility waivers (2012)	States were granted a reprieve from key provisions of NCLB.	

cost of $3.5 billion in the first year alone, with participating schools receiving approximately $2 million per year for up to three years.

The Obama administration sought to make good on the perceived failings of NCLB. NCLB required states to identify schools in need of improvement for failing to make progress toward the universal proficiency standard. This resulted in 38 percent of all schools failing to make AYP by 2011.[28] The Obama administration offered states new flexibility around identifying schools in need of improvement, focusing attention on the lowest achieving 5 percent of Title I schools statewide.[29] This brought substantial relief to states struggling under the weight of the sheer number of schools requiring intervention.

Moreover, recognizing that upward of 80 percent of schools identified for restructuring under NCLB chose the amorphous "other" option, the administration deliberately limited state and local discretion and required more ambitious turnaround strategies. As the program regulations for SIG describe, "After nearly a decade of broad state and local discretion in implementing, with little success, the school improvement provisions of ESEA, the department believes, for the purpose of this program, it is appropriate and necessary to limit that discretion and require the use of a carefully developed set of school intervention models in the nation's lowest achieving schools."[30]

The new approach to turnaround required districts to put in place contentious changes to schools. Based in part on Secretary Duncan's experience in Chicago, where his tenure included closing sixty schools and reopening a dozen others under new leadership, the administration's approach to turnaround was based on the widely held belief in reform circles that low performing schools are largely staffed by ineffective teachers and leaders.[31] As Duncan remarked on those reforms in a 2009 interview, "I was convinced that because students were performing at such . . . low levels that we, educators, were part of the problem."[32]

Schools subject to intervention would be required to put in place one of four improvement strategies:

- *Transformation.* Schools were required to replace the principal, adopt a teacher and principal evaluation system that accounted for student achievement growth, adopt a new governance structure, provide job-embedded professional development, institute comprehensive instructional reforms, and increase learning time.
- *Turnaround.* Schools were required to replace the principal and upward of half of the teaching staff, adopt a new governance structure, provide job-embedded professional development, institute comprehensive instructional reforms, and increase learning time.
- *Restart.* Schools were required to convert to a charter school or close and reopen under the management of a charter or education management organization.
- *Closure.* The district was required to close the school and enroll students in higher performing alternatives elsewhere in the district.

The programs also aimed to infuse dollars into local school systems just as many confronted the fiscal fallout stemming from the Great Recession. State funding per pupil dropped dramatically in the wake of falling tax revenues. Both RTTT and SIG helped local school systems stave off reductions in staff and other services. As one district leader noted, "The grant has been a stop-gap lifesaver to us in many ways, enabling us to continue moving forward when everything else is being cut."[33]

In some respects, the public supported the Obama administration's aims. In a 2009 poll asking how new federal dollars should be spent, support for improving low performing schools was second only to saving teachers' jobs among public priorities—36 percent versus 46 percent.[34] But history also suggests that the turnaround strategies embraced by the program were deeply unpopular among the public, given conflicts over firing teachers and administrators, charter conversions, and school closures.

The Obama administration's work on school turnaround had wide-ranging and disparate results. The programs brought fresh urgency to the plight of low performing schools, resulting in unprecedented attention from researchers and private consultants, as well as state and district administrators. Between 2009 and 2017, more than two thousand articles were written on turnaround in *Education Week*, compared to a mere six hundred in the prior two decades.

Among the eighteen states that were awarded RTTT grants, many responded to the Obama administration's efforts on school improvement by putting in place ambitious state-led turnaround strategies.[35] Tennessee leveraged its grant of $500 million to launch the Tennessee Achievement School District (ASD), a statewide turnaround district that would take over low performing schools and turn over their operations to nonprofit charter operators. While Tennessee developed new turnaround strategies, Massachusetts leveraged its grant to double down on its existing work supporting school improvement through school and district takeovers, as well as the launching of "Turnaround Corps"—a group of teachers and principals trained to improve low performing schools. Backed by supportive state legislatures, reform-friendly governors, and entrepreneurial state chiefs, Tennessee and Massachusetts embraced the kind of "transformative" change that the Obama administration sought.

More than fourteen hundred schools participated in the administration's SIG program, resulting in twenty school closures, fifty-eight charter conversions, and hundreds of teachers and principals losing their jobs in the name of improvement. Thousands of other schools were put on notice that persistent low performance would no longer be tolerated without serious consequences, a sea change from previous decades in which low performing schools may have been subject to public shaming, but were largely left alone.

But the impact of these initiatives on the schools and students that federal policy makers sought to help was uneven. Among the six rigorous evaluations of the SIG program, just two—California and Massachusetts—reported any positive impacts on student achievement, and in the case of California, those effects were quite modest given the costs of the program.[36] In early 2017, Mathematica released its long-awaited national evaluation of the program.[37] The report found that schools that received grants through the program were no more likely to post significant improvement in math or reading test scores, high school graduation, or college enrollment.

Case studies of implementation suggest that principal replacement did not always have its intended effects, either. While some schools' teachers reported benefiting from the infusion of new leadership, others struggled to adjust, citing lack of trust and adjustment to different leadership styles.[38] As one administrator reported, "A few places might have been better off if they had not had to change and go through a stop-start motion."[39]

Rural districts, which made up about one-fifth of the turnaround program, already faced shortages of qualified staff and SIG's replacement requirements added to their difficulty. As George Welsh, superintendent of a six-hundred-student district in Colorado, noted, "We didn't think that just firing half of our teachers and hiring whatever was available out there was necessarily going to be a higher-quality option than what we currently have."[40] In North Carolina, evaluators found that the program resulted in an increase in the number of inexperienced principals working in participating schools.[41] An evaluation of SIG in Texas found that the program had larger negative impacts on rural schools compared to their urban peers, likely reflecting the human capital challenges many rural districts face.[42]

These challenges were exacerbated by the short timeline on RTTT and SIG. Both programs were advanced as part of a broader national initiative to prop up state and local economies in the face of the Great Recession, and schools had just three years to design and implement their turnaround plans, including the expenditure of all awarded funds. As a result, state, district, and school administrators lacked the luxury of time to plan. Instead, they were, in the words of one district staffer, "building the plane as we fly it."[43] As the National Education Association reported, the lag between when states received federal funds and when they officially named schools to be awarded grants left some schools scrambling to put in place their turnaround plans just weeks before school started.[44]

In part as a result of these challenges, the Obama administration's efforts generated significant backlash among Democratic and Republican lawmakers as well as educators and administrators. Carlos García, the superintendent of the San Francisco Unified School District, openly worried that the program would reduce opportunities for innovation and disincentivize teachers and principals to take on the challenging work at low achieving schools.[45] Others voiced their concerns that the Department of Education's prescriptions were based more on a "hunch" than any evidence that the required models actually worked as improvement strategies.[46] In 2010, less than one year into implementation of the SIG program, Representative George Miller (D-California), Chairman of the House Education and Labor Committee, worried that the turnaround requirements were shortsighted: "You can . . . say you're going to turn around a school, you can reconstitute a school, you can close a school [but] it won't matter if you don't have [certain] ingredients in place . . . [including] collaboration, buy-in from the community, the empowering and the professional development of teachers."[47]

By 2015, policy retrenchment was on display as Congress worked to reauthorize ESEA through the Every Student Succeeds Act (ESSA). Under the new law, states regained substantial flexibility over school improvement and ED was explicitly barred from dictating specific turnaround strategies, marking a return to the state and local discretion that dominated school improvement prior to NCLB.

LESSONS LEARNED

The last two decades of federal education reform efforts have been shaped profoundly by the deceptively simple call to improve America's schools. Whether couched in a civil rights mandate or the desire to improve the nation's economic competitiveness, federal policy makers on the left and the right, Democratic and Republican, have embraced the idea that federal policy can and should fundamentally reshape educational opportunity in the United States. What can we learn from these efforts?

Lesson 1: Centralized Strategies Are Vulnerable to Problems

The Bush and Obama administrations sought to overcome the fragmented nature of education policy making in the United States—leveraging incentives and directives—to coerce and compel people to bring more urgency and creativity to their work. In a handful of cases they succeeded, with entrepreneurial state chiefs, local superintendents, and educators leveraging the political cover and money offered by the programs to deliver improved results for students. But for many others, the initiatives missed the mark, leaving wide swaths of educators and policy makers disaffected and far too many students still struggling.

The challenge of scaling effective turnaround strategies is aptly captured by what Richard Elmore called the "noble lie" of public administration.

Elmore argued that policy makers are unable to directly influence schools, and their efforts to do so, by prescribing permissible actions, are often ineffective because educators and administrators possess significant discretion and are constrained by countervailing organizational and political realities.

Where the administrations' initiatives found a receptive audience, they arguably found more success. In Massachusetts, where state chief Mitchell Chester, legislators, and districts had spent nearly a decade developing new strategies to support improvement in educator pipelines, school turnaround, and accountability, federal school improvement initiatives bore fruit. The impact of SIG on student achievement in Massachusetts rivaled the results attained by states' widely lauded, high performing charter schools.[48] Of course, Massachusetts may have achieved those results absent federal intervention, given state leaders' commitment to pursuing thoughtful improvement strategies.

But Massachusetts may be the exception that proves the rule. States, districts, and schools were not equally prepared to design, implement, and oversee the ambitious changes to staffing and school organization that the Bush and Obama administrations had sought. Weaknesses in state and district capacity, inadequate educator pipelines, and bureaucratic red tape made it difficult for schools to make good on their turnaround plans.

It is easy to chalk these challenges up to "implementation"—a notion that suggests that a stronger federal role could somehow resolve the problems that emerged. But that would be a mistake. Like all public policies, the school improvement initiatives launched by the Bush and Obama administrations depended on the commitment and capacity of other actors—state and district administrators, principals and teachers, families and community members. While policy can help to channel people's efforts toward common goals and create roadblocks to effective leadership, it is no substitute for entrepreneurial action.

Lesson 2: You Can't "Idiot-Proof" School Reform

If the Bush and Obama administrations overestimated the power of policy to support school improvement, they underestimated the importance of leadership at the school, district, and state level. Observing the weaknesses in the implementation of prior school improvement initiatives, both administrations sought to "idiot-proof" reform by restricting leaders to pursuing particular strategies rather than enabling them to develop transformative changes of their own design.

But while the initiatives effectively forced the hand of many state and local leaders to pursue politically controversial and disruptive changes to schools, they offered no guarantees that leaders would exercise the appropriate creativity and caution in their execution. All too often, schools lacked the resources and flexibility required to undertake the reforms that federal policy makers sought, but were labeled "failing" all the same. District and state leaders were also hamstrung, infused with a compliance mentality shaped in large part by federal mandates.

The initiatives also limited the actions of leaders who may have been positioned to make good on the promise of school improvement through homegrown strategies. Under NCLB, the focus on a narrow set of goals (AYP) resulted in vast numbers of schools getting swept up into improvement efforts, diluting the meaning of low performance and efforts to address it. A prescriptive set of escalating interventions diverted resources toward strategies that would later be proven ineffective. In the case of the Obama administration, schools were forced to make disruptive changes to staff, with little consideration of whether such moves were the right ones. Districts that lacked access to qualified replacements or saw promise in an existing principal could not use their better judgment to pursue an alternative approach, a fact that particularly hurt rural schools caught up in the programs.

The lack of attention to leadership not only compromised the effectiveness of the administrations' programs, it also offered cover to lackluster leaders, who could rightly blame federal policy makers for their failures to improve low performing schools, and undermined the political legitimacy of school improvement, as educators and the public equated it with efforts to close schools, enrich consultants, fire teachers, and expand charter schools.

The Bush and Obama administrations' efforts grew out of the perceived failures of leaving such work to the whims of local leaders. But neither did the administrations' approaches provide a remedy for these challenges.

Lesson 3: There Are No "Silver Bullet" Solutions

For some, the failures of federal school improvement efforts under the Bush and Obama administrations are a sign that traditional schools and districts are unable to improve, too burdened with the sclerosis that comes with long-established institutions. Instead, they argue we should focus on developing new structures, via chartering and other market mechanisms. For others, the limits of federal dictates are evidence of the primacy of educators, superintendents, and local school boards in determining how and what schools should improve.

It is ironic, of course, that those who deem federal school improvement efforts a failure argue that what ails American education can be solved via simple solutions, whether those are based in our faith in professionals or in our skepticism of them. Like turnarounds, the effectiveness of charter schools hinges upon actors whom federal policy makers do not control. And while it may be easier to set a new organization up for success, compared to reorienting a long-standing one, charter schools are not insulated from the political and other forces that can make or break any reform effort.

Like their critics, the Bush and Obama administrations engaged in a search for simple solutions to what ails low performing schools. These efforts have largely reflected a bias—toward whole-school improvement strategies rather than more discrete ones, and for rapid improvement rather than incremental progress. This has resulted in a predictable morass, with escalating calls for quick fixes that end in frustration and failure.

Federal reformers have paid much less attention to the messy work of improving curriculum, offering high-quality professional development, developing new pipelines of teachers and leaders, and transforming district central offices. While organizations like Summit Learning, Relay Graduate School, and 4.0 Schools are unlikely to take a failing school from bad to great, they can add to the toolkit available to school, district, and state leaders looking to improve education and expand students' access to quality educational experiences. Federal policy makers can provide financial support to such efforts as well as offer opportunities for researchers to study their impacts on students.

Lesson 4: People and Culture Matter in School Reform

Recognizing the institutional inertia that accompanies long-standing organizations like school districts and state education agencies, the Bush and Obama administrations sought to discipline school and system leaders through a mix of mandates and incentives. The idea was a simple one: without outside pressure, states, districts, and schools would choose the path of least resistance and continue to struggle.

But neither administration appreciated how important people are to school reform. Implementation of the administrations' school improvement programs was compromised by the complex, multilayered system of education governance, which required states, districts, schools, and, in many cases, contractors, to take on significant roles. For their part, states were charged with holding schools and districts accountable and overseeing implementation of new turnaround strategies. With few exceptions, states' oversight was weak at every point in the process. Districts were key intermediaries in the program, making principal appointments and shaping schools' operational flexibility, hiring and dismissal practices, and access to effective support. But many districts struggled to instigate and support evidence-based turnaround strategies. Schools ran up against rules that prevented them from expanding learning time or implementing a teacher evaluation system. Others were shortchanged by collective bargaining provisions that left them vulnerable to "last-in, first-out" teacher dismissals and less strategic approaches to teacher hiring.

Across the Bush and Obama administrations' school improvement programs, success was compromised by the reality that many districts lacked access to enough effective principals and teachers to support turnaround efforts. Much has been written about the human capital challenges facing Title I schools, but neither administration sought to address the substantial barriers districts face to recruiting more effective teachers and principals. With such replacements in short supply, the Obama administration's demand to put in place new leaders in low performing schools often did little more than "rearrange the deck chairs." As Caitlin Scott, a researcher at the Center on Education Policy, noted, "The money doesn't create new people. The problem of staffing a hard-to-staff school is more complicated, and we haven't really solved that problem yet."

Perhaps more than anything else, what unified the Bush and Obama administrations' approaches to school improvement was the bias toward policy as a lever for change. But *how* policies are carried out depends much more on the culture of professionalism that exists in state education agencies, school districts, and schools than it does on the rules promulgated by lawmakers and bureaucracies. Thus, as Frederick Hess has observed, "real change requires that the reform coalition focus much more attentively on the second half of the improvement agenda: cultivating and supporting teachers, principals, district leaders, and state officials willing and able to rethink old norms."[49] Federal policy makers, of course, cannot instigate culture change directly, but they can invest in new pipelines that prepare principals and teachers to lead the work, encourage states to revise licensing laws, and support fledgling efforts to better prepare state and district leaders to engage in the hard-knock work of politics and management.

Lesson 5: Research Too Often Leaves Policy Makers' Questions Unanswered

Researchers have long known that effective programs hinge on implementation and that variability in local contexts can make "what works" difficult to define with any degree of reliability. But the belief that evidence can be used definitively to design effective programs at scale remains deeply ingrained in both policy and research circles. An evidence-based approach to school improvement is not as simple as picking the "right" policy or program; it requires understanding whether initiatives have a chance of success in a particular context—given existing leadership, capacity, and political dynamics—and adapting the approach to deal with on-the-ground realities. An appreciation of these factors goes well beyond what policy analysts consider when they talk about "implementation" in education research.

Researchers should do more to examine not just whether programs are implemented with fidelity but also how effects vary across different organizational and political circumstances. While policy analysts like to discuss "point estimates," which describe the average effect of this or that, the real story in program evaluation rests in the variation. While ESSA has bolstered demands for evidence-based interventions, it has done little to address the misaligned incentives for researchers, which emphasize rigorous experimental methods to the detriment of research that would enable us to understand *how* and *why* programs work in some contexts but not others.

CONCLUSION

It is tempting to describe the Bush and Obama administrations as unique visionaries, casting aside previous approaches and instilling a new approach to school improvement, but that would be wrong. Their strategies represented an accumulation of nearly a century of reform efforts focused on "rationalizing" educational systems from above to make them more productive for both students and taxpayers as well as less subject to the political whims of entrenched interest groups. As Jal Mehta writes in *The Allure of Order*, "What began at the turn of the century as a movement from highly variable one-room schoolhouses to a district-level 'one best system' had by century's end become a national effort to use the power of the federal government to create uniformity across the nation's public schools."[50]

While the reform strategies under the Bush and Obama administrations differed in their particulars, they shared some common elements. Each sought to address gaps in local commitment and capacity by leveraging federal authority and resources. Through a logic of consequences, federal policy makers would push and prod states, districts, and schools toward more effective action.

There is little question that their efforts helped to shed new light on the challenges facing low performing schools and renewed urgency for resolving them. These are not trivial outcomes, given that for far too long these issues had been ignored by states and school districts. But neither administration was able to make good on its promise to significantly improve struggling schools or vastly expand the educational opportunities available to the low-income children and children of color assigned to them.

Any casual observer of school reform knows that discussions among advocates, policy makers, and other would-be reformers plays out as a clash of ideas, more focused on prescribing "what works" than on dealing with the nuance of policy design and implementation. But a failure to learn from the challenges that emerged through the most ambitious programs yet to tackle school improvement would be a mistake. As Karl Marx famously declared, "History repeats itself. The first as tragedy, the second as farce."

3

Incentives and Inducements

The Feds Fight Federalism

Patrick McGuinn

The presidential administrations of George W. Bush and Barack Obama witnessed unprecedented federal efforts to press states to adopt a number of education reforms around test-based accountability. During the 2000–2016 period, the US Department of Education (ED) utilized a variety of carrots and sticks to reward and sanction states according to their fidelity to the federal school reform paradigm. This chapter examines the scope and impact of these efforts and highlights key lessons about the potential—and potential limits—of federal efforts to use incentives and inducements to reshape state education systems.

The most striking feature of American governance is federalism—the allocation of constitutional authority across federal and state governments—and nowhere is its impact more profound than in education. Our multilevel and fragmented education governance structure and strong tradition of local control have made the creation of national policy in education—and national standards and assessments in particular—much more complex, both politically and administratively.[1] Yet persistent racial and socioeconomic achievement gaps, global economic competition, and the weak performance of US students on international tests have amplified the call for some common goals and yardsticks to measure our children's academic performance, as well as more ambitious efforts to improve teacher quality and turn around chronically underperforming schools.

The US Constitution does not give the federal government the power to command states to do anything in the area of education. As a result, the federal government has had to rely on incentives and inducements to get states to embrace federal education goals. Beginning with the National Defense Education Act of 1958 and the Elementary and Secondary Education Act of 1965, national policy makers have used the grant-in-aid system to prod states to improve their public schools. In order to claim their share of a growing pot of federal education funds, states have had to agree to comply with a wide array of federal policy mandates. These mandates initially focused on ensuring more equitable school funding and access rather than the academic performance of students and schools. A new federal focus on accountability for student achievement and school reform was outlined in the Improving America's Schools Act of 1994 and was given more "teeth" during the George W. Bush administration with the No Child Left Behind Act (NCLB) of 2001.[2] NCLB sought to use the increased federal mandates and spending to prod states to adopt academic standards and proficiency benchmarks, implement annual testing, and intervene in underperforming schools. The Obama years saw a continued focus on test-based accountability, but also the use of competitive grant programs like Race to the Top and Investing in Innovation (I3) as well as conditional NCLB waivers to encourage states to adopt Common Core, expand charter schools, and revamp their teacher evaluation systems. These developments fundamentally altered the relationship between the federal government and the states in education policy; states resented this new level of federal involvement and struggled to comply with all of the federal mandates and implement the reforms effectively.

BUSH AND NO CHILD LEFT BEHIND

The scope, specificity, and ambition of NCLB's mandates signaled something akin to a revolution in federal education policy. As written, however, the legislation was a complex mix of federal mandates and state discretion. Although states were required to put standards and tests in place and create a system for dealing with failing schools, they were also entrusted with setting the rigor of these reforms. Given these crosscutting currents, much depended on how the law was implemented by the Bush Department of Education, and how it handled states' requests for flexibility, extensions, and waivers. On this count, states hoped that the administration would be as amenable as the Clinton administration had proved to be in implementing the 1994 legislation. Deeming NCLB the most promising path to deliver the cultural shift in schooling it sought, however, the Bush administration took a hard line and pushed states to comply with the letter of the law. While this forced states to take the law's mandates more seriously than they otherwise would have, it unsurprisingly sparked vocal complaints among educators, who argued that the law's goals and timetables were unrealistic and that the resources and guidance provided were insufficient.

One awkward question was how the Bush administration would respond to states that pushed back against the law's requirements in the name of federalism. The administration faced a thorny choice: acquiescing and accepting the efforts to undercut NCLB's reach, or aggressively challenging states that threatened to forfeit federal dollars in order to opt out of the NCLB regime. In a decision that caused consternation among conservatives concerned about federal overreach and the integrity of states' rights, the administration opted to use every tool at its disposal to keep states in line. Given the noble promise of NCLB's pledge that every child would be proficient in reading and math by 2014, along with its belief that allowing states to backslide would launch the nation on a slippery slope and undercut its effort to transform schooling, the administration successfully brought substantial pressure to bear when Utah and Connecticut challenged NCLB in court.

The Bush administration's aggressive implementation approach succeeded in getting states to comply with federal mandates and intervene to a greater extent than ever before in districts with failing schools. As Phyllis McClure, a longtime member of the Title I Independent Review Panel, observed: "NCLB has grabbed the education community's attention like no previous ESEA reauthorization. It has really upset the status quo in state and local offices ... For the first time, district and school officials are actually being required to take serious and urgent action in return for federal dollars."[3] NCLB's requirement that states conduct annual testing and report student scores forced states to build new data gathering and dissemination systems and resulted in a greater degree of transparency in public education than ever before. Scholars Tiffany Berry and Rebecca Eddy wrote that the law had "transformed the landscape of educational evaluation" and was "redefining what evaluation is within the education evaluation community."[4] The pressure to produce rapid gains in student achievement also pushed states to innovate at an unprecedented rate. Though the pace and extent of innovation varied widely across individual states, nationwide the number and variety of alternative schools (charters, magnets, virtual schools), alternative routes for teacher and administrator licensing, and new approaches to instruction grew dramatically in the wake of NCLB. The number of charter schools nationwide, for example, grew from 1,297 in 1999 to 5,043 in 2009.[5]

By holding states clearly accountable for the performance of their public schools, NCLB also prompted state departments of education to expand their capacity to monitor local districts, provide technical assistance, and intervene where necessary.[6] The law—combined with the rigorous enforcement by the Department of Education—pushed states to rapidly and fundamentally transform their student testing, data collection, and district monitoring systems. ED closely monitored state compliance efforts on both the front end—through the use of detailed accountability plans that each state had to submit for review—and on the back end, through regular state reporting and federal audits.[7] ED's Office of Inspector General conducted audits of state policies and their compliance with NCLB mandates, and demanded that states make changes where necessary.

In implementing NCLB, the Bush administration fundamentally altered the orientation of the federal Department of Education—shifting it from its historical role as a grant maker and compliance monitor to a more active role as a compliance enforcer and agitator. The administration emphasized the importance of bottom-line results in student achievement, shifting the traditional focus from regulation and process. State education agencies, however, struggled mightily to comply with the law's programmatic mandates and meet its timetables for moving students to academic proficiency. A large number of schools across the country were identified as "in need of improvement" for failing to meet Adequate Yearly Progress (AYP) targets. As a result, however, even as states struggled to implement the standards and testing frameworks mandated by NCLB, they were also being forced to apply corrective measures to failing Title I schools (such as providing technical assistance and allowing students to choose a better school). In some states this was particularly difficult due to the large number of schools that had failed to meet AYP repeatedly and therefore qualified for more intensive corrective actions such as reconstitution.[8]

As intended, NCLB forced states and districts to focus more attention and resources on chronically low performing students and schools, though to widely varying effect. In their research on North Carolina, Thomas Ahn and Jacob Vigdor found that the most common restructuring action taken was to replace a struggling school's principal and that the change had a positive impact on student achievement.[9] Overall, however, a variety of concerns were raised about the design and implementation of the test-based accountability system at the heart of NCLB and the ways in which it fell short of its goals and produced unintended negative consequences in American classrooms.

Paul Manna has highlighted how NCLB created perverse incentives that led schools and states to adopt counterproductive compliance behaviors—such as teaching to the test, narrowing the curriculum, focusing on "bubble kids" rather than student growth, and lowering standards—which undermined NCLB's ultimate goals.[10] Despite the implementation and political challenges engendered by the law, one of its enduring legacies was the institutionalization of assessment and accountability in state education systems.

Though the lessons of NCLB were hotly debated, many observers highlighted the need for states to expand their capacity to support school reform and for the federal government to be less prescriptive about school turnaround measures. A 2011 RAND study concluded that "in providing both support and flexibility to states, the federal government might wish to consider both traditional inducements to support equity and other policy approaches to help build key state capacities where they are lacking; to induce innovation, evaluation, and dissemination of effective solutions as they arise; to develop independent expertise to help states; and to build networks to foster communication and problem solving."[11] One area of consensus about NCLB that emerged among researchers, and that would shape federal education policy during the Obama era, was that the law was too loose on standards and assessments and too tight on accountability. This enabled—even encouraged—states to relax their standards, proficiency targets, and/or tests (which precluded the collection of realistic and comparable achievement data) even as states were bound to implement a rigid (and sometimes inappropriate) timetable of federal remedies for struggling schools.

THE OBAMA EDUCATION AGENDA

While Bush had relied on the traditional formula grant system in ESEA (and the threat of losing those grants) to provide states with inducements to enact federal reforms, Obama took a different approach. Faced with divided control and partisan gridlock in Congress—which was not able to reauthorize ESEA, the largest federal education program, until his last year in office—the Obama administration opted to make education policy unilaterally from the executive branch with a creative, expansive, and controversial use of executive power.

Through the use of competitive grant programs such as Race to the Top (RTTT), School Improvement Grants (SIG), Investing in Innovation (I3), and the NCLB waiver process, the administration was able to incentivize states to enact important policy changes, particularly around charter schools, Common Core standards and assessments, school turnarounds, and teacher evaluation. The administration's aggressive push on school reform, however, eventually led to a political backlash against those same reforms and against federal involvement in education more generally, which resulted in an ESEA reauthorization (the 2015 Every Student Succeeds Act) that rolls back the federal role in K–12 schooling in important ways.

Race to the Top

As the Obama administration set out to craft its school reform blueprint, it faced both a significant political challenge and an unusual fiscal opportunity. The political challenge centered on the growing opposition by states (and many in Congress) to NCLB and coercive federal education mandates.[12] States had struggled mightily to implement the law, and while some studies show that it had a modest positive effect on student achievement, it did not generate as much progress in closing student achievement gaps as was originally hoped.[13] This context, combined with a Republican-controlled Congress, made it impossible for the administration to reach a compromise over the pending ESEA reauthorization and foreclosed (until the very end of its second term) the administration's efforts to codify its preferred school reform strategies in legislation. It would have to identify a different strategy for driving state education policy, and this is where the unusual fiscal opportunity played a crucial role.

The "Great Recession" that helped usher Obama into office in 2008 also led Congress to enact the American Recovery and Reinvestment Act (ARRA) of 2009 (colloquially known as the "stimulus bill"). The $800 billion program directed $100 billion in spending to education, the majority of which went to preserve teachers' jobs and fund existing programs. However, ARRA also set aside a smaller pot of $4.35 billion for "state incentive grants." The legislation provided little detail on the purposes of the grants or the process for distributing them and thus gave wide discretion to the US Department of Education. Secretary Arne Duncan ultimately decided that the grants would be distributed through a competitive state application process, which he called Race to the Top. RTTT—along with related $3 billion School Improvement Grant and $650 million Investing in Innovation funds for districts and nonprofits—was intended to provide a major federal investment to support promising educational reforms, and to reward states and districts at the "intersection of courage, capacity, and commitment," in Duncan's words. In

2009, ED announced that state applications would be graded on a five-hundred-point scale according to the rigor of the reforms proposed and their compatibility with four administration priorities: improving teacher training, evaluation, and retention policies; developing common standards and assessments; developing better data systems; and adopting certain school turnaround strategies.

The use of a competitive grant process to distribute such a large amount of federal education funds was innovative and unprecedented, as most federal funds have historically been distributed through categorical grant programs that allocated money to districts on the basis of need-based formulas.[14] States and districts in this traditional model received funding automatically based on their state educational needs (the number of poor, English as a second language, or special education students, for example), regardless of the performance of their schools or the alignment of state education policies with federal priorities. Under RTTT (as well as I3 and SIG), however, states had to compete with one another and received a grant only if they adopted (or promised to adopt) reforms that were compatible with federal goals and approaches.[15] The administration's guidelines for RTTT applications were "extraordinarily prescriptive" and incentivized states to enact policies that aligned with the Obama administration's education agenda.[16] Timothy Conlan and Paul Posner see this approach as part of the Obama administration's "hybrid model of federal policy innovation and leadership, which mixes money, mandates, and flexibility in new and distinctive ways . . . The model represents a blend of, but is different from, both cooperative and coercive federalism."[17]

Desperate for federal funds during a time of state budget crises, forty-six states applied during the first two rounds of the RTTT competition, with only Alaska, North Dakota, Texas, and Vermont declining to participate. Forty states applied in round one, which Tennessee and Delaware won with grants of $500 million and $100 million, respectively. Thirty-five states (as well as Washington, DC) applied for the second round of RTTT, with ten winners: Florida, Georgia, Hawaii, Maryland, Massachusetts, New York, North Carolina, Ohio, Rhode Island, and Washington, DC. The application guidelines also encouraged, and rewarded states for, engaging a wide variety of education stakeholders in the crafting of their applications. The *Washington Post* (2010) declared that RTTT "helped transform the national discussion on education," while the Policy Innovators in Education (PIE) network praised the way that "the competition spurred dramatic shifts in political will" and "created tremendous pressure on states to develop bold plans for school reform."[18]

RTTT's emphasis on expanding charter schools, adopting common academic standards and tests, and revamping teacher accountability helped open up a rift in the Democratic Party on school reform and changed the political climate around these controversial issues, paving the way for states to adopt new policies. The group Democrats for Education Reform declared that "the change unleashed by conditioning federal funding on bold and forward-looking state education policies is indisputable. Under the president's leadership, local civil rights, child advocacy, business, and education reform groups, in collaboration with those states and local teacher unions ready for change, sprung into action to achieve things that they had been waiting and wanting to do for years."[19]

RTTT succeeded in pushing states to enact a wide variety of education reform policies in order to make their grant applications more competitive or to fulfill the commitments they made in them. A 2011 Center on Education Policy survey of state education officials concluded that "nearly all of the dozens of ARRA-related reform strategies included in our survey are being acted on by a majority—often a large majority—of the responding states."[20] State actions on teacher quality reforms are illustrative in this regard. Despite recognition of the importance of teacher quality to educational outcomes and considerable research that questioned the efficacy of existing state teacher evaluation, tenure, and dismissal policies, before RTTT very few states had taken action to address the issue.[21] President Obama and Secretary Duncan effectively used the bully pulpit to draw attention to problems in existing state teacher evaluation and tenure systems and, combined with the incentives of RTTT and NCLB waivers, prompted an unprecedented wave of reforms. The National Council on Teacher Quality reported that thirty-six states (and Washington, DC) changed their teacher evaluation policies between 2009 and 2012.[22]

In the most in-depth analysis of the impact of RTTT conducted to date, William Howell found that in the wake of the competition (2009–2014), states on average enacted 68 percent of the "reform policies" it encouraged, while in the seven years before the competition (2001–2008) they averaged only a 10 percent adoption rate. Howell concluded that "the surge of post-2009 policy activity constitutes a major accomplishment for the Obama administration. With a relatively small amount of money, little formal constitutional authority in education, and without the power to unilaterally impose his will on state governments, President Obama managed to jump-start policy processes that had languished for years in state governments across the country."[23] States used their RTTT funds to implement a wide variety of new initiatives: Maryland trained a team of teachers and a principal from every school in the state on Common Core, Ohio districts hired former principals with strong track records to coach principals in struggling schools, Tennessee built an early warning data system to track student performance and alert teachers, and Hawaii increased the rigor of its graduation requirements.[24]

However, building the capacity at both the district and state education agency level to implement the reforms pushed by RTTT (and the NCLB waiver program) proved to be a major challenge across the country.[25] States and districts struggled to secure the financial, personnel, and technical resources to support schools with this work. In a 2011 survey of state education agencies (SEAs), Cynthia Brown and her colleagues noted that the wave of reforms had "put immense stress on agencies that were originally conceived as tiny departments primarily designed to funnel money to local school districts. Yet it is not at all clear that state education agencies are prepared for this demanding new role."[26] A 2011 Center on Education Policy survey found that operating budgets for a majority of SEAs had declined by 10 percent or more since 2007, and that "only a handful of states believe they have all three elements in place—adequate expertise, staffing levels, and funding—to carry out key American Recovery and Reinvestment Act (ARRA)–related reform activities."[27] While policy enactment is significant, educational improvements are unlikely to occur absent effective implementation of those policies, and it is clear that SEAs continue to face large capacity gaps as they undertake this work.[28] Some observers have argued that the Obama administration made a major strategic miscalculation with RTTT and NCLB waivers by pushing states to adopt multiple major education reforms simultaneously and to implement them concurrently on a short timetable, thus increasing the odds of implementation problems and political pushback.[29]

NCLB Waivers

NCLB was originally scheduled to be reauthorized in 2007, but disagreements between Congress and President Obama—and between congressional Democrats and Republicans—about the future of federal education policy resulted in the law not being revised and reauthorized until December 2015. In the interim, states struggled with the costs and consequences of implementing the law, as more and more schools failed to meet their NCLB-mandated goals of increased student proficiency (and 100 percent proficiency by 2014) and education leaders clamored for relief. As Kenneth Wong observed, "the Obama administration saw a policy window in the absence of ESEA reauthorization to advance some of its reform priorities."[30] It decided to act unilaterally, announcing an ESEA flexibility plan in 2011 that would enable states to apply to the US Department of Education for a waiver from NCLB's accountability provisions. In a speech announcing the program, President Obama stated: "I've urged Congress for a while now, let's get a bipartisan effort to fix this. Congress hasn't been able to do it. So I will . . . Given that Congress cannot act, I am acting." Elizabeth Mann observed that this made strategic sense: "The ESEA Flexibility waivers allowed the Obama administration to respond to increasing pressure to change the unpopular law but also helped them avoid another legislative battle in the immediate wake of the acrimonious ACA debates."[31]

ESEA contains a specific provision (section 9401) that permits education secretaries to issue waivers from federal regulations, and previous secretaries had used this authority regularly. What was new with these NCLB waivers was that the administration made the granting of them *conditional*, which was much more controversial and appears to be unprecedented in education. Secretary Duncan created a list of eighteen sets of policy commitments across four reform areas that states had to make in order to be eligible to receive a waiver: develop a plan for SEA systems and processes to monitor and assist district school improvement efforts; adopt college- and career-ready standards (such as the Common Core); develop a plan to identify and improve the bottom 15 percent of schools; and create teacher and principal evaluation systems "based on multiple valid measures, including student progress over time."[32] Members of Congress from both parties criticized the administration for attempting to legislate education policy from the executive branch, and called the conditional waiver program a violation of the separation of powers. Rep. John Kline (R-MN), for example, remarked: "In my judgment, [President Obama] is exercising an authority and power he doesn't have. We all know the law is broken and needs to be changed. But this is part and parcel with the whole picture with this administration: they cannot get their agenda through Congress, so they're doing it with executive orders and rewriting rules. This is executive overreach."[33]

Despite these reservations, most states were desperate to get out from under the NCLB accountability system and the majority of states applied for a waiver; as of November 2014, forty-three states had received them.[34] Significantly, the US Department of Education threatened to revoke a state's waiver if it did not meet the commitments in its application, and issued regular state-by-state monitoring reports on their progress. ED placed several states on warning status for losing their waivers and did in fact revoke the waivers of Washington (for failing to reform its teacher evaluation system) and Oklahoma (for rejecting Common Core).

As with RTTT, the application process for NCLB waivers succeeded in driving a significant—if widely varying—amount of education reform in states. An analysis of state waiver applications by the Center for American Progress concluded: "Overall, we found that states are proposing significant reforms compared to what was required or practiced under NCLB . . . Some states are pushing new ideas, many of which are promising or innovative, by ensuring all students graduate college- and career-ready, developing differentiated accountability systems, and improving teacher and leader effectiveness."[35] Fourteen second-round waiver applicants, for example, proposed to add subjects beyond reading and math (such as science, writing, and history) to their accountability systems. Additionally, many states (including Rhode Island) devised new school turnaround strategies, and a number of other states (such as Utah) began to incorporate student academic growth (rather than just proficiency) into their school rating systems. In another study of the waiver program's impact, Wong found that while "states made greater progress in meeting some of the federal expectations than others," on the whole the "administration has enjoyed substantial success in using the waiver process to leverage states to adopt policy changes."[36]

Common Core

Perhaps the most significant policy change spurred by RTTT and NCLB waivers was widespread state adoption of Common Core academic standards and its aligned assessments. Standards advocates believed that states needed incentives and support to build the systems necessary, but that a direct federal mandate (grant-in-aid condition) to adopt the Core would infuriate people across the political spectrum and likely doom the effort. The strategy that emerged was to cast the standards as "national but not federal" and have the federal government incentivize (but not require) states to adopt them. The carrots that the federal government used to encourage states to adopt the Core were the RTTT grant competition and the NCLB waiver application process. As noted in chapter 6 of this volume, this approach was remarkably successful—by 2010 forty-six states had adopted the Core and forty-four had adopted aligned assessments. Meanwhile, a new focus on college and career readiness also pushed state K–12 and higher education systems toward greater collaboration and alignment.[37]

As states moved toward full implementation of the new standards and assessments during the 2014–2015 school year, however, an anti–Common Core coalition gained strength. Some objections to the Common Core were shared across ideologies: a perception that the standards took a one-size-fits-all approach, created a de facto national curriculum, put too much emphasis on standardized tests, might threaten student privacy, and undermined teacher autonomy. Moreover, the Common Core was quickly linked to the emerging antitesting backlash. While the Core standards were separate from the new assessments—states can and have adopted the standards but not the tests—they became conflated in the public mind.

Tea Party adherents and others on the right viewed the Common Core as a dangerous—even unconstitutional—expansion of federal control into education and a violation of states' rights. The Obama administration's use of RTTT and NCLB waivers to encourage states to adopt the standards, and its funding of the two consortia that developed the aligned assessments, fed concerns that Uncle Sam was becoming the national schoolmarm. This involvement, along with the Obama administration's vocal and oft-repeated support for the Core, made it easy for opponents to cast it as a federal initiative. Despite the extensive media coverage, ad campaigns, social media activity, and legislative repeal efforts, however, as of spring 2015 forty of the original forty-five states that adopted the Common Core remained committed to them. As we have already seen, it is more likely that states will pull out of the two major assessment consortia (PARCC and SBAC), which may ultimately constrain the potential impact of the new standards on American education. States also witnessed unprecedented rates of students opting out of tests during the 2014–2015 academic year, and as of February 2017, only twenty-one states remained in the test consortia. It would be incredibly ironic if federal incentives and inducements designed to push states to embrace test-based accountability ultimately resulted in the undermining of faith in the entire idea of standardized testing.

Getting so many states to adopt (and retain) common standards is a significant accomplishment, but ultimately the story of the Common Core may be one of missed opportunity. To achieve the kind of systemic reform and educational impact that was originally envisioned, the standards need to be accompanied by concerted changes in testing, teacher prep, instructional materials, and professional development. The short-term boost in adoption encouraged by RTTT and waivers not only fueled political pushback but also crippled the coalition and agenda that were going to do all of these other things on a big scale. This suggests that the trade-offs of using carrots may not just be about creating political chops, but that there are also lessons about how those chops affect complex implementation realities downstream—potentially in ways that undermine one's larger objectives. RTTT and NCLB waiver carrots, for example, forced teacher evaluation reform activity to play out in political time, and in the same window as Common Core State Standards and new tests, which caused all kinds of complications. In this sense, carrots aren't just a spur to action, they're a spur to action *on certain timelines*—and typically jumble multiple reforms together in the spirit of taking advantage of policy windows.

How the use of federal carrots and sticks intertwines with the larger political and educational ecosystems also deserves further consideration. The interplay of inducements and incentives with the presidential bully pulpit and the activities of philanthropy that supersized federal activity can serve to curb criticism or pushback among the swath of mainstream education advocates, reformers, and pundits. The widespread absence of mainstream questioning on NCLB, RTTT, I3, and waivers, meanwhile, may enable policy makers to circumvent constructive criticism during the policy design stage and/or obviate the need to articulate and disseminate a rationale for the reforms to the general public.

The Every Student Succeeds Act

Congress finally passed the long-overdue reauthorization of NCLB in 2015, achieving bipartisan passage of the Every Student Succeeds Act (ESSA). Many observers saw the new law as a reaction against the Bush and Obama administrations' activism in education. Upon its passage, when asked about the future of the federal role in education, Senator Lamar Alexander remarked, "I think it will be very different. Everybody was really fed up with Washington telling 100,000 public schools so much about what to do and it was really creating a backlash on efforts to set higher standards, namely Common Core and teacher evaluation."[38] While the standards, assessment, and reporting mandates of NCLB remain, the law clearly reduces federal authority in some areas, particularly around accountability and what states have to do to turn around underperforming schools. There is also strong language in the law prohibiting the US education secretary from forcing or encouraging states to adopt any *particular* set of standards such as the Common Core.

The key takeaway here—and the big shift from NCLB—is that federal compliance monitoring of state accountability and school improvement efforts will be considerably reduced. ESSA also explicitly prohibits attaching conditions to federal education waivers, thus denying future education secretaries the tool that Duncan used to such effect. A federal focus on compliance auditing for civil rights violations, waste, fraud, and abuse will continue. Beyond this, however, the feds will have to rely on guidance more than enforcement to steer state accountability and school improvement policies, and states are not required to intervene in 95 percent of their schools. There is some irony here: while the Obama administration was able to successfully stimulate state policy change through the creative use of federal mandates, waivers, and grant competitions, the effort generated a backlash in defense of state rights and local control. As a result, ESSA very intentionally seeks to constrain federal power in education and to limit the kinds of incentives and inducements available to the US education secretary to try to influence state policy in the future.

Predictably, the reduced role of the federal government outlined in ESSA (and in the Trump administration's pronouncements) has been met with both praise and alarm, with some hopeful that increased state flexibility will return schools to local control and unleash innovation, while others warn that states are likely to respond by devoting less effort and fewer resources toward improving schools, and particularly those that serve disadvantaged students.[39] Thus, while many of NCLB's key components remain in place, and a significant role for the national government in K–12 education policy will continue, it is possible that we may well have witnessed the apogee of federal power in education.

LESSONS LEARNED

Lesson 1: Incentives and Inducements Can Spur Change

A key lesson of the 2000–2016 period is that federal incentives and inducements of the sort employed by the Bush and Obama administrations *can* generate significant state policy change and can do so in a relatively short period of time. It is also clear, however, that America's philosophical commitment to state rights and local control in education remains strong, and that federal ambitions for schools will always encounter political resistance and implementation challenges. In addition, getting states to enact preferred federal policy changes does not ensure that states will "own them" or remain committed to them over time. As Frederick Hess has observed, the federal government can force states to do things in education, but it cannot force them to do things *well*.

Lesson 2: Policies Must Address the Capacity Challenge

For policies to have their desired effect of improving student outcomes, however, they have to be implemented effectively, and this requires states to have capacity in their education agencies that is often lacking. As David Cohen and Susan Moffitt have observed, the federal government's ambitious goals in NCLB were not matched by sufficient attention to how teachers and administrators could realize these goals; there was a large disconnect between policy and practice.[40] NCLB (as well as Obama-era policies) ultimately forced states to change many of their educational practices, but political resistance and capacity gaps at the state level meant that these changes were often more superficial than substantive.[41] NCLB did not generate as much meaningful school improvement or progress in closing student achievement gaps as was originally hoped, making it abundantly clear that most state departments of education were ill equipped to monitor compliance with their own policies or engage in effective district- and school-level interventions.[42]

Similar capacity challenges were apparent as states struggled to implement the ambitious reforms outlined in their RTTT and NCLB waiver plans. The dozen winners from the RTTT competition formally amended their plans frequently—usually to scale back proposed reforms or push back timetables. A 2015 report by the US Government Accountability Office found that states encountered a multitude of challenges due to rapid policy adoption, short implementation timelines, and the lack of adequate capacity in their education agencies.[43]

Lesson 3: Reforms Must Resist the Temptation to Do Too Much Too Quickly

Political scientists like to talk about the significance of "policy windows," the rare and fleeting alignment of political forces that enables major policy change in a particular issue area such as education. When such windows open—as with Bush and NCLB in 2000 and Obama and RTTT a decade later—policy makers are tempted to try to enact as much of their agenda as quickly as possible before the window closes. The Bush and Obama reform agendas pushed states to undertake a multitude of different reforms related to standards, testing, accountability, choice, and teacher quality simultaneously and to implement them all in a short span of time. Each of these policy changes was a heavy lift on its own for states; packaging them all together compounded the implementation challenge. This approach exacerbated the capacity problem just described and ultimately helped to reduce the potential impact of the reforms and the political support for them.

The temptation to rush through open policy windows can also create political problems downstream if reforms are inadequately explained to the general public or if supportive political coalitions at the state and local level are not created. NCLB was widely seen (and resented) by state policy makers and citizens alike as a program pushed down their throats. The speed and process by which states adopted the Common Core and took on the Race to the Top application process without much public discussion or debate, though it initially seemed so effective, would ultimately generate anger and resentment and a perception of subterfuge that crossed party lines.

Lesson 4: The Politics of Accountability Is Problematic

Holding anyone accountable for school performance—whether students, teachers, or school administrators—is politically difficult and has no natural constituency. And this is particularly true for accountability for the educational performance of poor and minority kids, whose parents tend to have fewer political resources to advocate for equity. NCLB renewed doubts about whether states had the political will to address the problem of underperforming schools. States used their discretion under the law to manipulate their accountability systems by lowering their standards, making their tests easier, and/or decreasing their proficiency cut scores. Such actions were widely criticized for dumbing down the curriculum and undermining the law's school accountability system.[44] Similarly, many states used NCLB waivers (and ESSA plans) to create less ambitious and/or more ambiguous goals for closing achievement gaps.

Lesson 5: The State Role Has Been Invigorated

The Bush and Obama eras are rightly seen as a time of expanded (and unprecedented) federal activism in education. An important, if less recognized, legacy of this federal activism, however, is an invigorated role for state policy makers and state departments of education as drivers for educational improvement. While this obviously varies across the fifty states, as a whole states are much more deeply engaged in education reform than they were prior to 2000, and this engagement appears unlikely to fully recede even as federal mandates decline. NCLB held states (for the first time) accountable for the performance of school districts, while the design of the RTTT application process put governors and chief state school officers in charge of drafting state applications. By empowering these "education executives," RTTT may be speeding up what political scientist Jeffrey Henig calls "the end of educational exceptionalism" and elevating the importance of school reform debates in mainstream politics.[45] This appears to have accelerated the trend toward greater centralization of education policy making at the state level and, in particular, greater involvement of governors in school reform.[46]

Lesson 6: What the Feds Ask for, and When They Ask for It, Matters a Lot

The ultimate effectiveness of federal incentives and inducements depends a lot on timing and context, as states may be more willing and able to embrace federal ambitions in education at certain points in time than others. The Obama administration's grant competitions were able to leverage so much policy change because of states' dire fiscal situation during the recession; similarly, states were willing to make major promises to receive conditional NCLB waivers because they were desperate to get out from under the escalating changes required by the law's accountability system. Incentives are also more effective when implementation of reforms occurs immediately rather than downstream, such as with removing data firewalls or lifting charter caps under RTTT. More ambiguous, promise-laden commitments, such as reforming teacher evaluation systems, are more difficult for states to enact and sustain over time once the competition has ended and federal checks have been cashed.

CONCLUSION

The Bush and Obama administrations embraced an expansive view of the federal role in education, and one built on a test-based accountability framework. Bush used the greater spending and mandates contained in NCLB to induce states to undertake a massive reform effort aimed at reducing achievement gaps and turning around low performing schools. Obama, meanwhile, relied on the incentives of grant competitions and NCLB waivers to continue the accountability push and extend state reforms to new policy areas. Education reform is likely to be viewed as among the most significant domestic policy legacies of the two administrations. Their aggressive push on school reform, however, eventually led to a political backlash against test-based accountability and against federal involvement in education more generally, which resulted in an ESEA reauthorization (the Every Student Succeeds Act) that rolls back the federal role in K–12 schooling in some important ways.

However, ESSA for the most part is likely to return authority over education policy making *not* to the local level, but rather to the state level. A 2015 report from the Council of Chief State School Officers, for example, proclaimed that "regardless of this uncertainty at the federal level, state education leaders remain firmly committed to state accountability systems that support educators, parents, and students by providing useful information that leads to improved outcomes for all students."[47] While states have historically been relatively minor players in school reform, one of the enduring legacies of the Bush and Obama presidencies may well be the invigoration and expansion of the state role in education.[48] Going forward, states will now have considerably more latitude to determine their own education agendas, though also less political cover from federal mandates. What remains to be seen is if states have developed (or can develop) sufficient political will and administrative capacity to maintain the momentum that has built up behind education reform over the past two decades.[49] Precisely how states will utilize this newfound authority is unknown, but one thing is certain: flexibility from federal mandates will result in widely divergent state levels of commitment to school reform, a wide range of policy approaches, and widely varying levels of effectiveness in improving school outcomes across the fifty states.[50] That is American federalism at work, for better or worse.

4

Federal Efforts to Improve Teacher Quality

Matthew A. Kraft

In 1981, newly appointed Secretary of Education Terrel H. Bell convinced President Ronald Reagan to appoint the National Commission on Excellence in Education. The commission's landmark report, *A Nation at Risk*, first planted the seeds for a direct federal role in shaping the teaching profession in the United States. The report identified the poor skills and training of the current teacher workforce as one of four core causes of the "rising tide of mediocrity" in US public education. At the same time, the report warned that the "professional working life of teachers is on the whole unacceptable," and that serious shortages exist in key STEM fields. This call to arms was met with skepticism by President Reagan, who was committed to shrinking the already limited role of the federal government in education. Two decades later, however, Presidents George W. Bush and Barack Obama would answer this call by advancing major federal policy initiatives aimed at improving the quality of public school teachers in the United States.

Bush's and Obama's federal education reforms were remarkably similar in their goals and ambitions. Bush's No Child Left Behind (NCLB) Act and Obama's Race to the Top (RTTT) and NCLB state waiver programs leveraged federal funding and authority to address four broad areas: academic standards, data and accountability, teacher quality, and school turnarounds. This chapter focuses specifically on how these efforts have influenced the teaching profession. During Bush's and Obama's combined sixteen years in office, the federal government succeeded in fundamentally changing licensure requirements and evaluation systems for public school teachers. Reflecting on the successes and failures of these reforms provides important lessons about the potential and limitations of federal policy as a tool for improving the quality of the US teacher workforce.

TEACHER LICENSURE REFORMS UNDER BUSH

A Nation at Risk elevated concerns that many teachers were not well pre-pared or qualified to teach their subject matter. The report asserted, "Half of the newly employed mathematics, science, and English teachers are not qualified to teach these subjects." The creation of the Schools and Staffing Survey (SASS)—a federally funded national survey of schools and teachers, first administered in 1988—helped to bring this picture of poorly qualified and out-of-field teaching further into focus. Richard Ingersoll's analyses of the SASS data documented that a third of math teachers, a quarter of Eng-lish teachers, and a fifth of science and social studies teachers did not have a degree in their subject.[1]

Research at the time also demonstrated that states held widely different and often low standards for obtaining a licensure to teach in public schools.[2] Unlike many countries, where authority over public education is centralized at the national level, states in the United States have sole authority to estab-lish licensure criteria and grant licenses to teach in public schools. When Bush took office, less than half of all states required high school teachers to have majored in their subject area.[3] Even among the twenty-nine states that required teaching candidates to take a subject matter test, minimum scores were often set so low that nearly everyone passed.[4] States also commonly granted emergency or temporary licensures. In 2001, 6 percent of teachers nationally lacked full certification and in nine states more than 10 percent of teachers were uncertified.[5]

NCLB's Highly Qualified Teacher Provisions

President Bush signed NCLB, a reauthorization of the Elementary and Sec-ondary Education Act (ESEA), into law on January 8, 2002. The 670-page document included a set of Highly Qualified Teacher (HQT) provisions that were the result of a bipartisan compromise between the Republican administration and congressional Democrats led by Senator Ted Kennedy. The HQT provisions were intended to establish a set of standard licensure requirements across states in order for teachers to be considered high qual-ity.[6] The law defined "highly qualified" as meeting three broad requirements: 1) possessing a bachelor's degree from a four-year institution, 2) holding a full state certification, and 3) demonstrating subject area competence.

New entrants into the teaching profession were held to the highest stan-dards. The law stipulated that to be considered an HQT, new teachers had to demonstrate subject matter knowledge and competence in teaching skills. New elementary school teachers were required to pass a state examination covering reading, writing, math, and other areas of the basic elementary curriculum. New middle and high school teachers were given four options to demonstrate competence in their subject area: pass a state exam in their content area, earn an undergraduate or graduate degree in their subject area, accumulate the equivalent coursework of an undergraduate degree in their subject area, or attain an advanced certificate or credential. The law gave states greater discretion for certifying current teachers as highly qualified. Like new teachers, current teachers could meet HQT requirements by passing subject matter tests or obtaining the equivalent of an undergraduate degree in their subject. States were also allowed to certify teachers against a locally created "high, objective, uniform state standard of evaluation" (HOUSSE).

Lawmakers established an aggressive timeline for states to comply with these standards and provided federal funding to support implementation. All new teachers and paraprofessionals hired with Title I funds were required to meet HQT standards for the start of the 2002–2003 school year. These requirements were expanded to all core-subject teachers and paraprofessionals by 2005–2006. Total federal spending by the US Department of Education (ED) increased by 46 percent between 2002–2003 and 2005–2006 when the HQT mandate came into effect.[7] In fiscal year 2002 alone, more than $3 billion was made available as formula grants to states and local education agencies (LEAs) to be used for professional development, developing alternative routes to certification, helping teachers meet certification requirements, recruiting and retaining HQTs, testing teachers in subject areas, and creating programs for HQTs.[8]

The law also made several enforcement mechanisms available to the Bush administration. Six months after the law was passed, states were required to submit reports to ED with details of how they would meet HQT requirements. States then had to submit an annual report card detailing the professional qualifications of public school teachers as well as the percentage of teachers with emergency or provisional credentials. The law also included language requiring state plans to "ensure that poor and minority children are not taught at higher rates than other children by inexperienced, unqualified, or out-of-field teachers" and to disaggregate these statistics across schools in the top and bottom quintiles of poverty in the state.[9] As a core compliance mechanism, the federal government could choose to withhold Title

I funds from states that failed to meet these requirements. It also required schools to notify parents when their children had been taught for four or more consecutive weeks by teachers who were not highly qualified.

The effects of the HQT provisions

The core motivating principle behind the HQT provisions was both intuitive and widely appealing: teachers should know the material they teach. A national poll conducted by *Phi Delta Kappan* in 2002 found that 96 percent of respondents thought that teachers in the public schools in their community should be required to take a statewide competency test in the subjects they teach.[10] Examples of similar policies requiring potential primary and secondary teachers to pass an examination to enter the teaching profession can be found in fifteen of the forty-one member countries in the Organisation for Economic Co-operation and Development (OECD).

The HQT provisions resulted in some clear, if modest, successes. The percent of teachers teaching on state waivers dropped from 3.1 in 2003–2004 to 1.4 in 2007–2008.[11] The law also compelled states and districts to build new data systems tracking public school teachers' qualifications, which created an important new data source for examining the distribution of teacher quality. Finally, the law induced testing companies such as Educational Testing Service (ETS) to develop a new generation of tests to assess the basic knowledge, content expertise, and pedagogical skills of teachers.

These successes were undercut in many ways by ambiguity in the law, states' focus on compliance, limited federal enforcement, and unintended consequences. From the outset, the HQT provisions reflected a lack of understanding about the certification process and differences in local teacher labor markets. For example, states differed in whether they required middle school teachers to obtain an elementary or secondary teacher licensure. The degree to which teachers had to demonstrate content knowledge in their specific courses or their subject area more broadly was also unclear. Did high school science teachers who taught multiple subjects have to pass tests in chemistry, biology, and physics? Secretary of Education Rod Paige ultimately issued new guidance on certification flexibility for middle school teachers and high school science teachers, but never provided guidance on the certification requirements for special education teachers to be considered highly qualified.

Demonstrating content mastery for current middle school and high school teachers became an exercise in compliance that alienated teachers and did little to strengthen their skills. States overwhelmingly used their flexibility under the HOUSSE provisions to provide certified teachers avenues through which they could meet HQT standards in the course of their current professional duties. For example, certified teachers could meet the HQT standards by serving on a curriculum committee, mentoring a new teacher, leading an academic club, completing a National Board application, or attending conferences.[12] In many states, the bar was set so low on new state licensure and subject matter exams that nearly all teachers passed. Nationally, 96 percent of teachers passed all tests they took for their areas of specialization from 2003–2004 through 2008–2009.[13]

There were few, if any, actual consequences for states that circumvented the HQT standards through lax HOUSSE rules or that failed to make progress toward the goal of 100 percent of teachers being highly qualified by the end of 2005–2006.[14] It is not evident that Secretaries Paige or Spellings ever put a state on notice or warned a state of the potential loss of federal funding under Title I for failing to comply with the HQT provisions. States skirted even the parental Right-to-Know requirements by interpreting them as applying only to parents who requested HQT information, or by classifying only substitute teachers as not being highly qualified.[15]

Neither the executive branch nor ED focused attention on the HQT equity provisions that required states to report on and address inequities in the distribution of highly qualified teachers. These provisions were largely the product of bipartisan compromise, which allowed Congressman George Miller (D-CA) to include the language in the law. It was not until 2006 that ED even asked states to produce equity plans. The vast majority of these reports did little more than provide data found in state annual reports, and lacked targeted strategies for addressing the inequitable distribution of teachers.[16]

As a whole, there is very little evidence to suggest that the HQT provisions overall, or licensure exams specifically, have increased the quality of the teacher workforce. Licensure test scores are positively correlated with teachers' contributions to student learning, but only weakly so.[17] Most evidence suggests that the additional barriers to becoming a public school teacher imposed by licensure exams did more to dissuade higher-quality teachers from entering the profession than to keep less qualified teaching candidates out.[18] Licensure tests also created new barriers to important efforts to diversify the teacher workforce given that minority teaching candidates passed the exams at lower rates, on average.[19]

TEACHER EVALUATION REFORM UNDER OBAMA

The policy conversation about teacher quality evolved rapidly during President Bush's two terms in office. A growing body of empirical research on teachers emerged in this period that exploited new district administrative datasets linking students to their teachers. Three seminal findings served as signposts for the signature education reform initiatives of President Obama and his Secretary of Education, Arne Duncan: 1) the effects teachers have on student learning are large and vary considerably across teachers; 2) observable teacher characteristics such as those on résumés are at best weakly related to teachers' effects on student learning; and 3) teacher evaluation systems failed to differentiate among teachers despite large differences in effectiveness.

Research on teacher effects by William Sanders and June Rivers at the University of Tennessee's Value-Added Research and Assessment Center first captured the attention of policy makers at a national scale in 1996. Sanders and Rivers documented that a student who was taught by three consecutive top-quintile teachers gained over 50 percentile points more on state tests than peers taught by three consecutive bottom-quintile teachers.[20] Their research, along with that of Eric Hanushek, Tom Kane, and their colleagues, generated compelling evidence for what has become a stylized fact in education circles—teachers are the single largest school-based determinant of student achievement.[21] Researchers and policy makers interpreted these findings as evidence that ensuring students were taught by the best teachers several years in a row was enough to close racial and socioeconomic achievement gaps.

At the same time, new evidence cast doubt on input-based policies such as NCLB's HQT provisions. Studies consistently found only weak relationships between teachers' educational attainment, course taking, cognitive ability, or licensure type and their students' achievement gains.[22] Given these measurement challenges, policy makers saw new value-added models as a way to directly measure teacher output and better inform human resource decisions in schools.[23] School chancellors Joel Klein and Michelle Rhee were two national figures in the vanguard of this movement to reform district human capital practices in New York City and Washington, DC, public schools, respectively. Private foundations and philanthropic organizations, such as the Gates and Broad Foundations and the New Schools Venture Fund, invested millions of dollars to support these efforts in districts across the country. The release of *The Widget Effect* by The New Teacher Project

(TNTP) in June 2009 galvanized national attention on the failure of public schools to recognize and respond to differences in teacher effectiveness. The report used administrative data from twelve districts to document that nearly every teacher received a satisfactory rating.[24]

The growing momentum toward greater teacher accountability in the United States did not reflect broader international trends. The use of high-stakes evaluations as an approach to improving the quality of the teacher workforce varies considerably across countries. Several high-performing countries (e.g., Finland) place little emphasis on evaluations, while others (e.g., Singapore, Japan, and Korea) invest in teacher evaluation with a focus on informing teacher promotion and compensation.[25] Very few countries incorporate performance measures based on student test scores, relying instead on classroom observations by supervisors and often informal peer accountability.[26]

Race to the Top

A month after taking office, President Obama signed the American Recovery and Reinvestment Act (ARRA). While the bulk of the $115 billion for education funding was allocated to cash-strapped states and districts to help them avoid layoffs, $4.35 billion was allotted for a competitive state grants program. This program, known as Race to the Top, became the central education initiative of Obama's first term. The law required ED to award the full $4.35 billion in less than two years given that ARRA's purpose was to stimulate the economy.

The grant guidelines released by ED in November 2009 provided states with a detailed five-hundred-point rubric on which their applications would be judged. Points were allotted across four key areas: 1) Standards and Assessments, 2) Data Systems to Support Instruction, 3) Great Teachers and Leaders, and 4) Turning Around Struggling Schools. Across these four areas, Great Teachers and Leaders was given the most weight, with 27.6 percent of all possible points. Within this category, points were allocated across five reform areas: teacher evaluation, the equitable distribution of teachers, traditional teacher preparation, alternative teacher preparation, and professional development. Teacher evaluation criteria comprised the largest share, with 58 out of the 138 points.

The RTTT application rubric detailed specific evaluation system features that the Obama administration incentivized states to adopt. States could earn five points for measuring student achievement growth, fifteen points for implementing rigorous evaluation systems that incorporated student achievement growth and used multiple rating categories, ten points for conducting annual evaluations and providing feedback, and twenty-eight points for using evaluations to make decisions about professional development, tenure and promotion, compensation, and retention. Although these elements constituted only 11.6 percent of the total points possible, states passed new legislation overturning state laws and collectively bargained agreements that had previously prevented districts from linking teachers to their students' test scores.

Few states passed on the opportunity to secure hundreds of millions of dollars in additional federal grant aid during the Great Recession. Forty states, along with the District of Columbia, submitted applications to the first round of the RTTT competition in January 2010, just two months after the request for proposals was released. Some states contracted with outside consulting firms, such as Education First and McKinsey & Company, to draft their proposals within the short timeframe.[27] ED awarded grants only to Delaware and Tennessee, but encouraged applicants to reapply in June. Out of thirty-six applicants to the second round, nine states and DC were announced as winners in September 2010. The Obama administration succeeded in securing additional funds for the 2011, 2012, and 2013 fiscal years to conduct a third state grant competition and two rounds of district grant competitions. Seven additional states and twenty-one districts won competitive grants in these rounds. Across forty-six states and the District of Columbia, 615 applications representing over 1,689 districts entered the RTTT district grant competition.[28] In total, ED awarded $4.63 billion to state and district competition winners.[29]

The RTTT competition provided the Obama administration with a powerful lever for inducing states to commit to rapid and sweeping teacher evaluation reforms. This was not the first time the federal government had leveraged competitive grant programs to advance education reforms. For example, Congress established the Teacher Incentive Fund (TIF) in 2006 under Bush. TIF supported district incentive pay proposals designed to recruit effective teachers to high-need schools and reward teachers who received strong performance evaluations. Unlike during the Bush administration, the Department of Education under Obama used all available means through the RTTT grant competition to compel states to enact their proposed reforms. Moreover, Secretary Duncan and ED were strategic in their scoring of grant applications—they required most states to revise and resubmit applications if proposals were not closely aligned with the administration's vision of high-stakes teacher evaluation reforms. ED also actively monitored the progress of RTTT winners by requiring annual performance reports, conducting site-based visits in struggling states, and placing states on high-risk status if they did not meet the commitments in their grant proposals in a timely manner.[30] ED even temporarily withheld funding for Hawaii, Georgia, and Maryland because these states had not secured the support of state unions or LEAs in adopting new teacher evaluation systems.[31]

State waivers from NCLB

While the Obama administration oversaw the RTTT competition, states and schools continued to operate under the accountability structure created by NCLB. The share of schools failing to meet Adequate Yearly Progress (AYP) goals began to increase by double digits as the mandate of 100 percent proficiency in math and reading by 2014 approached. In 2011, 48 percent of schools did not meet AYP. Secretary Duncan warned that this number would surpass 80 percent unless the federal government took action.[32] The consensus on Capitol Hill was that NCLB was not working, but Congress's inability to reauthorize ESEA meant that schools were increasingly facing sanctions under the law.

Under Secretary Duncan's guidance, ED invoked section 9401 of NCLB to grant states flexibility in complying with the law. The administration offered states relief from NCLB's requirements in exchange for a commitment to pursue four education reform principles: 1) college- and career-ready standards, 2) state accountability systems for schools, 3) teacher evaluation reforms, and 4) reduced reporting requirements for schools and districts. ED's guidance and expectations around teacher evaluation reforms were a clear continuation of the priorities spelled out in the RTTT competition. States had to commit to adopting teacher evaluation systems that differentiated across at least three performance levels, used multiple measures to determine performance (including weighing student academic growth as a "significant factor"), evaluated teachers on a regular basis with clear and timely feedback, and informed personnel decisions for teachers using performance measures. Unlike NCLB and the RTTT grant competition, no federal funding was made available to support states in implementing the reforms required for receiving a waiver.

The Obama administration's approach to state waivers marked an important transition from using strong financial incentives under RTTT to leveraging the threat of increasingly burdensome sanctions under NCLB. States
were not required to apply for a waiver, but the alternative required them
to implement an increasingly acute set of corrective actions when schools
failed to meet AYP multiple years in a row. This included setting aside Title
I funding for tutoring programs and restructuring failing schools by dis-
missing the school administration and most of the staff. Between February
2012 and April 2014, forty-three states and DC were granted a waiver from
NCLB's provisions.

As with RTTT, ED under Obama actively enforced states' commitments
to the four principles outlined in their NCLB waivers. Several states, including Kansas and Oregon, were placed on high-risk status, while Washington's
waiver was revoked for failing to link teacher performance evaluations to
student growth measures. The waiver process continued to push states to
adopt and implement high-stakes teacher evaluation systems when public
support for such systems was eroding. From 2012 to 2014, public support
for using student performance on standardized tests as part of teacher evaluations had dropped from 52 percent to 38 percent.[33]

The effect of RTTT and state waivers on teacher quality

In many ways, the Obama administration succeeded in transforming the
way in which teachers are evaluated in the United States. When Obama
took office, teacher evaluation was an infrequent compliance exercise, with
few, if any, consequences tied to teachers' summative ratings. By the end of
Obama's second term, all but six states had radically reformed their teacher
evaluation systems to incorporate multiple performance measures, often
including value added to student achievement; to rate teachers on a scale
with multiple categories; and, in some cases, to tie these ratings to decisions
related to professional development, retention, and tenure.

These reforms resulted in several positive developments. Building on
progress made under NCLB, states that won RTTT awards, and many that
did not, invested in next-generation administrative data systems that provide a wealth of information to inform policy and practice. States also abandoned the binary checklists that assessed teachers on professional standards
related only tangentially to instruction, such as the cleanliness and organization of the classroom. Administrators now evaluate teachers with locally

adapted versions of research-based observation rubrics that focus on instructional quality and teacher-student interactions. These rubrics provide clear standards and a common language for discussing high-quality instructional practice.

At the same time, these new evaluation systems fell short of reformers' ambitious goals. Teacher evaluation reforms were championed as teacher improvement systems that would be used to identify and remove low performing teachers, support teachers' professional growth through observation and feedback, and attract and retain high performing teachers with performance pay. Although the proportion of teachers rated in categories below proficient increased to just over 4 percent, on average, the proportion of teachers rated in the lowest category, unsatisfactory, remained less than 1 percent under the new systems.[34] Interviews with principals revealed a variety of reasons for this, including the amount of time it takes to formally document unsatisfactory performance and concerns that schools will be unable to fill open positions with stronger candidates.

The new evaluation systems did succeed, however, at differentiating teacher performance at the top end of the distribution. Across states, an average of 37 percent of teachers were identified as highly effective, with considerable variation across individual states. Publicly recognizing exemplary practice is an important and nontrivial change to a professional culture that has eschewed differentiation. However, states rarely linked these new high-performance ratings to teacher compensation or opportunities for professional advancement. Only ten states adopted some type of merit pay program.[35] Even districts that were awarded grants to implement merit pay systems through ED's Teacher Incentive Fund commonly designed bonus systems with very low standards and small payouts, which served as de facto increases in base salary for most teachers.

Most RTTT applications and state rollouts of the new evaluation systems framed them as tools for promoting teacher development. Evidence has shown that rigorous evaluation supported by frequent observation and feedback can improve teacher practice and student achievement.[36] However, few states or districts funded or implemented systems capable of supporting teacher professional growth. Some states, particularly those that were compelled to adopt evaluation reforms in exchange for an NCLB waiver, lacked the buy-in and funding necessary to move beyond minimum compliance. Others tried but ran into substantial implementation challenges in scaling new evaluation systems. Because hiring outside evaluators or coaches was often prohibitively costly, districts gave administrators the added responsibility of conducting observations and providing feedback to teachers. This meant that administrators had to provide instructional feedback to teachers across grade levels and content areas irrespective of whether they had prior experience teaching these grades and subjects. Administrators had little time for conducting more than the minimum number of required observations, and post-observation conferences became infrequent and largely a formality.[37]

Recent research also reveals that high-stakes evaluation reforms decreased the number of new entrants into the teaching profession, increased the difficulty of filling vacant positions, and increased turnover among current classroom teachers. On one hand, this is concerning given teacher shortages in certain regions and subject areas as well as the negative effects associated with turnover on both schools and students. Studies show it costs between $2,000 and $8,000 to replace a teacher, and that turnover undercuts efforts to coordinate instruction and lowers student achievement.[38] At the same time, if evaluation reforms made teaching more attractive to high performing current and prospective teachers but less attractive to low performing teachers, then these patterns could result in a net gain in the quality of the teacher workforce. Recent research has found that evaluation reforms moderately increased the selectivity of novice teachers' undergraduate institutions.[39] Several studies have also found that turnover among current teachers has been disproportionately concentrated among low performing teachers.[40]

Progress on some elements of Obama's teacher evaluation reform agenda began to erode even before his second term ended. In an attempt to relieve pressure on states, ED created a waiver amendment process to request additional time for pilot-testing the new systems. Still, the number of states committed to including student growth measures as part of the evaluation system dropped from forty-three states in 2015 to thirty-nine states in 2017.[41] Moreover, the number of states requiring student growth to be the preponderant measure in teachers' overall ratings decreased from nineteen in 2013 to ten in 2016.[42] Political opposition to the Obama administration's use of NCLB waivers to advance teacher evaluation reforms culminated in the passage of the Every Student Succeeds Act (ESSA) in December 2015, which explicitly prohibited the Department of Education from mandating evaluation requirements as a condition of Title I funding or state waivers.

LESSONS LEARNED

Lesson 1: Federal Data Collection and State Reporting Requirements Are Valuable Practices

The federal government was responsible for the development of the data that, in many ways, shaped efforts to improve education policy under Bush and Obama. For example, the federally funded Schools and Staffing Survey produced compelling national statistics on teachers' lack of training in core content areas and the frequency of teachers working out-of-field. Most districts and states have invested in modern student information and human resource data systems to comply with NCLB reporting requirements. These new data systems made it possible for researchers to estimate individual teacher effects on student outcomes, which subsequently shaped the Obama administration's focus on teacher evaluation reform.

Annual reporting requirements under the Bush and Obama Departments of Education made states' progress toward employing highly qualified teachers and implementing teacher evaluation reforms both public and transparent. These reporting requirements influenced where state departments of education focused their attention and provided the federal government with a means of comparing states' progress. Under Obama, ED also expanded the Civil Rights Data Collection to include new measures, such as the percent of teachers in a district who are absent for at least ten days. Simply documenting that more than one in four teachers meet this definition of being chronically absent has generated considerable public pressure on schools to address teacher attendance.[43] The challenge is how to leverage these data and reporting requirements to advance reform efforts in a way that focuses on the underlying challenges rather than the metrics themselves.

Lesson 2: Competitive Grants Are Effective at Incentivizing Reforms

Both the Bush and Obama administrations used competitive federal grants successfully to incentivize states to undertake reforms. All but four states invested substantial time and money to submit applications to Obama's RTTT competition. States were willing to change laws and propose ambitious and politically controversial reforms for the chance to win awards that amounted to only 1 percent of annual state education budgets.[44] While the Great Recession amplified states' willingness to compete for federal grant dollars, such competitions can clearly motivate and provide cover for states to pursue ambitious reforms.

Competitive grant programs have several advantages. They are viewed favorably by politicians across the aisle given their voluntary nature. This is evident in the longevity of the TIF grant program, established under Bush, expanded under Obama, and continued under Trump as the Teacher and School Leader Incentive Fund. The voluntary nature of these grant programs also limits the effectiveness of those opposed to the reforms. The Obama administration effectively sidestepped initial political opposition to RTTT because teacher unions and legislators had few ways of organizing against it. However, failing to engage in interest-based discussions with this opposition proved shortsighted for the long-term success of evaluation reforms. Competitive grants are capable of catalyzing education officials to undertake major reforms, but more limited in their ability to support successful implementation.

Lesson 3: Reforms Have to Balance Unavoidable Conflict with the Importance of Buy-in

History has taught us that the success of education policy initiatives depends on the will and capacity of local "street-level bureaucrats" to implement reforms.[45] ED under Bush and Obama invested limited time and effort soliciting educators' diverse perspectives on policy reform initiatives. In the case of licensure reforms, the Bush administration benefited from a less ambitious goal that enjoyed near-unanimous public support. Public support alone, however, was not enough to secure successful implementation. Facing teacher shortages in hard-to-staff regions and subject areas as well as pressure from teacher unions, state officials ultimately set low bars and wide loopholes for current teachers to demonstrate subject competency. Imposing new content-standard requirements on veteran teachers was unlikely to succeed without also providing considerable support to teachers to meet these new standards.

The evaluation reforms advanced under the Obama administration faced even stronger opposition from educators. In 2010, a national poll by Education Next found that only 24 percent of teachers were in favor of using student growth measures to inform tenure decisions.[46] The irony of the RTTT grant competition was that the rubric included points for evaluation systems that "are designed and developed with teacher and principal involvement," while the prescriptive scoring rubric and short timeline simultaneously undercut these very efforts. States could compel districts to implement new systems, but they had no control over the scores principals gave teachers. Principals overwhelmingly assigned observation ratings that ensured all but a small percentage of teachers would receive an overall rating of proficient or higher under the new evaluation systems.[47]

It is hard to imagine ambitious reforms benefiting from the support of all the diverse constituents in the education sector. The lesson here is not to restrict reform efforts to popular approaches or watered-down changes at the margin, but to recognize that efforts to change the status quo are likely to be more successful when reformers involve diverse stakeholders early on in the design process. Federal teacher policy reforms suggest this is particularly true when reforms require changes to educational practices instead of technical or regulatory policy changes.

Lesson 4: Education Reforms Need to Be Responsive to Basic Labor Market Principles

The teacher policy reforms under Bush and Obama resulted in a number of unintended but largely predictable consequences based on basic economic principles. We know that labor markets differ substantially across local contexts. We know that raising the barriers and costs to entry into a profession will affect who chooses to pursue that profession. We know that nonpecuniary benefits such as working conditions and job security are important elements of a profession's overall compensation. Federal efforts to promote teacher licensure and evaluation reforms did little to anticipate and address the potential negative consequences of these reforms.

Uniform licensure standards set the bar too low in many local labor markets but too high in others. Requiring teachers to become certified in every subject they teach proved to be a substantial challenge for rural districts that often rely on teachers to teach multiple subjects. Hard-to-staff schools in disadvantaged neighborhoods faced similar challenges attracting and retaining highly qualified teachers. Licensure exams created a new barrier to entry into the teaching profession that was related only weakly to teacher effectiveness. Introducing high-stakes teacher evaluations caused fewer people pursue teaching as a career, likely because of the perceived loss of job security and professional autonomy for teachers.

Many of the negative consequences of federal teacher policy reforms could have been addressed directly through alternative policy designs or efforts to mitigate these negative effects. States might have been given the opportunity to offer districts temporary waivers from certain HQT requirements. Funds might have been made available for test-prep services and tutoring supports to help teachers pass licensure exams and take coursework in their subject area. States might have offset the introduction of high-stakes evaluation with new approaches to teacher compensation and investments in teachers' working conditions.

Lesson 5: Prioritize Clear Goals but Allow for Flexibility in Processes and Timelines

The goals of the Bush and Obama administrations were quite sensible: strengthening teachers' content knowledge and making human capital decisions based on job performance rather than seniority. These federal education reform efforts ran aground in many states because of their prescribed set of system structures and rapid, politically advantageous implementation timeline. Instead, ED under Bush and Obama might have pursued a more flexible approach that recognized states' different starting places and levels of internal capacity.

When RTTT began in 2009, there was not a single statewide evaluation system that employed the design features rewarded by the grant rubric. The administration's consistent pressure on states not to delay their reform commitments left little time for pilot testing and professional training. States that could not meet these ambitious timelines were threatened with the loss of grant funds or waiver approvals rather than supported in adapting their approaches and timelines. The high priority placed on test-score-based measures of teacher performance created major opposition to performance-based decision making in public schools. At the same time, the wide flexibility provided to states under the HOUSSE rules allowed them to make the HQT requirements under NCLB largely a paper compliance exercise for teachers already in the classroom. Striking the right balance between flexibility and follow-through is difficult, but critical.

CONCLUSION

The Federal Role for Improving Teacher Quality

Starting with the passage of ESEA in 1965, the federal government has had an important and growing role in shaping education policy. The successes and failures of federal efforts to strengthen teacher quality highlighted in this chapter do not suggest that a diminished role is more appropriate. It seems unlikely that a majority of states would have been more successful at improving the quality of the public teacher workforce or addressing the inequitable access to effective teachers in the absence of these federal efforts. What is unclear is whether the positive effects of these reform efforts could have been realized with fewer negative consequences if these administrations had taken alternative approaches. Lessons from these efforts illuminate ways in which the federal government can continue to leverage its position to improve educator effectiveness within the context of our decentralized education system.

Perhaps the most enduring effect of teacher reform efforts under Bush and Obama is the now widespread recognition of the central importance of teacher quality. This shift in perceptions has helped shape teacher policy in productive ways, such as reducing the use of seniority-based layoffs and transfer rights for tenured teachers to "bump" provisional teachers from their positions. District leaders and school administrators now have far more meaningful information about teachers' qualifications and performance relative to when Bush or Obama first took office.

Thirty-five years after *A Nation at Risk* was first released, the challenge of improving teacher quality remains as relevant now as ever before. Progress will likely be slow and uneven, but investing in teacher quality is among the most important commitments we can make as a nation.

Acknowledgments: I am grateful to Chad Aldeman, David Dunn, Rick Hess, Michael McShane, Mike Petrilli, Kate Walsh, Daniel Weisberg, Joanne Weiss, and Ross Wiener for the helpful guidance and insights they provided. Brendan Bell, Sarah Conlisk, and Anna Meyer provided outstanding research and editorial assistance. All errors and omissions are my own.

5

The Bush-Obama Agenda for Education Research and Innovation

Major Investment, Mixed Returns

Robert Pianta and Tara Hofkens

During the Bush and Obama administrations, an unprecedented amount of federal funds was channeled into improving student achievement by supporting education research and innovation. Starting with the Bush administration's overhaul of the Department of Education and extending to Race to the Top (RTTT) programs throughout the Obama years, over $3 billion was invested in education research alone. The investment—an exponential increase from administrations prior—is notable not just for the amount of money spent. It also represents an unprecedented effort to transform education outcomes from the top through a federally funded infrastructure designed to drive student learning improvements through the quality and accessibility of research and innovation.

The results were mixed at best: student learning held steady; the quantity and quality of research improved; major federally driven initiatives like teacher evaluation and Common Core failed operationally and politically; examples of successful innovation didn't scale or replicate; and in the end, Congress decided to devolve control of public education policy and programs back to the states, citing federal overreach as one of the main reasons. How and why did this ambitious project falter? What can we learn from the successes and failures of this unparalleled federal engagement in improving public education?

This chapter addresses these questions with a high-level overview and analysis of lessons learned from large-scale federal initiatives, the evolution of federal policy in education toward the Every Student Succeeds Act (ESSA), new models for research and innovation emerging in the field of "implementation science," and the tension between scientific rigor and the reality that educational processes, programs, practices, and policies are fundamentally localized. If the nation spends $3 billion on research designed to improve education, with little to show for it, how do we ensure the next tranche makes a difference? Can research and development in education provide traction on complicated problems in the same way it does in health? How is it that research has led to success in treating AIDS but not in ensuring that every third grader can read?

FEDERAL INVESTMENT IN EDUCATION RESEARCH AND INNOVATION: OERI TO IES

Prior to the Bush and Obama administrations, federal investment in education research and innovation was for the most part facilitated by the Office of Education Research and Improvement (OERI). Originally established in 1979 as the research arm of the National Education Institute (NEI), OERI aimed to improve student achievement by funding research and development (largely through national research centers) and by facilitating the translation and dissemination of scientific knowledge to educators through Regional Education Laboratories (RELs) and publicly available resources like the ERIC clearinghouse. In one sense, OERI attempted to provide a form of supply chain management for the production and distribution of education research and innovation, the nature and quality of which was largely determined by researchers themselves. The effort produced federally supported research initiatives on computer-based instruction, student motivation, and higher-order thinking skills, among others, which opened up these areas for consideration by educators and policy makers.[1] Ultimately, factors such as the lack of a vision for the quality and intent of federal funding, an overstretched OERI with limited oversight, and the sense that most educational research was small-bore and failed to connect to educators' actual practice contributed to a lack of confidence that federally supported research would result in positive change for students.[2] OERI, as an enterprise, was judged (by Congress and many investigators) to have produced research of low quality with little relevance or utility for addressing problems in education. One primary critique was that OERI-funded research was largely focused on theory and description and not on intervention and impact.[3] Furthermore, OERI research that *was* rigorous and relevant was often not used effectively or at all, either because the results were not accessible to educators or because they were not well synthesized or translated to practice.

To add to the doubts about OERI's impact, growing public dissatisfaction with student performance on standardized tests, and various "score cards" on the condition and progress of education, contributed to an urgent call for reforming the level and model of federal investment in education research and innovation. Starting in the Clinton years and throughout the tenure of OERI, statistics from national (e.g., National Assessment of Educational Progress [NAEP]) and international (e.g., Trends in International Mathematics and Science Study [TIMSS] and the Program for International Student Achievement [PISA]) standardized tests revealed that despite some modest gains, a large portion of American students failed to meet minimum national standards of proficiency and underperformed relative to their international peers on core subjects like mathematics and reading. The response to the public and political pressure to introduce accountability-based reform was to establish an infrastructure that would target federal funds to build an evidence-based understanding of "what works" to improve student learning, develop proven tools for improving performance, and provide information and supports to public schools for implementing effective (i.e., evidence-based) programs and practices. In short, OERI was dismantled and a new regime was formed.

In 2002, the Education Sciences Reform Act (ESRA) replaced OERI with the Institute of Education Sciences (IES). Unlike OERI, which worked under the mission to "provide leadership in the conduct and support of scientific inquiry," IES framed its mission in terms of impact—working to "provide scientific evidence on which to ground education practice and policy and to share this information in formats that are useful and accessible to educators, parents, policymakers, researchers, and the public."[4] IES structured federal investment in education research to emphasize specific problems of practice and produce causal relations between education inputs (e.g., curricula, teacher training, policies on class size) and student achievement, resulting in tools and processes that could be implemented at scale.

IES established fund distribution processes and standards that were markedly different from those of OERI. Infrastructure was developed to articulate problems meriting research attention (e.g., detailed requests for proposals), evaluate the quality of research proposals (e.g., standing scientific review panels and criteria for assigning merit), synthesize and disseminate research results for use in schools, and identify evidence-based tools and procedures for practitioners (i.e., What Works Clearinghouse). IES was a complete reengineering of federally funded education research and innovation.

The Bush and Obama administrations also fueled education research and innovation with an influx of funds that represented an unprecedented investment. After an initial budget of $135 million in 1974, the education research budget for the National Institute of Education was cut in half and then did not exceed $80 million until it was dissolved in 1985.[5] In 2000, toward the end of OERI, the total budget increased to around $275 million. In contrast, IES expenditures on research alone exceeded these numbers. Under the Bush administration, the IES awarded over $890 million in research grants.[6] Under Obama, funding for education research and innovation exceeded $3 billion.[7]

STRUCTURING FEDERAL RESEARCH INVESTMENTS TO IMPROVE ACHIEVEMENT

Both the Bush and Obama administrations believed that they could improve student achievement by investing in research and innovation that would direct, inform, and shape the policies and actions that affect children in schools. In order to do this on a national scale, both administrations borrowed the research and development (R&D) model used by the National Institutes of Health (NIH). This model involves a heavy investment in basic science, which describes how biological processes work and the conditions under which they vary. Scientists then manipulate these processes to prevent and fight disease. For example, scientists may create a drug or therapy based on evidence from basic science and then test its effects in a series of increasingly complex experiments involving random assignment to treatment and control groups. These randomized control trials (RCTs) enable researchers to evaluate if a treatment actually causes certain results, while eliminating confounding factors. Following successful RCTs, a potential treatment is sanctioned by the appropriate federal agency (e.g., the Federal Drug Administration) for availability to the public (commercialization). This was the template for the IES approach to R&D.

The NIH model of scientific inquiry is the gold standard for identifying solutions to medical problems and translating those solutions into practice and policy that successfully treat and prevent disease and promote good health. Given the complexity of health, health problems, and the health system, there was good reason to believe that the model for federal investment in research and innovation used in the NIH could also prove helpful in promoting better outcomes in public education. So the assumption that undergirded the Bush-Obama investments in research and innovation was this: a federal dollar invested in education with an NIH-like approach would yield benefits to K–12 children and their communities primarily in terms of improved achievement.

Thus, the goals of research investments for the Bush and Obama administrations were strikingly clear—to derive tools and solutions for education practice and policy that would improve student achievement. Coupled with the heavy influence of state standards assessments and accountability through the No Child Left Behind (NCLB) Act of 2001, the aims were even narrower—to drive improvements in students' performance on state standard tests (i.e., group-administered, often multiple-choice, achievement tests). The research infrastructure designed and implemented under the Bush administration, whether through IES or the ancillary efforts of the RELs, undoubtedly aimed to use scientifically derived tools (i.e., developed with the NIH model) to boost test scores and close gaps in those scores related to racial, income, or disability status. The research and accountability systems intersected in NCLB to drive evidence-based reform. And by emphasizing the use of "evidence-based solutions" in accountability frameworks, NCLB intended to drive a virtuous cycle of decision making toward the products of the reengineered and innovation-driven research infrastructure.

In this grand scheme, the role of IES was to generate evidence-based solutions that improve overall achievement and close gaps by supporting research on the causal impact of policies and programs (e.g., curricula) that target fundamental educational skills (e.g., mathematics and reading). In this system, dissemination of evidence-based tools is regulated through warrants for research products' causal impacts that are "certified" by the What Works Clearinghouse (WWC), a neutral-party repository for information about tools that work. Ideally, local education agencies (LEAs), states, and practitioners look to WWC when sourcing products and tools for use and have confidence that these tools meet standards for causal impact on student learning. Fundamentally, this model of research and innovation produces student achievement by "pushing" knowledge developed by scientists out to practitioners and decision makers.

THE OBAMA YEARS: SHIFTING THE R&D INVESTMENT MODEL

The Obama administration continued the Bush model of funneling federal investments in education R&D through the IES and REL infrastructure. As noted earlier, Obama and his Secretary of Education Arne Duncan directed an enormous sum to spend on improving educational outcomes for students in the United States. Having adopted the Bush approach of pushing evidence, causal effects, and research-based tools, they also recognized that the Bush investments had produced some proven tools that were not being implemented at a scale that could make a difference. Thus, the Obama administration added a few components that shifted the model of federal R&D investment.

First, the Obama Department of Education increased overall investment in education research and innovation by leveraging the stimulus package to create the RTTT and Investing in Innovation (I3) programs. Favoring proposals that took proven approaches into the field at scale (e.g., state- or districtwide implementations), the RTTT and I3 programs were highly intentional efforts to shape state and LEA activities around evidence. One could view the RTTT and I3 programs in some ways as expansions of those aspects of the NIH/public health model that focus on translating scientific discovery into practice; RTTT and I3 were investments through which promising educational interventions (deemed effective in RCTs) were either evaluated in much larger experiments or "brought to scale" (delivered at a population level).

The Obama administration also made a number of moves to target the connection between research and practice, shifting that relationship into a more bidirectional, if not practice-driven, framework. While remaining consistent with the goal structure of IES and the focus on rigor and causal inference, director John Easton promoted (and invested in) stronger partnerships among researchers and practitioners and decision makers in the field. These alliances were intended to elevate the influence of practitioners on research, such that the questions or conditions that research would consider were driven by consumers, not solely the province of scientists. For example, the Easton-led IES opened competitions for research-practice partnerships, in which university-based investigators might pair with a school district or state around a major educational challenge. This shift in the direction of practice-informed research—and the allocation of funds to these efforts—was a hallmark of the Easton IES and, in many ways, one of the forces driving the emergent field of implementation science.

Obama and Duncan also formed a close partnership with the Bill & Melinda Gates Foundation to address teacher effectiveness and raise standards for student achievement—widely regarded as two significant shortcomings of NCLB. Specifically, this close and strategic partnership between the federal government and a major philanthropy aimed to fund: 1) research to supply teacher evaluation tools that could be moved to the field through RTTT and I3 (i.e., the Measures of Effective Teaching study); and 2) the development of states' common achievement standards and assessments (i.e., Common Core State Standards).[8] Thus, Obama—perhaps closer to the "education president" than either of his two predecessors, who had also laid claim to that moniker—layered onto the standard IES model an effort to far more intentionally drive research findings and evidence-based tools into the field.

The combination of federal and foundation funds with early-stage effective tools produced through the prior IES investments resulted in an expanded model of federal support for research and innovation, reflected in the RTTT/I3/Gates Foundation framework, that was very focused on actively moving effective tools to the field at scale. This expanded model for characterizing the federal investment in R&D, although more closely embedded in the field (applicants to RTTT and I3 were SEAs and LEAs), remained fairly top-down. To illustrate, RTTT and I3 *required* the use of evidence-based approaches to various problems in education, and if applicants for these programs prioritized teacher effectiveness and higher standards, they were more likely to obtain funds. Moreover, the components of teacher evaluation were prescribed within the two funding streams—if an SEA wanted RTTT funding, it had to develop a teacher evaluation system that fit certain a priori criteria. RTTT and I3, along with the Gates partnership, were largely responsible for dozens of states' efforts to develop and implement systems for teacher evaluation that utilized some form of classroom observation and value-added assessment data, as well as for the assessment and curriculum development work related to the Common Core State Standards, which at one time had more than forty governors listed in support.

None of this structure is unusual; most funding agencies set priorities for funds and put in place a number of constraints for applicants that fit the agencies' preferences and priorities. But the fundamental challenge of bringing evidence-based tools to scale, even those with very strong evidence of causal impact on achievement, is that local conditions almost always prevail in education improvement and reform initiatives. Thus, not surprisingly, over time RTTT and I3 gradually relaxed the criteria by which applicants' adherence to certain priorities were evaluated. And the process for evaluating proposals with regard to the strength of causal evidence available for the proposed innovation was weakened and relaxed; there simply weren't enough experienced reviewers. Finally, political pushback from states, teacher unions, and eventually the public undermined any leverage the federal government could obtain by using the flow of funds as an incentive. In the end, this devolution of responsibility for dissemination of innovation and research-based practice from the federal government to the states was encoded in ESSA, which dismantled the federally driven accountability system of NCLB and many of the structures supporting the creation and push of evidence out from the federal level.

Notwithstanding the devolution of responsibility for policy making, accountability, and implementation to the states, federal funds still actively support research, development, and innovation activities in education. IES still shapes federal support for education research, and the goal/topic structure that was invented under Russ Whitehurst's direction in the first Bush term remains in place and still reflects the emphasis on controlled evaluations and a push model of inquiry and scale. There is more emphasis on research-practice partnerships and field-embedded experimentation, but the IES model still rests on an assumption that a proven program, curriculum, or tool, if adopted and used as prescribed, will produce the desired results.

WHAT HAPPENED?

As we evaluate the Bush-Obama investments in research and innovation, we set the context by considering achievement trends on standardized tests. This form of student performance was in part the genesis of the restructuring of IES and certainly the most prioritized indicator for federal investments. Then, we describe the features and effects of large-scale, federally funded research and innovation programs in terms of fund flows to those activities. Considered in the context of Bush-Obama models for federal research and innovation investments, aligning national achievement trends with specific funding programs provides a rough approximation of where we have been and suggests a roadmap of where we might go in education research and innovation.

The Economy as Context

To interpret the trends in student performance during the Bush and Obama administrations, it is important to first consider the economic context during the Bush-Obama administrations. For example, largely due to economic growth during the Clinton years, between 1990 and 2004 schools hired more teachers and support staff and student-teacher ratios fell 4.5 percent.[9] At the same time, family income rose, unemployment dropped, and there were notable improvements in other indicators of family and child health and well-being. Throughout this time, children's NAEP scores were mostly either relatively stable or slightly on the rise.

However, by fall 2007 the US economy was in a tailspin, a severe economic decline that had a significant impact on the public educational system and the families enrolled in it. As an increasing number of parents became unemployed (from 4.8 to 8.1 million in 2010), enrollment in public education increased at the same time that state and local funding for many public school districts declined.[10] While the number of teachers and school personnel working at public schools remained steady or slightly increased at the beginning of the recession, between 2008 and 2011, over 3.7 percent of teachers lost their jobs.[11] To reduce costs, schools also laid off teacher aides, support staff, and school administrators.[12] Salaries and incentives for teachers who remained employed were also reduced, limiting the ability of some school districts to recruit and retain high-quality teachers.[13] Educational programming was dialed back and, in some cases, instructional time was decreased (e.g., through reductions in public preschool programs).[14] As a result, many public schools had larger class sizes and relatively fewer resources for providing high-quality learning opportunities and individualized support for successive cohorts of children who were being raised under the direst economic circumstances seen in generations.

The impacts of the recession on the public education system undoubtedly shaped the extent to which federally funded research and innovation contributed to student achievement. First, the overall reduction in educational resources and opportunities in public schools changed the quantity and quality of learning opportunities in ways that directly affected how much students learn (e.g., cutting back on full-day kindergartens). Second, the recession squeezed public schools and families in ways that changed the opportunity and ability for education research and innovation to effectively support student learning. For example, research-based reforms targeted teacher quality and curriculum because these factors drive student motivation and achievement. But by diminishing the capacity of public schools to invest in, successfully implement, and sustain these reforms, the recession could have rolled back prior progress and made it far tougher to implement any new approach effectively. Furthermore, the recession contributed to more children experiencing economic hardship, housing instability, and the type of familial turbulence that can interfere with children's productive engagement in school—all of which could influence academic performance, or the effectiveness of reform efforts to support it, by changing the very nature and intensity of what it would take educationally for any given child to succeed.[15] That said, the investments during the Clinton years could have bolstered the chances of student success, which would then have carried forward into the Bush and Obama years. Attributing responsibility for the rise and fall of student achievement at this macro level is challenging, particularly given the cumulative nature of educational attainment and success.

The Evidence on Student Achievement: Population Trends in NAEP

Approximately every two years the National Assessment for Education Progress (NAEP) tests a nationally representative sample of fourth-, eighth-, and twelfth-grade students to assess what American children know and can do in reading and mathematics. Because NAEP tests have taken place for over fifty years, they provide an achievement context both during and before the Bush-Obama years. The federal goal is for all students to become proficient in the knowledge and skills taught at each grade level.[16]

NAEP trends suggest that federal investments in research and innovation could have contributed to achievement gains and/or forestalled what would have otherwise been expected achievement declines due to the economic circumstances. Reading and mathematics scores for fourth-grade students exhibit an initial visible gain after 2000 (perhaps a legacy of the Clinton years), followed by a consistent, albeit modest, improvement through 2015. Fewer fourth graders scored "below basic" and more students scored basic, proficient, or advanced in reading and mathematics from 2000 to 2015. Similarly, eighth-grade students exhibit a gradual increase in reading and mathematics scores that declines after 2013; however, the proportion of eighth-grade students scoring below basic in reading and mathematics remained essentially the same. The trends for fourth- and eighth-grade students are largely echoed in the results of TIMMS and PISA assessments as well.[17] In contrast, NAEP scores for twelfth-grade students exhibit almost no net change in reading and mathematics from 2002/2005 to 2015.

Importantly, standardized test trends during the Bush and Obama years indicate improvement in academic achievement in the areas where there was the highest level of federal investment in education research and innovation. For example, the WWC describes more research-based, proven interventions for reading and mathematics for elementary and middle grades than for high schools (forty-two and forty, respectively, compared to nineteen). The parallel between R&D efforts focused on evidence-based practice in reading and mathematics and trajectories of achievement in these subject areas at a time of incredible economic and social strain tentatively suggests that federally funded research and innovation may have shaped student achievement at a national level. Given the severity of the recession, it is reasonable to expect that student achievement would *decline*, and yet the trend in performance for fourth- and eighth-grade students across these years was modest and steadily *positive or sustaining*. From this perspective, it is interesting to ponder whether the investments in education research and innovation could have forestalled the decline otherwise expected due to economic circumstances, particularly among students in elementary and middle grades who may have attended schools or grades in which effective, research-based innovations were more likely to have made their way into the classroom.

Federal Investment Targeting Reading and Literacy

As suggested previously, perhaps there is no area of education in which a larger amount of federal (and state and local) resources has been devoted than that of early literacy and reading. Conceived out of the gate by the Bush administration, Reading First (RF) was a $6 billion program intended to ensure that every child learned to read (preceded by the America Reads Act, which was the Clinton administration's tutoring program). RF and its junior partner, Early Reading First (ERF), funded basic and applied research, program implementation, training, statewide assessments and screening, and curriculum development—the major components of a system through which research can and should influence practice. Importantly, the RF and ERF initiatives rested heavily on a robust basic science of literacy and language development, which had grown over an almost thirty-year arc to map the trajectory and mechanisms responsible for early literacy development.

RF and ERF rested on that science and were the mechanism through which that basic science of literacy development was translated into a set of robust and proven applications.

RF and ERF produced a suite of evidence-based tools (assessments, curricula, activities, training modules) and systems of field-based implementation resources (e.g., literacy coaches, curriculum specialists) that provided teachers with supports to take these tools into practice with fidelity to the proven models. Many states (e.g., Florida, Texas) used RF and ERF to invest in capacity building for further research and development and systems-level supports. And reading instruction throughout the United States changed to reflect the basic science and its application—classrooms focused on decoding and phonetically based approaches (in contrast to the prior generation of "whole word" models). These forms of instruction became the predominant focus of curriculum, training, and instruction for teaching literacy throughout the United States, and in many ways remain so today.

The results on student achievement have been mixed. Although RF contributed to first-grade students' ability to decode, the program does not appear to have significantly impacted reading comprehension in grades 1, 2, or 3, regardless of the state within which the program was implemented or the number of years that students were exposed to it. Not every child learned to read by third grade, but more children could decode words by third grade. Although modest in impact on student outcomes and conditioned by the economic context described earlier, the RF and ERF story is one of considerable public investment in research and an accompanying implementation support structure that does appear to have contributed to sustained change in the performance of the nation's schoolchildren. However, because decoding skills, while necessary, are not a sufficient competency for proficient reading, we still see notable gaps in reading performance in third grade and beyond, when comprehension becomes the goal of reading. Thus, it is possible that this reduction of a complex skill to a narrow skill—one not complemented by an equivalently intense and research-driven focus on language development, vocabulary, and conversation, which might have fostered stronger comprehension and broader literacy competence—eroded the ultimate legacy of the RF and ERF era.

Success for All

In addition to investing in highly focused curricular and classroom practice interventions such as RF and ERF, the Bush and Obama administrations also invested in programs that shape achievement through schoolwide supports. For example, a good deal of research evaluating the impacts of tools with strong causal evidence also very clearly identified that even the most effective curricular interventions required extensive operational support from the school in order to be delivered well across classrooms and grades. Success for All (SFA), among other intents, addressed this need for school-level support.

Originally developed in the 1980s in Baltimore public schools, SFA combines curriculum with schoolwide structures and supports that have been proven to be effective into a multicomponent "delivery system" for Title I elementary schools. The foundational SFA program is built around the implementation of a literacy curriculum that covers multiple elements (phonemic awareness, phonics, vocabulary, fluency, and comprehension) and emphasizes cooperative learning and cross-grade grouping based on reading skills. In implementation, SFA operates largely as an intensive professional development and time management program that includes teacher practices to monitor student progress and schoolwide reforms in order to address attendance, problem behavior, and health needs, and support parental involvement.

By the end of the 1990s, SFA had been implemented in elementary schools throughout forty-seven states. The program scaled back substantially at the start of NCLB, when Title I funds were routed to EF and EFA, and then resurged when it was awarded a $50 million I3 grant under the Obama administration. In terms of effects, SFA was particularly successful in supporting phonics among children with low preliteracy skills, but does not show significant effects for children who start kindergarten with good literacy skills or for any children's development of fluency or reading comprehension. And the efforts from the I3 scale-up grant revealed that schools need to have sufficient school personnel and budgetary support in order to participate in and successfully implement a comprehensive whole-school program such as SFA. Due in large part to the economic crisis previously described, the I3 implementation of SFA reached about half of its targeted enrollment of new schools (~450 of 1,000). Many schools opted not to participate because they did not have the resources to do so, and several schools that did participate did not implement some key components to the program, like the full-time on-site facilitator and the computerized tutoring program. In some sense, one lesson learned from SFA is that even with well-resourced supports for a highly focused and structured program that had been well tested, local variation and conditions overrode the effective dose of treatment and mitigated impact on students. This lesson is evident not only in large-scale efforts such as SFA, but also in countless other examples of well-researched and proven innovations developed during the Bush-Obama years. In the next section, we summarize and reflect on this and other lessons learned and the rise of implementation science as a complement, and perhaps alternative approach, to investing in research and innovation.

LESSONS LEARNED

Overall, the unprecedentedly large federal investment in education research and innovation during the Bush and Obama years paid off in some ways, although the evidence of benefits to children's learning or closing of achievement gaps remains elusive. Clearly, today there is a higher quantity and quality of research into factors that contribute to student achievement. To the extent that such research may, in the long run, generate actionable knowledge and scalable tools, then it could translate into benefits for children. The ideal of "evidence-based" practice has become part of the lexicon in public education, and although it is difficult at times to differentiate whether these claims are made on the basis of scientific merit or marketing, at least we talk about evidence. Infrastructure and initiatives developed at the federal level to provide sustained support to education research and innovation have contributed to several educationally promising programs, progressing from development to evaluation and scaling-up stages, and some of these tools (e.g., curricula in math and science) are now being used with many tens of thousands of students. And an infrastructure and set of standards now support efforts to synthesize, translate, and disseminate information about "best practice" to policy makers and educators. Without question, the United States has a more robust and scientifically respectable system of research, development, and innovation in education than it did twenty years ago.

Nevertheless, the more important indicator of the success of this federal effort is whether it has had a positive impact on student achievement. And instead of a cascade of impact (as might have been expected and/or hoped for from a several-billion-dollar investment), effects on student achievement have been elusive—a trickle of modest gains in the context of persistent underperformance, with large gaps between socioeconomic and racial groups. And there is reason to believe the meager returns are not just because of the coincident challenges imposed by the Great Recession.

As we examine the consequences of the past twenty years of federal investment in education R&D, four lessons surface: education is not like medicine; implementation matters; uptake is spotty; and fundamental questions remain open.

Lesson 1: Education Is Not Like Medicine

Perhaps one of the greatest lessons of the Bush-Obama R&D model is that education is different from medicine and health care in ways that make the NIH model of identifying and prescribing "doses of effective treatment" a poor fit for understanding and addressing underachievement in the stunningly varied localities in which US public education takes place. There are at least two ways in which the IES parallel with biomedical research and health care breaks down.

First, unlike in medicine, in which researchers identify putatively potent treatments that can be titrated in sufficient doses to effectively treat an illness across variations in people or circumstances, federally funded education research has failed to find highly potent interventions (to say nothing of minimally effective doses) of educational practices that improve student achievement among all (or even selected groups of) students. What works for a given student may not for others, and on average, effects are very small. This could be because the treatment itself is ineffective or weak, or because local conditions ultimately control impact. And because there is very little emphasis on the basic science of processes that produce achievement across different types of students in different contexts, results from RCTs in education are less grounded in strong theories and hypotheses of the basic mechanisms involved.

The second breakdown involves regulation of practice and application. Unlike in contemporary medicine, in which health care decisions and practices are tightly constrained and prescribed by regulations based on scientific inquiry, evidence and practice in education are much less closely linked. In education, the distance between what we learn from federally funded research and what students experience in a classroom is vast, divided by layers of regulatory processes at the state, regional, and district levels and the people and conditions that inhabit those levels. And there is little to no vertical alignment that would ensure high-fidelity implementation of a proven practice, for example in mathematics instruction. Even in schools or classrooms, despite incentives and mandates to implement evidence-based practice, administrators and teachers remain unaware of the approaches that have proven effective, implement them in idiosyncratic or incomplete ways, or are allowed the autonomy to opt out. In short, while the NIH-type infrastructure has generated more educationally relevant knowledge and potentially effective tools than ever before, these research-driven innovations are lost in translation when it comes to their use in schools across the country. Even the most promising and proven tools either sit on the shelf or are used in ways inconsistent with their design.

Lesson 2: Implementation Matters and Needs to Be Studied

To address these issues with translation, new forms of research aim to identify barriers and facilitators to effectively implementing interventions and to quantify the effects of these factors on the outcomes of intervention studies. This research, bundled under the umbrella of "implementation science," has yielded important information about factors that influence implementation of evidence-based approaches in schools, but has yet to address how to build systems that ensure better implementation. The recent rise of implementation science, most notably through the efforts of the Carnegie Foundation for the Advancement of Teaching, repositions the locus of influence in the research-to-practice translation and dissemination model reflected in the Bush-Obama approach. In this new framework, local practitioners formulate research questions and hypotheses and partner with investigators to design and conduct smaller-scale, rapid-cycle studies that evaluate the merit of hypotheses or impact of intervention prototypes. The process is iterative, rapid, and local, with the primary aim of building local capacity to develop solutions with evidentiary backing—a dramatically different approach than requiring locals to consume interventions proven effective elsewhere by others.

Not surprisingly, this recentering of influence in local settings for research and innovation parallels a recentering of accountability and responsibility for reform, as documented in the reauthorization of NCLB in the form of ESSA. In ESSA, authority for regulation and responsibility for producing results sits within SEAs and LEAs, with the federal government stepping away from the more prescriptive approaches to accountability and innovation seen under Bush and particularly Obama. It remains to be seen whether this recentering of authority, in policy or in research and innovation, is successful.

Lesson 3: Not Enough Is Known About How States and Localities Actually Use Research

The recent shift to understand implementation is in part predicated on an even larger challenge facing the R&D enterprise: Is there any evidence for actual uptake of research (findings, products) by educational practitioners and policy makers? Thus, even the very first step in an implementation process—being aware of results or promising, evidence-based interventions—is an open question. The WWC, initially conceived of as the nation's clearinghouse for relevant and useful information on research-supported educational practices and policies, is largely recognized as underutilized. This may be a function of the evidence pipeline—it takes time to build a body of robust studies across the hundreds of potential questions and applications for which educational practitioners may seek answers or recommendations.

And recent surveys also demonstrate that most education practitioners and policy makers receive information not directly from researchers or research products (such as journal articles), but from a broad and diverse array of intermediaries that translate and purvey research findings according to their own mission and aims. Actual practitioners and policy makers rarely, if ever, are exposed to original findings and results. This highly mediated process of translation, in the context of a research literature with major gaps in relation to the relevant problems of practice, can lead the potential consumers of research to discount its importance or applicability to their work, as well as its credibility. Importantly, the scientific, policy, and practice communities have identified this as a concern and are actively engaged in identifying and advancing solutions, but this will take time. As we saw in the cases of Reading First and Success for All, even the strongest and most robust evidence-informed applications fail to make their way into America's classrooms with fidelity.

Lesson 4: Big and Fundamental Questions Remain

The fundamental question under ESSA is whether American children learn more when the nature and quality of their education programming is managed at the federal or local level (or somewhere in between). Assuming at least a twenty-year run with ESSA-like regulation, the parallel question concerns the infrastructure and mechanisms needed to support a localized, capacity-building approach to research and innovation. Given the push-oriented model currently in place, what new or transformed structures and mechanisms are needed to flow federal resources to localized activities? What assurances will be important for maintaining the quality and rigor of research? What mechanisms are needed to address potential for generalizability and scale? Is there an alternative, a complement, or a variant of the current IES model that not only fosters strong, localized, authentic, and rigorous research that effectively translates into improved student performance, but also advances understanding and applicability of locally driven models across the widespread and varying needs of US school systems and classrooms?

CONCLUSION

In looking ahead to the next decade and beyond, we see a number of promising forces at play, which we suspect will fundamentally change the nature and (we hope) impact of research and innovation in education, with support from the federal government. We believe the Bush-Obama years are a cautionary tale. Big investments in a specific model of research and innovation proved marginal in impact for two reasons: we have too little solid knowledge of the basic educational processes that cause achievement, and the NIH model assumed that a decontextualized approach to developing and evaluating educational interventions would lead to tools that scaled. Put another way, if we don't know enough about how classrooms and schools work, then it is very difficult to design treatments that enhance their impacts. And as Tip O'Neill reminded us, local conditions override the very best central planning. The research and innovation vector of the Bush-Obama experiment ends with a bit of a whimper but leaves the elements of a transformed approach to research and innovation that could have promise going forward.

The shift to a focus on implementation, and the science of schooling and classroom processes inherent in that focus, is a fundamental change and one with considerable promise. Turning researchers' attention toward the dynamics of activity in educational settings, this shift will require a deeper conceptualization of the influences on learning and development, one that is far more connected to understanding and modeling the dynamics of change and much less wedded to evaluating average program impact. Such a shift will require methodologies that enable modeling the activity of complex systems over time and increasingly will have to accommodate disciplinary expertise and funding that span sociology and neuroscience. Fundamentally, we need to know much more about how schooling works and does not work as we simultaneously and systematically work to improve it.

This dual focus in aims—research for understanding and for improvement—carries an inherent tension. As this new research and innovation paradigm evolves, interventions will be organized around evaluating hypotheses on the mechanisms responsible for driving complex educational systems and processes, not solely around whether curriculum package X produces a bump in student achievement. Unless we recognize that the knowledge base describing educational mechanisms is woefully underdeveloped, we run the risk of not learning the lessons of the Bush-Obama experiment. This does not mean that the agenda of the new paradigm will not or should not include a robust program of evaluating potential interventions, but simply that research, development, and evaluation of innovations is embedded in a larger project of understanding what and how learning takes place in educational settings and systems. It also means that diffusion and dissemination of new knowledge and tools are most likely to operate best through networked and local mechanisms, not through top-down dictates. In this new paradigm, the need for building local capacity to conduct, understand, and interpret research will be tremendous.

This new paradigm will require funding and patience. It is investing in the long game in a sector known for wanting the right solution for everyone today. The federal government funds long-game research in all sorts of other areas, so the precedent for similar support for education research is established. Although perhaps too oriented around obtaining returns in a short time horizon and too limited in its focus on *what* works rather than *how*, the Bush-Obama experiment established the credibility of research in education. Ultimately, the Bush-Obama years will be remembered for building the foundation for a science of education that maps to the complexity and sophistication of the questions needing attention and answers.

Acknowledgments: We thank colleagues at the Center for Advanced Study of Teaching and Learning for their generous contributions to discussions of research and innovation. The research reported herein was supported by the Institute of Education Sciences, US Department of Education, through a Postdoctoral Training grant to the University of Virginia. The opinions expressed are those of the authors and do not represent views of the US Department of Education. Correspondence concerning this chapter can be addressed to Robert C. Pianta at rcp4p@virginia.edu.

6

Why Standards Produce Weak Reform

Tom Loveless

S tandards define what students will learn and when they will learn it, establishing common goals to guide an entire educational system's reform efforts. The attractiveness of the idea rests on its simplicity. Education policies of both the Bush and Obama administrations were predicated on a belief in standards-based reform, but affinity for standards predates these two administrations and extends beyond Washington. Standards-based reform originated in the states and has enjoyed nearly three decades of bipartisan political support.

This chapter argues that the Bush-Obama policies have exposed inherent weaknesses in standards-based reform. The weaknesses stem from the organizational and political obstacles that standards face in the transition from statements of ambitious learning goals, created in upper-level policy forums, to the student learning that takes place in schools.

HOW DID WE GET HERE? STANDARDS BEFORE BUSH AND OBAMA

Standards have evolved incrementally, with each successive iteration correcting a supposed flaw in previous versions. To understand key elements of the Bush-Obama approach to standards, one must consider the standards that came earlier. States created curriculum frameworks in the 1980s and early 1990s, delineating what was to be taught and learned in each subject. A 1992 survey found that thirty-five states had adopted curriculum frameworks in English language arts, and thirty-eight in mathematics.[1] Most states focused on minimum competency and basic skills, but a few stood out as exceptions.[2]

California State Superintendent of Public Instruction Bill Honig marshaled brand new curriculum frameworks (frameworks had existed since at least the 1960s) to overhaul K–12 subject matter, the state's California Assessment Program, textbook adoption, and professional development programs.[3] This multipronged approach, in which state policies are designed to reinforce each other in the pursuit of ambitious learning objectives, came to be known as systemic school reform or standards-based reform.

An influential 1989 article by Marshall Smith and Jennifer O'Day articulated the basic theory of systemic reform.[4] Smith and O'Day argued that the multilevel educational system produces policy fragmentation, reform efforts that overlap or contradict each other. They criticized 1980s state-level reforms for emphasizing "more of the same"—longer school days, increased graduation requirements, more testing, and an emphasis on learning basic skills. They criticized reforms attempting to restructure schools as episodic and uncoordinated, exhibiting a "project mentality" that tackled problems on a school-to-school basis. As a 1991 policy brief from the Consortium for Policy Research in Education explained, "The first step in developing a coherent system of instructional guidance is to work toward agreement on a core body of challenging and engaging knowledge, skills, and problem solving capacities as goals for all students. All state policies guiding instruction would be based on these goals, forming a consistent, supportive policy structure for school improvement."[5]

Professional Groups

Professional curriculum groups assumed an important role in standards writing in the 1990s as the US Department of Education (ED) funded several organizations to write national standards. ED repeatedly stressed that the standards were voluntary. The National Council of Teachers of Mathematics (NCTM) had released *Curriculum and Evaluation Standards for School Mathematics* in 1989. Although not funded with federal money, the NCTM standards became a model for other subjects. The Bush administration awarded grants for writing standards in science, history, geography, foreign languages, the arts, English, and civics.[6] The Clinton administration followed with Goals 2000, which called for voluntary national standards. Goals 2000 created a federal agency, the National Education Standards and Improvement Council (NESIC), to certify the standards crafted by subject matter organizations and the student assessments created by individual states. In 1996, with Republicans now in control of both houses of Congress—and with party members growing suspicious that NESIC's validation powers invited federal interference with state autonomy—legislation passed that abolished NESIC before even a single member had been appointed.[7]

Political Opposition

Political opposition to standards projects grew throughout the 1990s. The national history standards, released in 1994, spurred a backlash from conservatives who charged the document with political correctness. But the controversy transcended partisanship. A US Senate resolution condemning the history standards passed by a vote of 99–1. Other standards projects also struggled. The Department of Education cut off funding for the English language arts (ELA) standards in 1994, citing delays in writing and the vague wording of the standards in early drafts. The two organizations responsible for the standards, the National Council of Teachers of English and the International Reading Association, continued the project using their own funds. When the ELA standards finally appeared in 1996, they drew harsh criticism. An editorial in the *New York Times* acidly criticized the jargon-filled standards, the review beginning with: "A curriculum guide for teaching English has just been released in a tongue barely recognizable as English."[8]

Even support for the seemingly nonpolitical NCTM math standards wavered. As new textbooks and materials in accord with the NCTM standards appeared in classrooms, charges surfaced that the standards promoted "fuzzy math," calculator use over computation skills, and a constructivist education philosophy embracing many century-old, child-centered practices of progressive education that had always been viewed warily by the public. In one of the earliest examples of the internet's potential for political organizing, two groups that included scientists and mathematicians—many of them lifelong Democrats—founded Mathematically Correct in California (1997) and HOLD (Honest Open Logical Decisions) in New York City (2000) as websites for advocating resistance to NCTM-style math reform.[9]

Lessons for Standards in the Twenty-First Century

As the new century dawned, several standards projects had been battered politically, but the basic idea that standards could improve education remained strong. The theory was right, a common argument asserted, only the details of implementation had gone wrong. The Bush and Obama administrations attended to the lessons learned from earlier projects as they designed their own standards-based reforms.

It was not enough to promise "voluntary" standards, as the federal government had to be kept far away from—or at least out of view of—the standards. The word *national* also had to be handled delicately; better to differentiate "national" from "federal" and stress the state-level origins of standards-based policies. The NCTM standards taught that political support cannot be taken for granted, even if standards documents are greeted with widespread acceptance upon their initial release. Standards must focus on content, not pedagogy. They should define specific expectations for learning skills and knowledge in each grade, not promote esoteric educational principles or embrace a particular philosophy.

Bush's and Obama's policy makers generally agreed that standards should focus on challenging material and seek ambitious accomplishments, not merely the acquisition of basic skills or minimum competencies. Additionally, standards must have real consequences attached to them to move the system. Simply encouraging states to take "corrective action" with failing schools, as 1994's Improving America's Schools Act had done, allowed many states to avoid adopting meaningful accountability systems.

Federalism and the Bush and Obama Approach to Standards

As governor of Texas in the 1990s, George W. Bush had embraced and extended the standards-based policies of preceding governors in his state, both Democratic and Republican. When he took office as the forty-third president of the United States, Bush brought Texas school reform with him. The Bush 2000 presidential campaign used the candidate's education record as an issue to illustrate "compassionate conservatism," with the hope of prying away centrist voters and weakening the Democratic Party's longstanding political advantage on domestic issues. Once in office, Bush's rhetoric promoting the No Child Left Behind Act of 2001 (NCLB)—that the nation must end the "soft bigotry of low expectations"—wedded ambitious educational standards to the cause of civil rights. Closing gaps became a national goal. As Patrick McGuinn documents, this argument proved important in convincing powerful liberals in the US Senate, including Senator Ted Kennedy, to relinquish opposition to testing and accountability.[10]

NCLB increased federal involvement in K–12 education, a matter historically—and constitutionally—left to the states. But the new law gave a nod to federalism. States would be free to adopt their own standards, to create their own tests, and to decide for themselves where to draw the line defining "proficient" student performance. The requirement that states enforce a

[handwritten: what about students with special need?]

goal of 100 percent student proficiency in reading and math by 2014 meant that a steadily rising number of schools fell short. By 2007, public support for the law collapsed.

The Obama administration took a different approach to federalism. Adopting common college- and career-ready standards, meaning the Common Core State Standards (CCSS), was one way for states to gain points in the competition for 2009's Race to the Top funds. Starved for revenue during the Great Recession, states could be forgiven for mistaking this incentive as nonoptional. As years passed without the reauthorization of NCLB, Secretary of Education Arne Duncan offered waivers to states seeking exemption from the most onerous provision of the law: the requirement of 100 percent proficiency. In exchange for waivers, states had to sign on to a list of reforms favored by the administration, including college- and career-ready standards and teacher evaluation systems that included student test scores. Many Republicans accused Duncan of using waivers to impose an unlegislated reform agenda on the states. Conservative support for Common Core sharply declined. Michael Petrilli, a Republican supporter of Common Core, urged Duncan to help the CCSS effort "by declaring that the federal government is going to stay a million miles away from the Common Core."[11]

The Bush and Obama administrations respected federalism rhetorically when describing standards. But the actual result was different. The federal role in K–12 education was larger in 2017, when Barack Obama left office, than in 2001, when George W. Bush entered. Standards-based reform played an important part in both administrations' expansion of influence and centralization of power.

Public Opinion

[handwritten: what about teacher opinions?]

The public likes standards in education. The popularity of the general idea has remained stable over decades. A 1989 Gallup Poll, for example, found 70 percent of the public in favor of requiring local schools "to conform to national achievement standards and goals" and 77 percent supporting tests to determine if students meet the standards. Nearly three decades later, the 2017 *Education Next* poll also found widespread support.

Table 6.1 reproduces the results of several *Education Next* polls on standards. Two trends are evident. The surveys presented random samples of respondents with two versions of the same question, one asking if they supported "Common Core standards" and the other simply "standards." The widespread popularity of CCSS in 2013, with 65 percent in favor and only

TABLE 6.1   *Education Next* polls on standards, with and without Common Core name, 2013–2017

Position	Prompt	2013	2014	2015	2016	2017
With name	Support	65	53	49	42	41
	Oppose	13	26	35	42	38
Without name	Support	NA	68	54	56	61
	Oppose	NA	16	30	28	20

Note: Question with name omitted was not asked in 2013.

13 percent opposed, fell sharply in subsequent years. By 2017, support registered 41 percent and opposition 38 percent. But support for the generic notion of "standards" remained strong, with 61 percent in favor and only 20 percent opposed.

Although opposition to CCSS may have peaked in 2016 and may now be plateauing, the Common Core brand has clearly taken a hit. By 2014, conservative opposition had led legislatures in three states—Indiana, Oklahoma, and South Carolina—to rescind earlier adoption of the standards. Dozens more states revised their standards (only superficially) or changed the name to exclude any reference to Common Core. The erosion of support that had occurred with NCLB was now facing Common Core. Also as with NCLB, political controversy threatened to overshadow the key question of whether Common Core was having an effect on student achievement.

RESEARCH ON THE EFFECT OF STANDARDS

This section summarizes research on the effect of standards on student achievement. The discussion is organized chronologically, starting with standards-based reform in the 1990s and ending with Common Core.

Standards-Based Reform in the 1990s

In the early days of NCLB, two studies examining National Assessment of Educational Progress (NAEP) data from the 1990s suggested standards-based reform could be used to boost student achievement.[12] Importantly, both studies should be understood as evaluations of standards in conjunction with accountability systems, not of standards alone. The analyses compared states that sanctioned schools based on low test scores with states not employing such sanctions. Twelve states had school accountability systems in 1996; by 2000, a year before NCLB was enacted, the number had grown to thirty-nine. All of the accountability states had adopted standards or frameworks. The tests that identified failing schools were written to reflect the standards, but the studies modeled only the accountability regimes, not the tests or standards themselves, as potential causal factors.

Martin Carnoy and Susanna Loeb included student and school accountability provisions in creating an index reflecting the intensity of accountability for each state. Higher NAEP scores were associated with stronger accountability systems. Eric Hanushek and Margaret Raymond's study was limited to school accountability. They found that states adopting consequential school accountability—that is, accountability with teeth—were more likely to make gains from fourth to eighth grade on NAEP than states without consequential accountability.[13]

what consequences?
who did the affect?

No Child Left Behind

As NCLB matured, several researchers investigated the effects of NCLB by examining variation in state performance on NAEP. A study by Thomas Dee and Brian Jacob exploited the fact that while many states had test-based accountability in the 1990s, NCLB forced the remaining states to adopt standards in reading and mathematics, to test student progress in demonstrating proficiency with the standards, and to hold schools accountable for the results. As with the pre-NCLB studies, it is the final policy element of accountability—in this case, the introduction of NCLB-style accountability—that served to differentiate the states in the analysis. Dee and Jacob found statistically significant, positive effects for NCLB on fourth-grade math scores (effect size of 0.23). Gains in eighth-grade math were positive and nearly significant (effect size of 0.10); no significant effects were found in reading in either fourth or eighth grade.[14]

no longer voluntary

Manyee Wong, Thomas Cook, and Peter Steiner also used variation in NAEP scores to evaluate NCLB's impact. They compared national public school performance to that of Catholic schools, the latter presumably outside of NCLB's influence. In addition, they modeled the stringency of state accountability systems by comparing the number of schools declared at risk of sanctioning. The study found consistently positive effects of NCLB on fourth- and eighth-grade math scores but no effect in reading.[15]

ENG is not as easy to grasp as math concepts, deeper comprehension & understanding needed

Wong, Cook, and Steiner caution that their findings apply to No Child Left Behind as a whole; they do not tease apart the various elements of the law.

That warning underscores the problem with drawing inferences regarding the effect of standards from the NCLB research. Standards are foundational to NCLB. Despite that, evaluating the end effects of NCLB—or, as the pre-NCLB studies do, the end effects in states with standards-based accountability systems—captures the impact of multiple policies, not just standards.

Efforts to isolate the effects of standards have been sparse. A 2009 analysis by Russ Whitehurst investigated whether the quality of a state's standards is related to its performance on NAEP.[16] Whitehurst used ratings of state standards produced by two organizations, the American Federation of Teachers (AFT) and the Fordham Institute, and NAEP scores from 2000 to 2007 (both the longitudinal gains and the cross-sectional scores for each administration of NAEP). He found no correlation between the quality of state standards and NAEP scores. Whitehurst also disaggregated the state NAEP scores of white and black students and still found no statistically significant correlation. States with weak standards, at least in the eyes of AFT and Fordham's evaluations, scored about the same on NAEP as states with strong standards.

The Lead-Up to Common Core

The *2012 Brown Center Report* (BCR) presented an analysis attempting to predict the effects of Common Core.[17] It confirmed Whitehurst's 2009 finding—that the quality of state standards bears no relationship with student achievement—using NAEP data from different years and employing a different set of demographic controls.

One section of the BCR study focused on test score variance. The "common" part of Common Core addresses between-state differences in standards, not differences within states. After all, students in all fifty states in 2012 had been educated under common standards since the advent of NCLB in 2002—and in many states, long before that. The assumption is that state-level learning differences are driven by differences in students' exposure to educational factors shaped by state standards. High-quality, common standards would lead to a good education for all by boosting achievement in low performing states.

The idea may be intuitively attractive, but where variance appears in test scores raises doubt. The standard deviation of NAEP scores within states is four to five times larger than the standard deviation of state means. What does this say about standards' potential reach? Massachusetts and Mississippi report NAEP means about twenty-five points apart. Some believe that common standards can ameliorate such a difference. But, as shown in table 6.2, the average within-state standard deviation is larger than twenty-five points. Every state has a mini–Massachusetts-Mississippi contrast within its own borders. In some cases, mini–Massachusetts-Mississippi contrasts can be found within school districts, within schools, and, yes, even within classrooms. And those contrasts exist despite students receiving an education under common standards.[18]

The BCR study concluded that the Common Core State Standards would have a negligible impact on student achievement. The quality of state standards is not correlated with state NAEP scores; the level at which states define proficiency on state tests is also largely uncorrelated with NAEP scores; and the amount of test score variance between states is dwarfed by the variance within states, the latter four to five times larger than the former despite within-state variance already having been "treated" by common standards.[19] It is important to emphasize that these shortcomings are not exclusive to Common Core. They apply to all standards.

A study with an optimistic outlook for Common Core was published later in 2012. William H. Schmidt and Richard T. Houang of Michigan State University (MSU) rated states' mathematics standards for their similarity to the CCSS math standards (CCSS-M) and compared the ratings with states' 2009 NAEP eighth-grade math scores.[20] The ratings drew on the authors' work analyzing scores on international math assessments, which produced the theory that high achieving nations scored at the top of international league tables because of the focus, rigor, and coherence of their math standards.[21] The MSU study employed a rubric showing that CCSS math standards were similar to the standards of top-scoring nations in focus and coherence. They then rated state standards using the same rubric and calculated a proximity score reflecting the congruence of state standards with CCSS-M.

TABLE 6.2   Size of between-state and within-state standard deviations (SD)

Grade/subject	Between-state SD	Within-state SD	Multiple (within/between)
Fourth grade/reading	6.6	34.7	5.3
Fourth grade/math	6.3	27.8	4.4
Eighth grade/reading	6.5	32.9	5.1
Eighth grade/math	8.5	34.8	4.1

Note: Standard deviations expressed in NAEP scale score points, 2009 assessments.

The authors regressed 2009 state NAEP scores on the proximity scores and a set of demographic controls. The initial regression produced no findings of statistical significance. An analysis of residuals suggested dividing the states into two groups: thirty-seven wealthier, higher scoring states (Group A) and thirteen, less wealthy, lower scoring states (Group B). Modeled separately, the two groups produced statistically significant results, indicating that 2009 state NAEP scores were related to the similarity of state math standards to CCSS-M. Schmidt and Houang hypothesized that the two groups reflected differences in the implementation of standards (Group B facing more severe resource constraints and demographic challenges) and concluded that the findings, in terms of Common Core, offered "a vision of what can be"—that is, a vision of what Common Core standards could accomplish if implemented appropriately.[22]

Effects of Common Core

In a February 2017 article, Morgan Polikoff argued that it may be too early to tell whether Common Core has had any effect.[23] He cited several examples—among them, studies of small high schools, vouchers, NCLB, and School Improvement Grants—in which early findings were either partially or fully reversed by later evaluations. It takes time to implement complex policies, and Common Core, seeking to tweak several downstream parts of the educational system, probably requires more patience than most policy efforts before a valid evaluation can be conducted. In addition, no one knows when standards are fully operational, in the sense of pinpointing when a fair amount of time has passed for judging whether their intended changes have actually taken effect.

Nonetheless, early research of standards has its virtues. Opportunity costs in terms of time and resources arise in the early days of implementation. The key activities that Common Core supporters relied on for successful implementation of the standards—development of tests, creation of curriculum materials, and professional development of teachers—were well under way, if not completed, by 2013. Billions of dollars and hundreds of millions of educators' hours have gone into the CCSS effort. In 2018, it's too late to get that money and time back or to redirect them toward other endeavors. When Common Core was first being debated, supporters surely knew that mid-course corrections might be necessary. A mid-course correction is impossible if the direction in which one is heading mid-course is unknown.

The *Brown Center Reports* of 2014 through 2016 presented several studies of Common Core using NAEP scores, and they possess all of the limitations of evaluating standards in the early phases of implementation. They are by no means conclusive. Moreover, they cannot discern causal effects, only the changes in NAEP scores associated with groups of states sharing particular characteristics. As with the aforementioned studies, including the Schmidt and Houang analysis embraced by Common Core advocates, gauging the effect of Common Core requires analysis of state variation in some aspect of the reform. The BCR studies created implementation indexes to model how states differed in implementing Common Core.

First presented in the 2014 BCR, the 2011 implementation index is based on responses to a 2011 survey by federal budget officials asking how states spent funds from the American Recovery and Reinvestment Act of 2009. States reported if they had engaged in four activities: 1) adopted CCSS; 2) provided, guided, or funded professional development on CCSS; 3) provided curriculum/instructional materials for CCSS; or 4) worked with a consortium to develop assessments aligned with CCSS. States responding affirmatively to all four activities were categorized as "strong implementers" of CCSS (nineteen states). States indicating that they had not engaged in any of the activities (five states) were designated "non-adopters." The remaining twenty-six states were categorized as "medium" implementers; that is, they had adopted CCSS but had not engaged in all facets of implementation.[24]

The 2014 study found that from 2009 to 2013, strong implementation states gained 1.9 NAEP scale score points in eighth-grade math; the medium implementers gained 1.0 points; and the non-adopters gained 0.6 points. The 1.3 scale score advantage of strong implementation states over the non-adopters is quite small (about 0.035 standard deviation). Most of the advantage appears in 2011–2013, the second half of the four-year interval, which offers a sliver of encouragement for CCSS. It seems reasonable to assume that more CCSS states would have begun implementation after 2011 rather than before 2011. Thirty-three states and DC had adopted CCSS by August 2010, and another twelve states by June 2012.[25]

The same analytical strategy was employed in later studies, updating the initial analysis using the most recently released NAEP data and employing a second index of implementation. The second index was based on responses to a 2013 survey of chief state school officers on their state's plans for implementing CCSS. States with plans to complete "classroom implementation" of the Common Core ELA standards by the end of the 2012–2013 school year were designated "strong" implementers (eleven states); states that had not adopted CCSS or had rescinded adoption were classified as "non-adopters" (seven states); and the remaining states were placed in the "medium" category (thirty-two states).

The *2016 Brown Center Report* examined the relationship of state implementation to NAEP scores in fourth-grade reading and eighth-grade math. The results were similar to the 2014 BCR study. Only trivial differences, 1.5 NAEP scale score points or less, were detected in the NAEP scores of strong implementers of CCSS and the scores of non-adoption states.

This chapter utilizes a new analysis. Table 6.3 shows the score differences from the two models.[26]

The data in table 6.3 use regression-adjusted NAEP scores, calculated by Matt Chingos and Kristin Blagg of the Urban Institute, to report demographically controlled changes in state scores. Chingos and Blagg adjusted state NAEP scores for racial composition, the proportion of students identified for free and reduced lunch, special education, English language learner programs, and age at testing. The data compare average growth on NAEP in strong implementation states with growth in the non-adoption states. Cells with positive values favor the strong implementers; cells with negative values favor non-adopters. The findings are consistent with the previous analyses using unadjusted scores, detecting only tiny differences between strong implementers of CCSS and non-adopting states. The largest difference favoring strong implementation states—found in the bottom row of the column, "Entire six years (2009–2015)"—is only 0.6 NAEP points.

TABLE 6.3   NAEP scale score change, difference between strong CCSS implementation states and non-adopters (average change in demographically adjusted score, 2009–2015)

Grade/subject	Implementation index model	Entire six years (2009–2015)	Most recent interval (2013–2015)
Fourth grade/reading	Imp11	−0.1	−1.7
	Imp13	0.0	−2.4
Eighth grade/math	Imp11	−0.3	−2.3
	Imp13	0.6	−1.1

Note: Positive values favor states with strong implementation of CCSS; negative values favor non-adoption states.

All of the comparisons of NAEP score changes in the most recent interval (2013–2015) favor non-adopters of CCSS (ranging from 1.1 to 2.4 scale score points).

As mentioned earlier, the first analyses suggested that strong implementers of CCSS held a slight advantage in the early days of implementation. The later analyses, including the one reported in table 6.3, suggest that after 2013 the trend reversed. The advantage was now turning toward the non-adopters of CCSS. It's important to note that for all states, regardless of whether they had warmly embraced CCSS or developed their own standards, NAEP scores were stagnant from 2009 to 2015. The charge from NAEP critics that Common Core is responsible for holding back US achievement is not supported by this analysis.

LESSONS LEARNED

In most states, standards-based reform has existed for at least three decades. The Bush and Obama administrations premised their education policies on the potential of standards to improve schools and boost student achievement. The Bush administration's vehicle for standards-based reform was NCLB. Research indicates that NCLB produced modest positive effects on student achievement—confined mainly to math and with no significant effect on reading. The Obama administration embraced the Common Core. To date, eight years after the Common Core State Standards were released and adopted by a vast majority of states, no causal evidence exists on their effectiveness in boosting student achievement. The exploratory analyses presented in this chapter suggest minimal effects, perhaps slightly positive in the early years of implementation but then fading over time. More rigorous analyses are needed to confirm or reject this hypothesis.

The Bush-Obama record with standards is disappointing. Research suggests that standards—even clear, ambitious, and elegantly worded standards—are weak instruments for raising student achievement. Nevertheless, out of this disappointment have emerged several lessons for future policy makers and researchers.

Lesson 1: Political Support Matters and Supportive Coalitions May Not Last

Public support for standards reaches its apogee when standards are first considered, as an aspirational idea in their most general form, lacking curricular details and shorn of accountability—in other words, a reform without substance or costs. Once standards are written, adopted, and begin to influence educational activities downstream, support declines. Over time, NCLB and Common Core became tainted brands. Considering that NCLB's support plummeted after accountability systems began labeling schools as failures, support for CCSS may erode further once accountability tied to CCSS tests takes effect. The public loves their local schools and thinks they are just fine. Accountability linked to standards-based tests is for other schools.

Political coalitions that support standards during the design phase are difficult to maintain. What gets the political right excited about standards is holding the public school system accountable for student learning. That's why Chester Finn and Mike Petrilli like standards. What gets the Education Trust excited is being able to promote an equity agenda for disadvantaged kids. They focus on closing gaps. What gets professional groups excited is reorienting curriculum and instruction toward the ideals of progressive education: higher-order thinking, learning "how to learn" over learning facts, conceptual understanding, project-based learning, heterogeneous groups, and so on. That's why proponents of balanced literacy, twenty-first-century skills, and constructivist math like standards. All of these groups construe the word *standards* in accord with their respective worldviews—worldviews that do not always overlap.

Lesson 2: Standards-Based Reform Is Top-Down and Mechanistic

Standards advocates portray education reform as an engineering problem. Improvement will arise from getting all of the system's pieces working in sync in pursuit of ambitious goals. Setting standards is what professional educators and upper-level policy makers do; the work that goes into attaining standards is done downstream by someone else—and often referred to simply as "implementation." Standards advocates regard the political and organizational contexts of schools and school systems as potential allies in implementing goals, overlooking that they also have the power to undermine the linkages between standards and the curriculum, instruction, and assessments that standards seek to forge.

Standards are regulatory. The fundamental difference between minimal and maximal regulation is germane to a discussion of education standards. Standards that attempt to ensure that every American child is college- and career-ready are maximal. USDA regulations are minimal. They do not guarantee that we can all have filet mignon every night for dinner, or even a meal that tastes good. They do guarantee that the food supply will be safe and reasonably devoid of "yuck factors," ingredients that most people would prefer not to eat but won't kill them. Yuck factor standards are minimal. That's why the FDA publishes a handbook setting acceptable levels for insect parts, rat hairs, mouse droppings, maggots, and other disgusting "natural or unavoidable defects" showing up in our food.[27] Setting those levels at zero would shut down the food supply. Utopianism rarely makes good public policy.

Lesson 3: Curriculum Matters, but Standards Do Not Guarantee More Effective Curriculum

As pointed out earlier, implementation of standards involves their impact on downstream educational activities—what happens in schools and classrooms. Improving curriculum is one of those downstream events.

The effects of curriculum programs can vary significantly, as was demonstrated through a randomized control trial of first- and second-grade math curricula conducted by Mathematica Policy Research. The study today remains one of the only experimental evaluations of K–12 textbooks. The four programs in the experiment covered essentially the same topics. Students in three of the programs (Math Expressions, Saxon, and Foresman-Addison) scored about the same, but all three outscored the fourth program (Investigations) by a statistically significant amount (effect size of about 0.22). A student at the 50th percentile who received instruction in Investigations in first and second grade would have scored at the 59th percentile if taught from one of the other programs.

Curricular alignment to CCSS refers to whether a curriculum adheres to Common Core standards. Alignment is not synonymous with quality. Alignment evaluations, typically conducted by expert panels rating textbooks, answer the question of whether texts address the topics embodied by standards; they do not address a text's impact on learning. Two texts may teach the same topic, with one doing it well and one doing it poorly. If that topic is addressed in CCSS, both texts are in alignment.

A serious threat to alignment arises from a practical reality of classrooms: everything that is taught is *not* learned. Teachers attempting to teach a new concept will notice that some kids don't have easier, prerequisite skills or knowledge. Since it makes no sense to teach the more difficult concept, they will try to get those kids on pace by reteaching the easier material. That is what any good teacher would do, but it renders the class curriculum out of alignment with the prescribed curriculum. When these slippages occur year after year, misalignment grows.

CCSS writers are hopeful that standards can avoid slippage, or at least diminish the chances of it occurring. There are fewer topics in each grade. The pace of instruction is slowed down to devote more time to each standard. But the fact remains that grade-based standards assume that students possess the prerequisite knowledge to tackle each grade's new learning. CCSS supporters believe that students will be better prepared to transition from grade to grade, but that's a belief, one not supported by empirical evidence, and by no means assured. In a 2017 poll in three states—Texas, Ohio, and Kentucky—teachers were asked to rate a list of ten challenges they face implementing college- and career-readiness standards. The top two responses were "a wide range of student abilities," with 71 percent describing it as a moderate or major challenge, and "inadequate student preparation in prior grades," with 62 percent rating that as a moderate or major challenge.[28]

The same potential for misalignment arises on the other end of the achievement spectrum, with high achieving students who already know the standards for their grade. Why waste time and bore students by teaching them something they already know? The CCSS math standards offer a single course in eighth grade that includes some algebra, but it is not an Algebra I course—that's reserved for ninth grade. Following the adoption of CCSS math standards, enrollment of eighth graders in Algebra I began to decline, falling from a peak of 48 percent in 2013 to 43 percent in 2015. The decline reversed a steady increase in eighth-grade Algebra I enrollment that had been going on since the 1990s. Many educators consider acceleration of some students (but not all) as antithetical to the "common" in Common Core. If all students can't take Algebra I in eighth grade, this point of view reasons, nobody should be allowed to take it.

The alignment studies may have exacerbated the difficulty of getting good materials for high achievers into classrooms. Singapore Math, a curriculum long admired by the gifted and talented education community for advancing students quickly through challenging material, scored poorly for alignment in the reviews of EdReports.org.[29] A common complaint of the evaluators was that Singapore taught content too early. Teaching content ahead of its designated time violates the CCSS notion of curricular coherence.

Lesson 4: Standards Can Be Used in Efforts to Change Pedagogy

Early research on standards recognized that external standards faced a difficult task in changing how teachers teach. Andrew Porter discussed the inherent tensions of promoting professionalism and teacher autonomy with "telling teachers what to do."[30] Porter's admonition to leave pedagogy to the discretion of teachers was reinforced by the failure of the 1990s standards projects, which were chock full of pedagogy. The Common Core website is emphatic: "Teachers know best about what works in the classroom. That is why these standards establish what students need to learn but do not dictate how teachers should teach. Instead, schools and teachers will decide how best to help students reach the standards."[31]

Jason Zimba, one of the primary authors of the CCSS math standards, commented, "Standards shouldn't dictate curriculum or pedagogy. But there has been some criticism recently that the implementation of CCSS may be effectively forcing a particular pedagogy on teachers." Indeed, press accounts documented teachers complaining about pressure to change their teaching. Emmanuel Felton, in a 2014 *Hechinger Report* story, reported, "The Common Core wasn't necessarily supposed to change how math is taught, but in many schools that's exactly what's happening." Later in the article, Phil Daro, one of the lead writers of the Common Core math standards, is quoted: "The Common Core is silent about how to teach. When we wrote the standards we were prohibited from addressing how to teach, that's not what standards are supposed to do."[32]

So what happened? In reading and mathematics, the 1990s were riven by curriculum battles between traditionalists and progressives. Standards embody political compromises, and the compromises manifest themselves in negotiated wording. Serving a role similar to the communiqués issued after meetings of world leaders, standards are orchestrated to emphasize common ground. But the common ground erodes once standards are converted into curriculum and instruction. Differences papered over with rhetoric are exposed. Dog whistles signal to local educators that imposing pedagogical restraints on teachers may be compatible with the standards after all.

Here's an example. *Engage New York* published what it called "twelve pedagogical shifts demanded by the Common Core State Standards," six in math and six in English language arts. The term *pedagogical shifts* spread like wildfire. Teacher-blogger Barry Garelick, a critic of Common Core and math traditionalist, observed, "[E]ven before the ink dried on the Common

Core standards, proponents of Common Core talked about 'The Shifts' as if they were, [or] are, enforceable parts of the standards themselves." Garelick has devoted several blog posts to describing the progressive instructional practices on which he has received professional development, all in the service of implementing Common Core.[33]

CONCLUSION

There is a wonderful story (and almost certainly a myth) about a comment made by Premier Zhou Enlai during Richard Nixon's historic trip to China in 1972. Asked about the historical impact of the French Revolution, Zhou was reported to have responded, "It's too early to tell."[34] The comment quickly circulated as affirmation of the Chinese leader's legendary ability to take the long view on world events.

Common Core supporters have urged a long view on standards. Michael Kirst, chair of the California State School Board, named 2020 as the year when the beneficial effects of Common Core might be first apparent.[35] That's ten years after most states adopted the standards. The second graders of 2010 will graduate from high school in 2020. There may even be a longer wait. If Common Core is to be judged by its impact on college and career effects, such outcomes cannot be measured until several years after 2020.

Common Core sits in a public policy purgatory. We don't know if it's working; we don't know when we will know if it's working. The policy still has supporters, but its detractors are also numerous. As of 2018, the research on CCSS has been dominated by descriptive accounts of implementation (i.e., what's going on) along with an effort to build a knowledge base that will help local educators implement CCSS (i.e., how can we do this better). That is a reasonable research agenda, but given the track record of standards-based reform, perhaps it's time to consider an additional hypothesis: that standards simply don't work.

Federal Support for Charter Schooling

A Presidential Priority

Anna J. Egalite

O n January 8, 1790, the nation's first president delivered his State of the Union address to Congress. Curiously, among the list of topics addressed—national defense, the economy, immigration, and others—George Washington referenced education. Traditionally a responsibility of state and local governments, education is not typically regarded as an area that is ripe for leadership from the same public official who is also charged with serving as commander in chief, head of state, the nation's top executive, chief diplomat, legislator, and the face of a nation. Yet, as William Howell notes, Americans yearn for presidential leadership in education nonetheless, and presidents have responded by devising creative mechanisms by which they can insert their education priorities into state and local education policies.[1] Among modern presidents, George W. Bush and Barack Obama stand out for having made federal support for charter schooling a domestic policy priority and for finding creative ways to assert their leadership in a policy domain for which, at first glance, the president lacks obvious constitutional authority.

Charter schools represent a new kind of public institution that is mission-driven, decentralized, autonomous, lean, and quick to adapt to a changing environment. Performance contracts grant charter school leaders greater flexibility over curriculum, staffing, textbooks, scheduling, budgeting, and other administrative and curricular decisions but hold schools to strict accountability standards in return. Crucially, from a governance perspective, the charter school model represents a separation of policy oversight and decision making from service delivery. Today, there are almost seven thousand charter schools enrolling an estimated 3.1 million students. In seventeen US cities, charter school enrollment represents 30 percent or more of the total school-aged population.[2] Although Los Angeles has the highest number of total charter students (more than 150,000), the most charter-dense cities in terms of enrollment share are New Orleans (92 percent charter) and Detroit (53 percent charter). The only states that lack a single charter school are Montana, North Dakota, South Dakota, Nebraska, Kentucky, West Virginia, and Vermont.

The popularity of the charter school model in the United States is mirrored by contemporaneous efforts in other nations, such as the United Kingdom's "academy schools," which are publicly funded but independently operated schools that enjoy more freedom than schools that remain under the control of the local authority. Established in 2000, academy schools do not have to follow the national curriculum or respect a prescribed budget or school calendar. As of March 2016, about five thousand of the twenty-four thousand total schools in England were academy schools.

THE CHARTER SCHOOL LANDSCAPE IN THE UNITED STATES, PRE-2001

The nation's first charter school law was signed in June 1991 by Minnesota governor Arne Carlson. California passed its charter school law a year later, followed shortly by Colorado, Georgia, New Mexico, Massachusetts, Michigan, and Wisconsin. Elevating what started as a grassroots idea molded by Ray Budde, Joe Nathan, Albert Shanker, and Ted Kolderie to the federal policy agenda, senators David Durenberger (R-MN) and Joseph Lieberman (D-CT) were instrumental in passing the first federal charter school law, which President Bill Clinton signed as part of the 1994 reauthorization of the Elementary and Secondary Education Act (ESEA). Congress appropriated just $6 million for the Public Charter Schools discretionary grant program in 1995, but that figure rose steadily in the ensuing years, reaching $190 million by 2001.[3] By the time Clinton left office, the number of charter schools had increased from a single school in Minnesota to over two thousand schools in thirty-seven states plus the District of Columbia.

For context, the nation's first private school-choice program started around the same time as charter schools, with the establishment of the Milwaukee Parental Choice Program in 1990. Today, there are sixty-one private school-choice programs in operation across the country, enrolling almost 180,000 students. This is just a drop in the bucket relative to the three million students currently enrolled in charter schools. It is interesting to compare the modest growth in publicly supported private school-choice programs across the country with the explosive growth in the charter school sector over the same time period. This chapter explores what role the federal government played in promoting charter schools and what advice and intuitions can be gleaned from that experience.

FEDERAL PROMOTION OF CHARTER SCHOOLS UNDER BUSH AND OBAMA

Both the Republican and Democratic presidents examined here responded to public demand to make education a top-tier national issue by revealing bold plans to expand the federal role in education. Although a number of their other education reforms have faced harsh criticism for expanding Washington's footprint in a heavy-handed manner, insufficient attention has been paid to their role in making the expansion of charter schooling a national priority. Promoting charter schooling allowed the reformers to "go big," while keeping their ambition narrow. It allowed for authentic and localized co-creation of an education reform, genuine engagement of communities, and state-by-state conversations about what implementation should actually look like. In contrast, federal promotion of concurrent education reforms, such as the Common Core State Standards, involved a prescriptive package of reforms—standards, testing, and accountability—that quickly became a nationalized bundle of grievances.

Federal promotion of charter schools under these two presidents was twofold: they used the lure of federal dollars and flexed the federal government's regulatory power to exert outsized influence on the development of these publicly funded but privately operated schools. Their largest investments were through the Charter Schools Program (CSP) and the Credit Enhancement for Charter School Facilities Program (Facilities Program), which are summarized in table 7.1.

CSP grants are intended to promote the establishment, development, and expansion of charter schools. Although the CSP has existed since 1994, back when only seven states had even passed a charter school law, both Bush and Obama expanded the program with a significant infusion of federal dollars. In 2002, President Bush's Department of Education awarded $198 million through this program, a figure that increased to $211 million by 2008. One

TABLE 7.1   Charter schools grant programs administered by the US
Department of Education

Program name	Description	Notable developments under Bush	Notable developments under Obama
The Federal Charter Schools Program (CSP)	Created in 1994 as an amendment to the Elementary and Secondary Education Act, the CSP is a competitive grant program that provides financial assistance to support the planning, program design, implementation, replication, and expansion of charter schools. The CSP also supports the dissemination of charter schools' most successful practices.	In FY 2002, Bush's Education Department awarded $198 million in CSP grants. In FY 2008, annual funding had increased to $211 million.	The Obama administration oversaw the investment of over a billion dollars in the CSP between 2009 and 2015. Since 2010, the program has set aside funding specifically for the replication of high performing CMOs.
The Credit Enhancement for Charter School Facilities Program	Created in 2002, this program aims to enhance charter schools' credit so they can access private and other sources of nonfederal capital to acquire, construct, and renovate school facilities.	This program was created by the Bush administration in FY 2002. By FY 2008, $739 million had been invested.	Funding increased from $8.3 million in FY 2009 to $16 million in FY 2016.

Note: Four other federal programs can also offer facilities-related support to charter schools: the State Charter School Facilities Incentive Grants program (closed since 2014); the Public Assistance Grant Program operated by the Federal Emergency Management Agency; the US Department of Agriculture's Community Facilities Programs; and the New Markets Tax Credit Program and the Qualified Zone Academy Bond Program, both operated by the US Department of the Treasury.
Source: US Department of Education, "Welcome to ED's Charter Schools Program," https://www2.ed.gov/about/offices/list/oii/csp/index.html.

of the most significant early CSP awards occurred in September 2005, when Bush's Education Department awarded $20.9 million to the state of Louisiana in the wake of Hurricane Katrina. These funds were used to reopen existing charter schools, finance the creation of ten new charter schools, and expand existing charter schools to accommodate more students. By the last year of the Bush administration, charter school funding had reached $211 million.

When Obama entered the Oval Office in 2009, he increased funding for the CSP by about 60 percent so that by the conclusion of his presidency, federal support for charter schools had climbed to $333.2 million. In 2013–2014 alone, nearly half of all charter schools in the country benefited from federal grant money. Explaining the rationale behind the Obama administration's expansion of federal investment for charter schools, Secretary of Education Arne Duncan said, "Too often, charter school successes are isolated and don't have an impact beyond the walls of their own buildings . . . We're helping [charter] schools to scale."[4]

The Facilities Program, on the other hand, was created in 2002 to help non-profit organizations and charter organizations leverage their own finances to create, renovate, or expand charter school facilities. Between 2002 and 2008, the Facilities Program directed $739 million toward 207 charter schools. In 1999, then-Governor George W. Bush had proposed such a program during a campaign speech at the Manhattan Institute Luncheon in New York, where he spoke about a "charter school homestead fund" that could be drawn upon to finance charter school startup costs. Upon assuming the presidency in January 2001, President Bush's blueprint for education reform restated his desire to provide startup funding for charter schools. By the time the House–Senate conference reached an agreement on the No Child Left Behind legislation in December 2001, the legislative language that had been agreed upon included federal dollars to finance the startup costs associated with the creation of new charter schools. Congress ultimately approved $25 million to support a Facilities Program and in September of that year, the Department of Education announced its intention to provide facilities grants to groups in Massachusetts, New York, North Carolina, and Washington, DC.

Federal funding for the acquisition, construction, or renovation of charter school facilities is a significant lever for promoting charter school growth because, unlike traditional public schools, charter schools cannot issue bonds backed by property taxes. Further, the short-term nature of a charter agreement makes such investments look like a credit risk to lending institutions. The Facilities Program leverages federal dollars to reduce the perception of financial risk by guaranteeing debt undertaken to finance facilities so that private lenders and investors are more likely to provide financial support for charter schools.

In addition to directing federal grant aid to support charter schools, both presidents employed complementary strategies to boost the proliferation of charter schools, such as Bush's signature education reform, the No Child Left Behind Act (NCLB), and Obama's competitive grant program, known as Race to the Top (RTTT). Thus, the impressive expansion of charter schools throughout both presidencies reflects the combined impact of

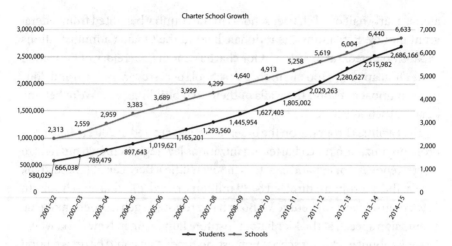

FIGURE 7.1   Growth in charter schools and charter school enrollment, FY 2002 through FY 2015

Source: National Alliance for Public Charter Schools Data Dashboard

federal investments and each president's complementary policies (figure 7.1). By the time Bush left office, approximately forty-three hundred charter schools were educating 1.3 million students across the country. This growth trajectory continued under Obama so that by fiscal year 2015, the most recent year for which we have data, those figures had climbed to over sixty-six hundred charter schools educating 2.7 million students.

THE EFFECT OF PRESIDENT GEORGE W. BUSH'S EDUCATION POLICIES ON CHARTER SCHOOLS

Saturday, January 20, 2001, marked an uncertain beginning to the presidency of George W. Bush. The Texan had lost the popular vote by half a million ballots, the outcome of the election was ultimately determined by the US Supreme Court, and his frequent verbal gaffes had already made him the laughing stock of late-night television. Nonetheless, his policy ideas had been substantive enough to persuade the public to vote against the incumbent party, despite eight years of strong economic growth. Addressing this seeming contradiction, Bush likened prosperity to a drug, warning Americans that prosperous times can dull a country's sense of urgency and empathy. "The path of least resistance is always downhill. America's way is the rising road," he said upon accepting the Republican presidential nomination on August 3, 2000. True to his word, he selected education policies that rejected complacency, disrupted the status quo, and shone a spotlight on achievement gaps.

Bush's support for charter schools was consistent with his general conviction that "freedom—economic, political, and religious—is the only fair and productive way of governing a society."[5] He was also enamored by the potential of charter schools to promote innovation in education. "Charter schools encourage educational entrepreneurs to try innovative methods. They break up the monopoly of one-size-fits-all education. These diverse, creative schools are proof that parents from all walks of life are willing to challenge the status quo if it means a better education for their children. More competition and more choices for parents and students will raise the bar for everyone."[6]

In running for the presidency, he maintained the claim that "local people should control local schools," yet there was no denying the reforms he was pursuing would dramatically increase federal involvement in education. To square this circle, the "compassionate conservative" focused on the unacceptably low achievement of racial minorities. Reflecting on the legacy of NCLB as his presidency wound down in November 2008, he said, "[NCLB] focused the country's attention on the fact that we had an achievement gap that—you know, white kids were reading better in the fourth grade than Latinos or African American kids. And that's unacceptable for America."[7] By spotlighting racial achievement gaps and using those data to justify advancing both public and private school choice, his signature school reform, NCLB, marked the start of a new vision for the federal role in education policy.

No Child Left Behind

A thirty-page legislative blueprint of the No Child Left Behind Act was presented to Congress on January 23, 2001. Made possible by bipartisan collaboration led by President George W. Bush, Senator Ted Kennedy, and congressmen George Miller and John Boehner, the thousand-page reauthorization of the Elementary and Secondary Education Act passed the House in May 2001 with 384–45 votes in favor and sailed through the Senate in June, where the vote was 91–8 in favor. Signed into law on January 8, 2002, NCLB came with a massive injection of federal dollars for education. In the year after the passage of NCLB, federal appropriations for education increased from $42.1 billion to $56.2 billion, a 34 percent increase. The core principles of the plan focused on standards, testing, local control, and choice. The school choice option was introduced in the following way: "American children must not be left in persistently dangerous or failing schools. When schools do not teach and will not change, parents and students must have other meaningful options."

In the negotiations preceding NCLB's passage, private school vouchers were quickly abandoned, but the law elevated the status of charter schools by supporting the CSP, by authorizing the Facilities Program, and by mandating that students attending public schools determined to be "in need of improvement" for two consecutive years could switch to a higher performing traditional public or charter public school. Chartering aligned with NCLB's push for transparency and accountability for disaggregated standardized test score data and, by simultaneously building the capacity of state education agencies to build longitudinal student data systems, NCLB made it more feasible for charter school supporters to keep score and demonstrate the efficacy of this reform for improving outcomes for high-needs student subgroups. Disaggregation in data collection efforts across the universe of all public schools remains especially influential. School performance data are frequently incorporated into school report cards to promote transparency, ensure accountability, and inform parent choices in the charter school marketplace.

Nonetheless, at the conclusion of Bush's time in the White House in 2009, his signature education accomplishment had fallen out of favor and his successor was charged with reauthorizing the nation's K–12 education law. With Democratic majorities in Congress, widespread frustration with NCLB's increasingly inflexible mandates, and bipartisan momentum for education reform, President Obama faced the choice of making a clean break from his predecessor's education policy paradigm or perpetuating it by furthering the expansion of charter schooling.

THE EFFECT OF PRESIDENT OBAMA'S EDUCATION POLICIES ON CHARTER SCHOOLS

When Illinois senator Barack Obama formally announced that he was seeking the Democratic nomination for president in February 2007, he promised a sharp break from the policies of the previous administration. He assured voters that "a different future is possible," but—unlike his promises about health care, national defense, energy policy, and others—his education policies actually looked a lot like those of his predecessor, reaffirming the previous administration's commitment to charter schools and hinting at continuity of federal support for such schools.

When Obama entered the White House in January 2009, forty states plus the District of Columbia had charter school laws, and there were approximately forty-six hundred charter schools in operation across the country serving 1.4 million students; by 2014–2015, there were more than sixty-six hundred charter schools. This 44 percent growth was no accident. In each of his signature education reforms, Obama prioritized the growth of charter schools, making no secret of his support for the schools of choice his Republican presidential predecessor had also promoted: "Our children only get one chance at an education, and charter schools demonstrate what is possible when States, communities, teachers, parents, and students work together."[8]

Race to the Top

The economic crisis served as a focusing event for Obama to incentivize cash-strapped states to adopt his administration's preferred set of education policies. The window of opportunity opened by the American Recovery and Reinvestment Act (ARRA) in February 2009 resulted in $100 billion being set aside for education and, although the bulk of that money was used to preserve teacher jobs, $4.35 billion was set aside for a competitive categorical grant program "designed to encourage and reward states that were creating the conditions for education innovation and reform; achieving significant improvement in student outcomes, including making substantial gains in student achievement, closing achievement gaps, improving high school graduation rates, and ensuring student preparation for success in college and careers; and implementing ambitious plans in four core education reform areas."[9] The design of the RTTT competition granted significant discretion to the Arne Duncan–led US Department of Education, which privileged the administration's preferred educational policy proposals and thus strategically incentivized state policy making. This strategy was most successful in the case of clear-cut policy shifts, such as encouraging states to lift caps on charter schools. Over the course of three rounds of applications, all but four states applied for an RTTT grant.

States improved their odds of winning grant funds under this competitive grant program if they committed to holding charter schools accountable for students' standardized test scores, offered equal funding to both charter and district schools, and allowed school districts to actually establish charter schools of their own. What was remarkable about the competitive approach by which the relatively small amount of RTTT funds was distributed, and the outsized public profile associated with the initiative, was the way in which all states—even those that did not win grant funds—were motivated to adopt the administration's preferred policies. It is unlikely that policy changes such as the lifting of charter school caps would have occurred if not for the lure of federal funds.

Only two states—Tennessee and Delaware—won grants in the first round of RTTT, but forty states plus the District of Columbia had submitted applications and had committed to changing their education policies to make their states more attractive to charter schools and thus improve their odds in later rounds. Take North Carolina as a case study. After failing to win any grant funding in RTTT's first round, school choice advocates spoke out about the way in which the state's application was handcuffed because of the existing charter school cap: "We missed a big opportunity, but lawmakers have time during the upcoming short session to position North Carolina more competitively before the second round of applications are due," said Darrell Allison, president of a local school choice advocacy organization.[10] State legislators responded as the administration had hoped: "It is inexcusable for North Carolina to leave $400 million on the table," said State Senator Larry Shaw (D-Cumberland). "I'm sure my colleagues would agree that charter school legislation must be at the top of the agenda when the General Assembly reconvenes in May." By June 2011, the bill to lift the charter school cap was approved by the North Carolina General Assembly and signed into law by Governor Bev Perdue.

The surge of legislative action in North Carolina was not an isolated response. Legislators across the country acknowledged that RTTT had impacted their deliberations, breathing life into policy proposals that had gotten little traction up to that point. Moving beyond anecdotes to analysis, the University of Chicago's William Howell examined the number of relevant education reforms adopted as state policy in the aftermath of RTTT's announcement.[11] This included policies enacted by a state legislature, governor, school board, or other state governing agency. Howell's analysis revealed that the administration's plan to stimulate state-level policy making was a success. In the five-year period from 2009 to 2014, winning states enacted 88 percent of the reform-oriented education policies incentivized by RTTT. What is more surprising is that *losing* states enacted 69 percent of these policies, and states that had *never even applied* for the competition adopted 56 percent of the policies prioritized by the competition.

ESEA Flexibility Waivers

As RTTT funding ran out and a Republican-led Congress struggled to reauthorize ESEA, the Obama administration devised an unprecedented, creative workaround that would allow it to continue to push its education policy agenda. By the fall of 2011, NCLB's 2014 deadline for 100 percent proficiency was fast approaching. Almost half of states nationwide were failing to make Adequate Yearly Progress toward this ambitious goal and were being penalized for their failure. Instead of offering competitive grant funds to incentivize state school reform efforts, as it had done with RTTT, the administration leveraged the promise of relief from the federal education law's most onerous targets and sanctions in exchange for adoption of its preferred education reform initiatives. Technically legal under section 9401 of ESEA, the conditional waiver strategy was a success. Ultimately, forty-two states plus the District of Columbia applied for and received an ESEA flexibility waiver.[12]

ESEA waivers had both direct and indirect effects on charter schools. The direct effects were apparent—as public schools, charter schools were bound by these waivers in the same way as traditional public schools. Their teacher and principal evaluation system had to be consistent with the criteria described in the state's waiver application; they were expected to meet "college-and career-ready standards," to take aligned assessments, and to meet "annual measurable objectives" proposed by the state. If a charter school fell short of these objectives, it would be identified as a "priority" or "focus" school and required to implement the specific interventions for underperforming public schools that had been approved under the waiver.

An indirect effect of ESEA waivers is that many states took advantage of the waiver application process to promote stricter standards for charter school performance, making it difficult for underperforming charter schools to evade public scrutiny. For example, testifying before the Senate Committee on Health, Education, Labor, and Pensions in February 2013, then–commissioner of education for New York John King explained, "The flexibility Waiver application gave New York the opportunity to clarify and reinforce accountability expectations for the State's public charter schools."[13] In writing its waiver application, King explained, New York sought to codify the expectation that charter school authorizers would rely on rigorous standards for academic and operational outcomes.

New Jersey also used the waiver process to reinforce standards for charter school quality, adopting a "no interventions" policy. Although the ESEA flexibility waiver required states to identify the lowest performing traditional public and charter public schools and intervene to improve student outcomes, the New Jersey Department of Education opted to automatically close any charter schools that received the "priority" or "focus" label, enforcing a stricter standard for underperforming charter schools than for failing traditional public schools.

The School Improvement Grant Program

Another program that received a significant financial boost under President Obama was the School Improvement Grant (SIG) program. Congress authorized $125 million for the program in 2007, which increased to $546 million in 2009, but the most notable infusion of federal dollars came under President Obama as a result of the 2009 ARRA, which ensured a total appropriation of $3.55 billion for School Improvement Grants. Selected schools won as much as $6 million over three years to adopt one of four approved school intervention policies. The vast majority of schools (96 percent) selected the "transformation" or "turnaround" models, which did not require the existing school to close, to convert to a charter school, or to hand over the keys to a charter or education management organization. A US Department of Education report released at the closing bell of the Obama presidency revealed that implementing a SIG-funded model had no impact on student test scores, high school graduation, or college enrollment rates.[14]

Although the official evaluation of the expensive federal SIG program had disappointing results, it is interesting to track the indirect impacts of this program on state-level policy making. Take, for instance, the case of district and school transformation efforts in North Carolina. In February 2016, the state board of education adopted a new policy concerning reform options for persistently low performing schools, offering just four models for school improvement: transformation, restart, turnaround, and school closure.[15] In other words, although there was no requirement or incentive to do so at that time, North Carolina adopted as state policy the exact four models that had been permitted under the federal SIG program. This copycat education policy is unlikely to result in dozens of charter school takeovers of failing public schools, however, as the restart model implemented in North Carolina does not require a charter school takeover. Instead, the restart schools are granted charter-like exemptions from state statutes and rules, but their governance model is left untouched so that the school district ultimately retains control of the school. To date, over one hundred traditional public schools in North Carolina have been identified as "restart schools" and granted freedom over operational decisions including their school calendar, teacher hiring, and curriculum. Thus, rather than boosting the number of charter schools in the state, the North Carolina restart model arguably boosts competition among schools by offering a "charter-lite" alternative.

In sum, federal funding and policy inducements under both presidents led to the dramatic expansion of variants of the charter school model over this time period. In the next section, we track corresponding changes in American public opinion on charter schools.

PUBLIC OPINION

One reason for the impressive charter school growth witnessed in recent decades is the bipartisan appeal of a reform that pushes control over education out of school districts and into the community. On one side of the aisle, Democratic activists have pointed to the empowering nature of this reform for traditionally underserved communities; on the other side, Republican supporters have been swayed by its potential to disrupt district monopolies through the introduction of choice and competition. Beginning in the summer of 2007, the journal *Education Next* and the Program on Education Policy and Governance at Harvard University began a national survey of US adults to track public opinion on key education policy issues. As figure 7.2 demonstrates, public opinion on charter schools during the final two years of the Bush presidency was neutral to positive, with only 14 and 16 percent of the public expressing an outright opposition to the formation of charter schools in 2007 and 2008, respectively. The rest of the public was approximately evenly split between supporting this type of education reform (44 percent in 2007 and 42 percent in 2008) or having no opinion either way (42 percent in 2007 and 41 percent in 2008).[16] Over the course of Obama's presidency, support grew until a plurality of Americans responded favorably to charter schools starting in 2013 (51 percent support) and continuing through 2016.

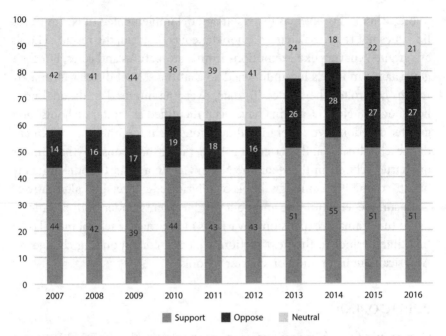

FIGURE 7.2   Public opinion on charter schools, 2007–2016

Source: The annual *Education Next* poll of public opinion

It may be the case that growth in public support for charter schools over this time period was part of a halo effect resulting from a popular president's endorsement. When the 2009 *Education Next* poll was in the field, President Obama was in a honeymoon period, with approval ratings above 60 percent. Even though the majority of the public had yet to make up their mind about whether or not they supported charter schools (44 percent reported being undecided), researchers noticed that when a randomly selected subset of the poll sample was told of the president's support for charter schools, approval ratings for this education reform jumped by 11 percentage points.[17] In sum, having an education reform–oriented Democrat in the White House dampened the possibility that leading Democrats in the House or Senate would speak out against charter schools and reduced the incentive for politically powerful interest groups, such as teacher unions, to mobilize around this particular issue.

LESSONS LEARNED

What lessons can be learned from the growth of charter schools under the forty-third and forty-fourth presidents? There are several.

Lesson 1: School Choice Is, by Definition, Messy

Although Bush's and Obama's other education priorities have been criticized for being aggressive and overly prescriptive, their promotion of charter schools—which are decentralized by definition—actually encouraged the messiness that federalism promotes. Many of the charter school policy changes these leaders incentivized—such as lifting state caps on charter schools—were clear-cut, targeted policy shifts that were well suited to federal influence. If the federal government wants to see charter schools spread, it will be most effective when it adopts this approach; that is, help charter schools get established by providing startup funds and incentivizing states to make the regulatory environment welcoming, then back off. This way, the federal government can avoid adopting a managerial role and navigating the excessive entanglement that can result when nuanced regulatory decisions are not left to the states. Future administrations would be well served by focusing on fostering transparency, addressing inequities, and collecting common data, but humbly deferring to the states on what specific charter school regulation, accountability, oversight, funding, and implementation should look like in action.

Lesson 2: State Priorities and Federal Priorities Are Not Always the Same

The second lesson is to make sure top-down federal directives do not crowd out state-led innovations. RTTT focused states' attention on nineteen federal priorities, but individual states may have been better off prioritizing alternative education policies, many of which would have directly benefited charter schools. Take, for example, the establishment of unified enrollment systems that streamline school application processes across multiple school sectors, which were not prioritized under RTTT but are now slowly spreading across choice-rich states and cities such as New Orleans, which uses "OneApp"; Denver, which uses the "SchoolChoice" system; and the District of Columbia, which uses "MySchoolDC." These systems address the problem of various application deadlines and uncoordinated application processes, which can be overwhelming for families and frustrating for school officials attempting to predict future enrollment. Aside from the obvious efficiency concerns of wanting to maximize the opportunity for the highest number of students to be matched to their preferred school, this problem also raises equity concerns because advantaged families are better positioned to gather the information needed to coordinate multiple applications. A unified enrollment system reduces the burden on families by centralizing all school applications across a city. This means there is just one application portal for all school options (public, private, and charter), one reliable source for comparative school information, and one application deadline. Data from New Orleans suggest the OneApp is fulfilling its promise of promoting efficiency, transparency, and fairness: in 2015–2016, 75 percent of applicants were assigned to one of their top three school choices.

Another obvious candidate for state-led innovation is the precarious state of teacher pension plans, which threaten to derail education finance systems in multiple locales. Estimates suggest that teacher pension plans across the country currently face a $500 billion shortfall and that for every dollar directed into state plans, on average, $0.70 must be used to pay down existing pension debt instead of funding benefits for new members.[18] In addition to these stunning unfunded liabilities, most teachers actually get a bad deal from their state's pension plan. Just one in five teachers receives full benefits upon retirement. Investing energy toward reforming pension plans for new hires could dramatically improve such statistics, aiding teacher recruitment and retention efforts.

Lesson 3: The Feds Can Play a Constructive Role in Research and Development

It is highly appropriate for the federal government to fund rigorous charter school research and disseminate information about successful practices. Led by the research firm Mathematica, the first randomized control trial of charter school effectiveness was funded by the US Department of Education. Experiments of this nature are often termed the "gold standard" because they rule out the possibility that results are influenced by selection bias. Published in 2010, this high-profile and well-regarded evaluation included observations from 2,330 students in thirty-six charter middle schools across fifteen states.[19] It revealed null impacts on student achievement overall, but reported positive impacts on math scores for low-income and lower achieving students. The significance of this study is that it allowed both supporters and opponents to reconsider their positions on a contentious reform in light of the first piece of causal evidence of charter schools' effectiveness.

Other experimental evidence of charter school effectiveness from high-poverty areas has replicated this pattern of findings, often relying on funding from private philanthropies. As a result of these investments, we know that the positive impacts of charter schools in high-poverty areas like Boston and New York City are significant and large.[20] In particular, charter schools associated with the KIPP (Knowledge Is Power Program) network—known for its "No Excuses" model, which emphasizes reading and math skills, features an extended school day and year, and enforces strict behavior standards—have produced dramatic gains across the board, with the largest effects observed from students with limited English proficiency, special educational needs, and lower initial achievement levels.[21]

An increase in research funding to study contemporary charter schools and incorporate more diverse outcome measures would be a highly appropriate use of federal tax dollars, and would allow groups of researchers to better examine new developments, such as the use of personalized learning models that make use of learning "playlists," competency-based progression, flipped classrooms, and flexible learning environments such as those modeled by Summit Public Schools, Rocketship Education, and KIPP Empower.

Lesson 4: Build Robust Coalitions by Introducing Ideological Diversity

Lawmakers must respect partisan differences if they are to secure the passage of a charter school bill by building allies across the aisle and accommodating diverse perspectives in pursuit of a common goal. In May 2017, for example, Republican and Democratic lawmakers in Colorado collaborated on a significant school finance bill that required public school districts to share voter-approved tax increases known as *mill levy overrides* with charter schools. The first of its kind in the United States, Colorado's House Bill 1375 was made possible because of the efforts of lawmakers on both sides of the aisle.

Education reform coalitions comprising strange bedfellows must tread carefully, and the apple cart may tilt if one group clearly frames the charter school issue as part of a larger agenda that might be at odds with the philosophical perspective of their collaborators. For advocates on the left, the charter school movement is part of a larger social justice agenda built around fairness, justice, and equity, and a way to give voice to disenfranchised groups seeking better opportunities. President Obama packaged his education reform efforts with this in mind. Speaking to the NAACP, his secretary of education described education as "the civil rights issue of our generation."[22] For advocates on the right, however, the movement is centered on the dignity of choice, the preservation of liberty, and a belief in the efficiency of a market as the best delivery system for public education. President Bush lauded the idea of holding educators accountable for mediocre schools by empowering families to flee. But if charter school bills are to make it over the finish line, each side must accommodate the other, which means abandoning group-think and carefully balancing the ideological diversity of reform coalitions.

Lesson 5: Limit Uncle Sam's Influence on Charter School Authorizers

Under Secretary Arne Duncan, the US Department of Education adopted a hands-on approach to overseeing charter school growth and quality assurance by attempting to expand the federal influence on charter school authorizing practices. It is not clear whether this has been helpful or if the federal government overstepped the mark by attempting to influence state-level political dynamics of charter authorization during this period. Fulfilling a profoundly different role than central-office bureaucracies, charter school authorizers are responsible for providing oversight of a school's academic, operational, and financial performance. They do not provide any educational services themselves; rather, their purpose is to ensure that high-quality services are provided by defining the accountability expectations, the degree of autonomy charters are permitted to exercise, and the general environment in which these schools operate. Guidance issued by President Obama's Department of Education focused on test scores as a primary quality indicator, on par with oversight of fiscal and operational management, pressuring states to ensure that authorizers were shutting down the lowest performing charter schools as judged by this metric.[23]

In July 2010, Secretary Duncan remarked: "As we look to shut down and turn around the 5,000 lowest performing schools around the country, about 200 of those happen to be charter schools, and that to me is absolutely unacceptable ... I think you need to do the same around authorizers, where you have states or districts that are much too lenient in who they approve and much too lenient in who they allow to continue to operate. I think you need to have a list of good authorizers and bad authorizers and very clear criteria about what it takes."[24] By pressuring states to privilege test scores over other evaluation criteria, Uncle Sam may have tilted the scale against

other indicators of school quality in favor of more easily quantifiable measures of math and reading achievement. The problem with this? Research
shows that the same charter schools that were shown to have unimpressive
average impacts on test scores had significant impacts on far more consequential, longer-term outcomes, including high school graduation, college
attendance, college persistence, and even earnings in adulthood.[25] Thus, if
authorizers are pressured to base their perceptions of charter school quality on test scores exclusively, they risk overlooking impacts on the long-run
outcomes that families ultimately wish to maximize.

CONCLUSION

Education policy has traditionally been a province in which US presidents
have been unable to exercise much independent authority. Supported by
limited constitutional authority, they have commonly used the bully pulpit to issue proclamations and draw attention to memoranda and influential reports. Yet both Bush and Obama bucked that trend, testing creative
approaches that would allow them to align federal funding and policies to
facilitate major growth in the charter school sector. Although their guiding principles may have differed—Bush, the compassionate conservative,
committed to "government if necessary, but not necessarily government";
Obama, the unflappable progressive urging hope and change so that government would work "on behalf of the many, and not just the few"—the education policies they promoted were similar, as were the means by which they
pursued those policies. Over a sixteen-year span, they led a major expansion
of the federal role in education that had not been experienced since the 1960s.

Changes in charter school policy over the course of the Bush-Obama era
present a good barometer of changes in the scope and character of the federal
role in education. Both presidents oversaw a Washington-centric education
agenda and made a substantial investment in the development of charter
schools. Between 2007 and 2014, the US Department of Education's Charter
Schools Program distributed grants totaling $1.5 billion to fund the plan-
ning, startup, and replication of charter schools across the nation. Given the
federal investments and policy inducements outlined here, charter schools
are clearly better off for it.

How will history remember these two presidents? Bush's signature education policy has drawn the ire of critics on both sides of the political spectrum for its overly ambitious goals and unattainable timeline. Obama has

been criticized for not respecting the boundaries of the presidency and for dramatically expanding the federal government's footprint. His administration induced states to enact its preferred education reforms by using unconventional means that relied on a generous, immodest interpretation of the statutory and regulatory power of the executive branch and aggressive policy implementation. Yet, despite these criticisms, both presidents' promotion of charter schools, in particular, has been game-changing. These publicly funded schools of choice represent a decentralized reform that aims to better serve families through choice and competition, empower citizens by flattening hierarchies and pushing control out of centralized bureaucracies into the community, and reframe the government's role as one focused on monitoring quality and overseeing accountability. The expansion of charter schooling on their watch has been a responsible and fruitful direction for presidents to exert their influence.

8

Challenging, Building, and Changing Capacity in State Education Agencies

Sara E. Dahill-Brown

During the presidential administrations of George W. Bush and Barack Obama, the federal government demanded a great deal from state education agencies (SEAs). To comply with No Child Left Behind (NCLB) and compete under Race to the Top (RTTT), SEAs had little choice but to play a larger role in both implementing and innovating new policies and programs. Across the board, these new responsibilities called for a shift away from the monitoring and compliance work that consumed much of SEA attention up to that point. In most states, escalating federal expectations pushed against the limits of SEA capacity. Agencies had to learn new information, master new skills, overhaul internal structures, and reimagine external partnerships. These challenges fell on SEAs that had long been experiencing fiscal and staffing shortages, which became more acute when the Great Recession decimated state coffers.

This chapter examines how preexisting capacity and limited resources shaped state responses to expanding federal requirements, and how SEA capacity developed between 2002 and 2015. Lessons emerge from this examination regarding the impact of federal policy on SEA capacity, and the role of SEA capacity in education reform. Broadly, failing to consider and invest in capacity undermined reform. Capacity matters in kind as much as in amount, and most states lacked the necessary capacity to lead the ambitious, systemic reforms mandated under NCLB and RTTT. As SEAs struggled to meet ambitious goals, comply with accelerated timelines, and adapt to a highly specific vision of reform, limited capacity contributed to subversive and incomplete implementation efforts. These failures sowed distrust, complicating future reform attempts. In spite of all this, SEAs were successful in building new capacity, especially with regards to statewide longitudinal data systems (SLDS), a project that was in many ways consistent with preexisting organizational capacity but also well funded through federal grants. Most SEAs also strengthened external partnerships, and many restructured around core goals—shifts that may signal more fundamental agency transformations.

However, the process of building SEA capacity must be understood as continuous and variable. Data systems involve constant and careful attention to data security, while new external partnerships require SEAs to manage complex networks and become more strategic political operators. Looking forward, the 2015 Every Student Succeeds Act (ESSA) walks back many of NCLB's provisions, creating opportunities for SEAs to build and extend capacity in more diverse ways. In so doing, the law offers up the possibility of a break with the singular vision that characterized education reform and shaped SEA efforts during the Bush and Obama years, though it must be acknowledged this charge falls on SEAs that continue to operate with limited resources.

DEFINING CAPACITY FOR EDUCATION REFORM

Within the fields of education and public policy, *capacity* refers to the ability of an institution to effectively implement and design programs, craft and enforce regulations, and efficiently deliver services. In short, capacity refers to an organization's ability to perform its central functions, translate abstract policies into concrete actions, and achieve critical goals—not whether or not it actually does these things, but whether or not it has the tools necessary to do so.[1]

Policy makers and researchers often break capacity down into a series of dimensions: fiscal, human, organizational, and external. Fiscal capacity includes revenues and monetary assets. Human capacity refers to an agency's staffing levels but also knowledge, skills, and experience. Organizational capacity describes infrastructure, formal and informal systems, technology, and institutional culture. External capacity describes relationships, trust, and outside support. Political will and legal authority can be regarded as components of external capacity, though some view them as distinct from capacity.[2]

SEA revenues, budgets, and staffing levels can be interpreted as critical benchmarks that signal whether or not an agency possesses the basic resources necessary to do its work. Yet capacity is not simply a question of numbers. Resources like money and staff matter in much the same way that spending in schools matters. How money is spent and what type of expertise the staff possesses—for example, whether they are oriented toward performance or compliance—are critical elements of capacity. To be effective institutions, SEAs must have *enough* capacity, and they must have the *right* capacity. What constitutes enough, and what constitutes right, will vary depending on the challenges SEAs are confronted with and the goals they are working to accomplish, whether it be building a new data system, delivering technical support, or administering assessments. For instance, under NCLB, states that reported identifying more schools as failing to meet Adequate Yearly Progress (AYP) were also more likely to report that they had insufficient capacity to implement the law.[3]

Though dividing capacity into separate dimensions for the purposes of analysis can help to identify challenges and needs within an institution, all aspects of capacity are interrelated. Limited fiscal capacity may mean too few staff, underqualified staff, too few training opportunities, and problems with recruitment or retention. Even the impact of money will be moderated by other aspects of capacity. For example, overly rigid organizational infrastructure might prevent money from being spent wisely or raise internal barriers to reallocating resources when an agency is faced with implementing a new project or program.

PRE-NCLB SEA CAPACITIES

To understand the capacity challenges that confronted SEAs during the Bush and Obama presidencies, it is helpful to reexamine how they became such critical institutions. Until the 1960s SEAs tended to be anemic agencies with little in the way of fiscal, human, or organizational capacity. By and large, they were maintained by skeleton crews and charged with few responsibilities, such as administering small grant programs and gathering simple descriptive statistics concerning enrollments and budgets.

This began to change when federal laws made new grants available to the states, first through the National Defense Education Act of 1958 and then with the passage of the landmark Elementary and Secondary Education Act (ESEA) of 1965. The expansion of SEA capacity was a deliberate aim of federal leaders; Title V of the ESEA devoted $25 million to building agencies so that they would be capable of implementing federal educational programs well into the future. In this way, the federal government facilitated an accelerated buildup of SEA capacity across every dimension. Administering ESEA and the Education for All Handicapped Children Act of 1975 gradually transformed SEAs into the institutional "guardians of 'equal opportunity'" for children with special needs, those who belonged to racial and ethnic minority groups, and those from low-income families.[4]

This focus on addressing disparities reinforced agency involvement with school finance reform, which eventually gave way to a focus on academic opportunities and outcomes. When attention to curricular reform intensified during the 1980s, in the aftermath of the *A Nation at Risk* report, SEA leaders and staff actively pressed for higher quality and more uniform curricula. State legislatures and SEAs raised graduation requirements, drafted standards, and began to implement standardized assessments. However, SEAs did not typically engage the internal workings of schools and districts. Therefore, SEAs expanded the scope of their activity using the familiar tools of regulation and compliance monitoring.

SEAs' mode of engagement with schools and districts shifted more decisively in the 1990s as state legislatures and the federal government intensified efforts to promote standards-based reforms. By 2001, thirty states had enacted a standards and accountability program. In eighteen of those thirty states the implementation year for these systems was 1998 or later, meaning that prior to NCLB, SEAs had not been afforded much time to transition to their new roles.[5] Moreover, very few state accountability systems included strong provisions, analogous to the ones implemented nationwide under NCLB.

Thus, at the time that NCLB was enacted, even though accountability policies were on the rise and SEA authority was growing, there remained a significant gap between what most agencies had the capacity to do and what the law required of them. Most SEAs were still functioning primarily as conduits for state and federal dollars, implementers of some state policies, licensure bodies, and enforcers of federal mandates. Their human, organizational, and external capacities were critically limited in light of what was expected of them during the Bush and Obama presidencies.

NCLB: ESCALATING DEMANDS, LIMITED CAPACITIES, AND DIVERSE POLITICAL CLIMATES

In the United States, schools have long been expected to serve as the cornerstone of the American Dream; they are the public institutions held most accountable for safeguarding equal opportunity, economic vitality, and a vibrant democracy. NCLB's rhetoric elevated these aspirations to new prominence, while its policies and programs escalated the demands confronting SEAs. In January 2002, surrounded by schoolchildren and a bipartisan coalition of supporters, President George W. Bush signed NCLB into law. It called upon states and school districts to turn around struggling schools, improve academic achievement among low-income and minority students, and increase the quality of the teaching force.

A report from the Center on Education Policy (CEP) likened this shift to going from a relatively straightforward position as a monitor to becoming an architect responsible for the design, construction, and operation of an entire system.[6] The high demands and fast implementation timeline of NCLB seemed to assume states already possessed the necessary capacity to improve student achievement and reduce achievement gaps—that, given the proper federal incentives, SEAs could simply reorganize existing capacity. For all but a few states, this was not the case. Many lacked the financial, human, organizational, and external capacities necessary to implement NCLB, particularly to design accountability systems and to support struggling schools.

Declining Fiscal and Human Capacity During the Early 2000s Recession

Entering into NCLB, SEAs around the country operated with vastly different financial resources, both overall and adjusted per pupil. Arnold Shober points out that during the fiscal year of 1998–1999, the Colorado Department of Education performed its core activities with a budget of about $205 million, while the Iowa Department of Education operated on a budget of about $302 million, and the Ohio Department of Education wielded a budget of roughly $2.2 billion. On a per-pupil basis, Ohio's SEA budget was double that of Iowa's and five times that of Colorado's.[7] These differences in access to fiscal resources were important for NCLB's implementation, because even though Title I grants jumped roughly 18 percent in the first year of NCLB, the additional funds covered only part of the law's many programmatic requirements, and subsequent increases would match more closely with inflation.[8]

During the 1990s, the American economy had experienced its longest period of uninterrupted growth. Consequently, as NCLB was being negotiated in Washington, DC, reporters speculated about what a smaller surplus might mean for the pending congressional negotiations over ESEA's reauthorization.[9] Instead, the 1990s technology boom faded, the dot-com bubble burst, and the country's economy was deeply shaken by the terrorist attacks of September 11th. These events manifested initially as a dip in revenue for Washington, DC, but emerged as full-on crises for all but a few states. By the end of October 2001, states found themselves facing significant deficits: $1.6 billion in Arkansas, $14 billion in California, $773 million in Delaware, to name just a few. The governor of Connecticut called a special legislative session to address a projected shortfall of $300 million, while Alabama and South Carolina made unprecedented cuts to aid for schools in the middle of the school year.[10] Difficult budget conditions persisted as stock market indices fell through the first quarter of 2003, and unemployment peaked in June.

Governors and legislators often viewed SEA budgets and staff as prime targets for cutting back during this lean time, because reducing a bureaucratic agency did not anger important political constituencies. In a survey conducted by the CEP during 2006, twenty-one SEAs reported that fiscal constraints, including deficits, slashed agency budgets, and programmatic cuts, had led to struggles during the first years of implementing NCLB.[11]

In that same survey, more than thirty states reported that inadequate staff presented a significant or moderate impediment to implementing required assessments and administering assessments to English language learners. More than forty states indicated that staffing shortages greatly or moderately limited their ability to monitor schools in improvement and that they had too few staff to provide adequate technical assistance to districts with schools in improvement. For this last requirement, it was striking that not a single SEA reported that staffing numbers were adequate to perform this new task. Staffing shortages also had a significant effect on SEAs' ability to monitor supplemental education service providers.

In a number of states, including Illinois, New York, and Georgia, the decline in SEA staff continued during NCLB, but was part of a longer trend stretching back at least into the mid-1990s. Staff reductions of 20 and 30 percent were not uncommon.[12] One state reported a decrease from 1,600 staff to just 275 in the span of five years.[13]

Staffing shortages and limited expertise exerted a disproportionate constraint on less populated states with smaller agencies. For many of the critical tasks required by NCLB (developing robust standards and assessments, for instance), the cost of initial work was not substantially less for states with smaller student bodies. However, staff were fewer and federal allocations were substantially smaller. In a very limited way, smaller scale offered an advantage in terms of monitoring; SEAs in less populated states were less likely to report that they struggled to keep track of schools identified for improvement, given that they oversaw a smaller number of schools districts. Yet they reported greater difficulty in leveraging those close connections to provide technical assistance to schools and districts.

Misaligned Expertise and Organizational Capacity

Inadequate staffing at SEAs was largely, but not entirely, a function of budget shortfalls. Shortages were compounded by organizational constraints. For example, lack of fiscal capacity resulted in uncompetitive salaries, but legislatures also imposed strict regulations on hiring that hindered bringing on new employees. SEAs especially struggled with recruiting and retaining highly qualified staff who possessed skills in data and analytics.[14]

SEAs were better organized and equipped to implement some aspects of NCLB than others. For instance, licensure and credentialing programs for teachers were adapted quickly to reflect new requirements that teachers be "highly qualified." This was an administrative task in keeping with the traditional work of SEAs, and a majority of districts were in compliance by 2006–2007. At the same time, relatively few states undertook the work of administering professional development or supporting schools and districts in helping teachers to meet the requirement, so poorer districts and difficult-to-staff areas often struggled to comply with this part of the law.[15] Some referred to progress toward universally highly qualified teachers as merely "a victory on paper."[16]

Several studies found that SEAs did, on the whole, make substantial progress toward developing robust assessment programs and information systems. This may have been because the technical work of data gathering and reporting was mostly consistent with work that SEAs had long undertaken, even though NCLB demanded a larger-scale operation. However, the work of supporting schools identified as needing improvement fell outside of most SEAs' prior experience and expertise. This work was often tacitly done, deferred, or outsourced to regional education service agencies (RESAs), districts, or even schools themselves.[17]

Prior experience with accountability turned out to be an especially important aspect of SEA capacity throughout NCLB's implementation. Some states had only the most basic of data systems in place, while others were already using unique identifiers for students to track academic progress over time.[18] In analyses of early NCLB implementation, states that had already implemented consequential accountability tended to set lower, more easily met thresholds for proficiency on state assessments.[19] Over time, as more schools entered into improvement status, state proficiency standards were often lowered.[20]

Transforming and Growing External Capacity

Tasking states with monitoring struggling schools and administering sanctions to schools and districts in improvement encouraged hierarchical relationships between SEAs and districts, challenged traditions of local control, and sometimes provoked a sense of distrust on the part of local leadership.[21] On the other hand, confusion among districts and schools meant that state leaders not only were expected by the law to provide support to districts and schools, but also were fielding more and more bottom-up requests for guidance.[22] In response, SEA staff described themselves as adopting a more "customer service" style of engaging with schools and districts.[23]

SEAs also sought out and strengthened partnerships with external organizations and nonprofits. The Colorado Department of Education, which has historically operated on a lean budget, has worked closely with the Colorado Education Initiative since 2007 to supplement its long-term planning capabilities by articulating ambitious goals, tending to stakeholders, and identifying opportunities for improvement.[24] The Missouri Department of Elementary and Secondary Education began to rely more heavily on regional professional development centers.[25] This work was especially necessary for smaller SEAs. New Hampshire, Vermont, and Rhode Island, three of the smallest states in the country, formed an assessment collaborative, the New England Common Assessment Program (NECAP) in response to NCLB (Maine also joined in 2009).

Resistance, Subversion, and Adaptation

NCLB was passed with bipartisan support at the federal level and welcomed in most states. SEA leaders in particular anticipated that many of the law's provisions would lead to improved academic outcomes for students.[26] Some SEA leaders even viewed the law as leverage to bring reticent legislatures on board with reforms they had long supported.[27]

However, the law also encountered fierce, vocal resistance from a few states and stakeholders who expressed reservations about the extent of testing required under the law and the blunt nature of the AYP measure of school performance. Utah and Vermont both threatened a court battle, and the State of Connecticut sued the federal government, arguing that the law constituted an unfunded mandate. This bold pushback was fleeting—Utah and Vermont never brought suits, and Connecticut's case was eventually dismissed—but the objections were symptomatic of conflicts that would crystallize with time.

As NCLB was implemented, the law ran up against the realities of limited or misaligned local and state capacity, and it became difficult to distinguish between acts of resistance motivated by political disagreements with the law's methods, and adaptations made in good faith of necessity. Evidence suggests that both of these motivations affected implementation decisions, though reports were more likely to highlight the sensational story of bureaucratic shenanigans and gamesmanship.[28]

At least twenty-three SEAs chose to backload academic growth expectations—that is, holding schools and districts to achievement standards that increased very slowly in the first five to seven years of the law and then accelerated as the 2013–2014 school year drew closer.[29] Since NCLB was scheduled to be reauthorized after five years, states that opted for this strategy were essentially betting that the law would be replaced before accelerated growth targets trapped them into identifying large numbers of schools as failing.

States also employed favorable measures of dropout rates and graduation, scheduled tests early in the school year to minimize their potential impact on classroom instruction, and tinkered with the minimum enrollment numbers necessary to trigger reporting the achievement of students in subgroups (thus dampening their impact on school accountability ratings).[30] Real instances of fraud emerged among supplemental education service providers, who were certified by SEAs and then contracted with local districts to provide tutoring whenever schools were identified for improvement.[31] At the local level, exposés about cheating among teachers and administrators proliferated, with particularly high-profile cases emerging in Houston and Atlanta.[32] SEAs may have been inept supervisors, or simply overtaxed.

THE GREAT RECESSION, RTTT, AND PERSISTENT CHALLENGES TO SEA CAPACITY

2007 stands out as a critical juncture for SEAs. Federal and state leaders were gearing up to negotiate a reauthorization of NCLB. Discontent with AYP and the growing number of schools identified for improvement was widespread. Yet frustrations were tempered by the expectation that the law of the land, then five years old, would soon change. Instead, successive crises disappeared millions of jobs and billions of dollars from the economy, and the number of schoolchildren affected by homelessness, unemployment, and poverty skyrocketed. Reauthorizing NCLB ceased to be a priority for Congress, and the state tax revenues SEAs relied upon and delivered to public school systems evaporated, almost overnight.

Efforts to reauthorize NCLB were supplanted by negotiations over the American Recovery and Reinvestment Act (ARRA, or the "stimulus bill"), and then the Patient Protection and Affordable Care Act. More than $67 billion of ARRA's education fund was used to prevent teacher layoffs, school closures, and supply shortages. States had to certify their commitment to the administration's educational goals, but the funds were disbursed via the usual formulas and required little creative work from SEAs.[33] However, within ARRA, $4 billion was set aside for the Race to the Top competitive grant competition, intended to support comprehensive, innovative reform efforts. Substantial grants were awarded to Delaware and Tennessee in the first round of the competition; ten more states won sizeable awards in the second round; and an additional seven states were provided small grants to support their work.

After the competition closed, Secretary Arne Duncan announced a waivering process through which states could apply to earn relief from some of NCLB's accountability requirements. In exchange for flexibility, SEAs needed to propose detailed alternatives to NCLB's accountability and embrace the administration's education reform priorities: incorporating student outcomes in teacher evaluations and implementing turnaround strategies for low performing schools. Waivers required much of the work of RTTT, but came with no additional federal dollars.[34]

Scarce Fiscal and Human Capacity During the Great Recession

Because RTTT arrived at a vulnerable moment for state school systems, it was met with a clamor that might not otherwise have been so substantial. Even with billions of dollars in federal aid allocated to public schools through ARRA, state governments were confronting major shortfalls, and the prospect of any additional funding was too important to pass up.[35] Every state other than Alaska, North Dakota, Texas, and Vermont applied during at least one round of the competition.

Throughout the financial crisis and recovery, SEAs consistently reported having too little money and too few staff. Surveys and interviews conducted by the American Institutes for Research and the Wallace Foundation found that even in 2008, SEAs felt stretched.[36] ARRA's stabilization aid provided only temporary funding that fell away within two years, so it staved off the worst of the crisis but left most states still needing to resolve shortfalls and uninterested in funding bureaucratic agencies.[37] In 2012, twenty-six of thirty-seven surveyed SEAs reported decreases in their operational budgets between the 2010–2011 and 2011–2012 school years. Thirteen anticipated another decrease in 2012–2013; twenty-four SEAs reported reducing their staff.[38]

In several states, cuts were notable for their magnitude. During 2011, the Texas legislature voted to allow a more than $4 billion cut to the state's public schools budget. By December of that year, more than twelve thousand teachers and support staff had been laid off, and more than six hundred school districts were suing the state.[39] The Texas Education Agency (TEA) lost 36 percent of its operating budget, and in a single year the agency went through two rounds of layoffs, bringing the total number of positions lost to more than three hundred.[40] Commissioner of Education Robert Scott, who presided over the bulk of these layoffs, found himself torn between coaxing school leaders throughout the state—as well as his subordinates at TEA—to make do with less, or petitioning legislators to restore vital funds. Frustrated by the lack of forthcoming aid for the schools and the agency, as well as the increasing weight and cost of high-stakes tests in Texas, he publicly stepped down from his leadership role.[41]

SEAs reported innovating around funding and staffing deficits; nonetheless, some work was delayed, left undone, or just partially completed as a result of these limitations. This seemed particularly apparent with the transition to the Common Core State Standards (CCSS). Across all the areas of CCSS implementation, only one-quarter of surveyed states reported having adequate funding, staff, and expertise to carry out their responsibilities.[42] State-level shortfalls were magnified by insufficient capacity at the local level, which often resulted in confusion among the teachers and school leaders trying to make sense of the new standards.[43]

The Development of Organizational Capacity Around Reform Priorities

In addition to budget cuts and staffing reductions, SEAs continued to struggle with organizational capacity mismatched against the priorities of the Obama administration. Though transformed relative to where they had been at the start of NCLB, many SEAs remained poorly structured in relation to the tasks that RTTT set before them. Federal funding continued to nurture internal silos that separated federally funded and state-funded programs— even when they were aimed at the same ends.[44] Hiring processes slowed down new projects, and even SEAs that received extra funding through RTTT were affected. Slow hiring and contracting contributed to delayed timelines and scaled-back scopes of work.[45]

In surveys in 2012 and 2013, SEA staff from more than forty states indicated that school turnaround was a high priority for their agency. However, they also indicated that supporting turnaround was extraordinarily difficult and that they lacked the necessary expertise—which is unsurprising, given that there is little consensus on what works among researchers.[46] A similar pattern was observed with CCSS, where more states reported having the capacity to develop and implement assessments, but far fewer had the necessary tools to develop curricula.

Nonetheless, states reported making progress toward building and preserving administrative capacities and expertise connected to school turnaround and improvement. In 2007–2008, only twenty-one states reported having either a designated turnaround office or SEA staff specifically focused on turnaround assistance; by 2012–2013 that number had risen to forty-three. Similarly, in 2007–2008, just twelve states reported having the capacity to monitor and report on the requirements for School Improvement Grants; by the 2012–2013 school year, forty-six states reported having this capability.[47]

Engagement with Stakeholders, Interstate Coordination, and External Partnerships

Recognizing that RTTT asked a great deal of state agencies, major associations held webinars and published guides to support their efforts, another way in which external capacity evolved under RTTT, waivering, and the implementation of the CCSS. Organizations like the Council of Chief State School Officers and the National Governors Association became more active providers of coordination and support to agencies, allowing them to share experiences with one another and often acting as liaisons to federal leaders. These organizations also supplemented state research capacity and produced policy analyses as well as implementation guides.

SEAs have increasingly relied on external partners to support challenging technical work. During the application process for RTTT, the Bill & Melinda Gates Foundation provided a quarter of a million dollars for each state in the form of consulting services to supplement state capacity, part of a larger pattern of philanthropic efforts to support long-term planning, research, and reform. In both 2012 and 2013, roughly 90 percent of SEAs reported consulting with an external agency in search of support for their turnaround efforts. The most commonly consulted partners were federally supported centers and labs, but also institutions of higher learning and regional or county offices.[48] Many states relied on outside providers in particular to drive turnaround efforts.[49]

Maximizing the potential of statewide longitudinal data systems is partly contingent on strong external partnerships with institutions of higher learning and other research organizations, though there are significant barriers to establishing and maintaining those partnerships. The SLDSs, for instance, do not collect data in a format researchers prefer and may often fail to gather variables researchers view as critical; SLDSs gather data based on what federal and state laws require. Agencies may further face political and privacy barriers to making data available, and researchers' goals and timelines may not overlap well with SEA needs.[50]

Politicized Agencies and Backlash

RTTT, CCSS, and waivers brought many SEAs into closer contact with state legislative bodies—at least thirty-four states enacted or changed laws and policies during the eighteen-month competition period of RTTT so as to be better positioned when submitting applications.[51] However, SEAs in many states adopted CCSS under their own authority—decisions that were subsequently taken up, scrutinized, and in a few instances reversed by a number of state legislatures, who openly suggested that SEAs and the federal government overstepped their authority and subverted democratic processes.

External partnerships also created opportunities for undue influence— or at least the perception of it. Tennessee, which won a large, first-round RTTT grant, engaged in extensive outreach and relied on external consultants to supplement agency capacity. However, results were slow to arrive, and many community stakeholders felt that their contributions and ideas were dismissed by outsiders who had little long-term stake in the state's school system.[52] Indeed, SEAs leading numerous systemic reform efforts found themselves responsible for a number of interrelated implementation processes with the potential to inspire backlash. The blowback against CCSS, for instance, was not simply contained to the new standards, but expanded outward to affect other, connected projects.[53] To an extent, SEAs could point to the coerciveness of federal policies and use it as a kind of political cover, allowing the federal government to bear the brunt of public frustration.

However, as SEAs came into closer contact with traditionally partisan institutions and organizations, conservative antipathy toward the federal government, and toward big government more broadly, was gaining momentum. Tea Party activists' ire was often directed at policies perceived to be associated with the federal government, including CCSS, so SEAs working to implement the standards became swept up in these partisan conflicts.[54] Moreover, the Tea Party movement not only drove strongly conservative candidates into both houses of Congress, but also contributed to increased partisan polarization in state governments.[55]

Republican predominance in state governments was consolidated throughout this period, reaching a new high in 2016 when the party managed to win unified control of state legislatures in thirty-three states. These victories highlight a growing divide between Democratic- and Republican-controlled states but also ensure that tax cuts are likely to be at the top of many red-state policy agendas, which may exacerbate budget shortfalls for SEAs in states where they are enacted. Diminished budgets may also increase instability and uncertainty as conflict over limited education funding increases.[56] Kansas, under the leadership of Governor Sam Brownback, may offer a preview of this phenomenon. Though the state government had long been conservative, it became more strongly so with the influence of Tea Party candidates during 2010 and 2012. A large, statewide tax cut translated into a substantial budget shortfall in the state's school system. The state legislature has since repealed tax cuts; the state supreme court has declared the school finance formula to be unconstitutional; and the Kansas State Department of Education has found itself in the news and often in the middle of contentious budget battles and litigation.[57]

LESSONS LEARNED

NCLB signaled the beginning of an era in which education reform would be more prominent on the agendas of national and state leaders. Yet the lofty rhetoric that so effectively captured the country's imagination also obscured very real challenges that accompanied a top-to-bottom transformation of state school systems. In the sixteen years since NCLB's passage, the importance of capacity for implementation—and the potential for political fallout when capacity is not considered—has become abundantly clear. In spite of this, it is equally clear that some of the successful efforts from this period demonstrate that SEAs can be strong partners in advancing reform, although there is an ongoing need to develop capacity, with more careful attention to the particular barriers and assets in each state.

Lesson 1: Ambitious Demands and Resource Constraints Yield Adaptive and Subversive Implementation Efforts

Throughout the Bush and Obama presidencies, SEAs were repeatedly asked to take on an increasingly diverse and challenging array of responsibilities. Under NCLB, SEAs had to work toward the goal of 100 percent proficiency, and under RTTT, SEAs were expected to close achievement gaps at an unprecedented pace. By defining success in such ambitious terms, SEAs could only come up short. In the case of school turnaround, SEAs were tasked with an endeavor that not only was resource intensive, but for which there was—and remains—little in the way of robust knowledge regarding how to do the work well.

At the same time, the majority of SEAs were coping with major staffing shortages, budget cuts, and uncertain funding streams. This combination fostered implementation efforts that were adaptive at best (meaning that SEAs attempted to stay faithful to the spirit of the law even though they implemented it in a way that differed from the designers' vision), and subversive at worst (meaning that SEAs took advantage of flexibility to undermine or avoid the work envisioned by designers).

This was particularly well documented when SEAs deliberately established low thresholds for proficiency during NCLB implementation. While this choice invited negative press coverage, as it appeared that states were deliberately gaming the law, it may have been a smart strategic decision in an environment of scarce capacity. A low threshold for proficiency meant identifying fewer schools as needing improvement, which in turn allowed SEAs greater flexibility in targeting limited resources to support schools that were struggling the most. States that had identified more schools for improvement were more likely to report that their capacity was overwhelmed by the need for support.[58]

Regardless of the particular rationale behind such choices, unrealistically high expectations all but guaranteed fraught implementation processes.[59] Though it may not be unreasonable to ask public institutions to do more with a little less, there are also limits to how far this can be taken, given the scope and significance of SEAs' work.

Lesson 2: Top-Down Policy, Inadequate Capacity, and Flawed Implementation Undermine Future Reform

The policies of the Bush and Obama administrations, and the implementation processes they engendered, undermined state and federal partnerships, fractured coalitions, and instilled a generalized skepticism toward reform, as well as toward the SEAs responsible for carrying it out. Heightened antipathy toward top-down policy processes, growing partisan divides, and pervasive distrust create an environment in which legislative negotiations are likely to break down and implementation is likely to provoke backlash.

Frustration with federal leadership took root when NCLB overrode state-designed accountability systems (or the lack thereof), grew as the perversities of AYP became clear, and intensified when the US Department of Education used the Great Recession to demand extraordinary academic progress and significant policy change via RTTT and NCLB waivers. Public opinion coalesced around the narrative that federal leaders had unfairly strong-armed states by leveraging vast resources against more limited capacity, stoking a resentment that was most pronounced in strongly Republican states, but shared by many Democrats. It contributed to the halting reauthorization of NCLB and fueled widespread resistance to the CCSS.

At the state and local level, NCLB's high expectations, and the limited capacity of state and local agencies, created negative feedback as flawed implementation progressed. By setting low standards for proficiency, SEAs were likely attempting to manage demands on their capacity, or making the defensible—albeit political—choice to safeguard local district control. Nonetheless, these choices meant they appeared to be playing games and shirking their responsibility to improve outcomes for children. Narratives about cynical gamesmanship were compelling and became more widespread over time, casting doubt on states' commitments to disadvantaged students. Moreover, these stories intermingled with concerns about overtesting, narrowing curricula, school choice, and the growing number of schools identified as failing by AYP.

Lesson 3: SEAs Are Well Positioned to Advance Some Systemic Reforms with the Correct Supports

Under NCLB and RTTT, SEAs began to reorganize around key goals, redesign accountability systems, and establish and make use of SLDSs. Successes in these arenas highlight potential avenues for effective partnerships between federal and state governments: drawing attention toward inequalities, creating incentives and opportunities to plan and reorganize, and providing concrete guidance for highly technical infrastructure projects.

Patrick Murphy and Monica Ouijdani emphasize that monitoring and reporting does represent important progress, explaining that "it has become much more difficult to overlook or ignore underperforming schools" as a result of SEA efforts.[60] In addition, roughly half a billion federal dollars in combination with SEA efforts have scaled up SLDSs. This new infrastructure can support smarter accountability systems, and dramatically expands possibilities for more rigorous disaggregation and analysis of individual student data. A number of states have already leveraged these SLDSs to build early-warning systems that can provide schools and districts with timely information about students who may be at risk of dropping out.[61]

SEAs nonetheless continued to seem more comfortable with administrative and compliance-oriented work rather than projects in direct support of classroom teaching and school improvement. This tendency resulted from a combination of factors: institutional history and culture, the rapid growth of SEA responsibilities, constraints on funding and staffing levels, lack of flexibility in allocating resources, difficulty attracting and retaining talented staff, and the coerciveness of federal policy. This was clearest with regards to school turnaround. Even the most advanced state interventions were not up to the task, and the work was complicated by the fact that there were few proven strategies for turning around struggling schools.[62] In close studies of agency budgets, Patrick Murphy, Monica Ouijdani, and Ashley Jochim found that in most states the proportion of staff focused on monitoring and administration was larger than the proportion of staff focused on turnaround, support, and improvement.[63]

Lesson 4: SEAs Can Strengthen External Partnerships to Supplement Internal Capacity

Both NCLB and RTTT compelled SEAs to expand outreach efforts and reimagine external relationships with various stakeholders (school districts, nonprofits, and even other states), converting some relationships into more hierarchical ones and spurring new and innovative collaborations in other instances. In part, this was driven by federal pressure—particularly during the Obama administration—to demonstrate coalition building. However, the comprehensiveness and complexity of the systems and programs that SEAs were tasked with designing and implementing meant that stakeholder engagement offered a valuable supplement to SEA expertise, providing access to local knowledge and establishing critical partnerships to support implementation efforts.

During the RTTT competition states were required to show both that diverse state and local stakeholders were afforded the opportunity to weigh in on plans, and that they supported state reforms. In applications, states had to demonstrate that there was a network in place to complete and support the planned projects. SEAs had to then serve as coordinating agencies. Many agencies also held listening tours or created online systems through which concerned citizens and organizations could weigh in on reform plans.[64]

Lesson 5: New Responsibilities and New Capacities Create New Challenges

New SLDS infrastructures highlight longstanding barriers to conducting research and bringing evidence to bear on policy decisions. Using the data that have been gathered to conduct rigorous studies may be beyond the internal capabilities of many SEAs, and the data included in SLDSs may still be inadequate to answer some of SEAs' most pressing questions. Moreover, SLDSs require constant attention to issues of data security. Millions of student records and data are held by states and districts, and these public information systems are not updated regularly or adequately protected.[65] Complicating efforts to preserve data security is the fact that student data are highly mobile, since SEAs are constantly collecting data from districts and sharing it with interested stakeholders and consultants. Additionally, SEAs' authority over data are contingent on state and federal laws that are subject to change.[66]

Similarly, partnerships with foundations, nonprofit organizations, and others introduce new challenges for SEAs. For instance, key elements of planning and implementation for RTTT were carried out by consultants, who later disappeared. So, while reliance on temporary workers was a way to cope with the fact that funding streams were fluctuating, it compromised institutional memory later on. SEAs that continue to develop external partnerships will have to manage contracts, maintain large networks, negotiate political conflicts, and develop systems that preserve institutional memory, coherence, and consistency.

Lesson 6: Priorities for Building Capacity Should Reflect Each SEA's Specific Context

Finally, some states struggled more than others with their new roles and responsibilities, whether due to smaller staffs, less experience with accountability, or more schools being identified as struggling and in need of support. The nature of a federal system is such that there will always be variation among states and local districts. For instance, matching staffing numbers from 2011 against K–12 enrollments from the 2010–2011 school year indicates that agency size is driven partly, but not entirely, by enrollments. More populous states reported larger staffs within their agencies on average, as illustrated by the fitted line in figure 8.1. However, agency size varied even among states with relatively similar populations—Florida and New York, for example. Notably, larger SEAs, relative to enrollments, appear mostly in southern states.[67]

SEAs operate in different political and cultural contexts, where the balance of power between states and districts varies, and so may need to perform larger or smaller roles. Researchers who have closely studied SEAs agree that some aspects of education reform work—maintaining longitudinal data systems, for example—should rest primarily with state agencies. Joanne Weiss and Patrick McGuinn have suggested that an SEA's essential roles should include articulating a vision, establishing priorities, and setting

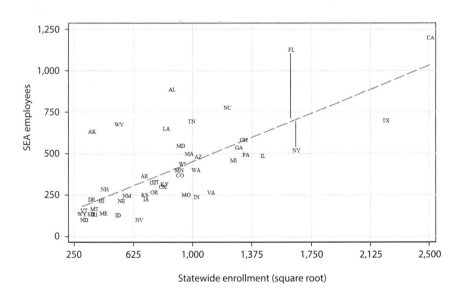

FIGURE 8.1 SEA staffing levels by enrollment (2010–2011 school year)

Sources: Cynthia G. Brown et al., *State Education Agencies as Agents of Change: What It Will Take for the States to Step Up on Education Reform* (Washington, DC: Center for American Progress, American Enterprise Institute for Public Policy Research, and the Broad Foundation, 2011); US Department of Education, National Center for Education Statistics, "Common Core of Data," https://nces.ed.gov/ccd/

goals; implementing standards and assessments; designing and operating accountability systems; administering federal and state funding programs; and developing communication systems that function both to disseminate and take in information.[68] Andy Smarick and Juliet Squire offer a similar list of essential responsibilities for SEAs.[69]

There are, however, divergent recommendations about whether "bigger, stronger, smarter, and more active" SEAs are needed to lead systemic reform.[70] Weiss and McGuinn are open to that potential, emphasizing that SEAs may or may not take a hands-on approach to turning around low performing schools and providing professional development, depending on state context and available resources. Smarick and Squire caution strongly against investing in SEA capacity, suggesting that agencies should instead limit their responsibilities, contract out operational work, and consider creating or partnering with external entities to take on more creative functions like research and advocacy.

Patrick Murphy and Lydia Rainey describe multiple approaches SEAs have adopted in their efforts to support school improvement: taking direct control of schools, building district capacity to support schools, or restructuring the incentives shaping school and district choices. Each of these requires different configurations of internal and external capacity. Murphy and Rainey are careful to emphasize that research offers too little evidence to strongly recommend one strategy over another.[71] Thus, while SEAs can and should continue to learn from one another, there is no single, best way to build capacity.

CONCLUSION

In the years since the Great Recession, state education budgets have rebounded substantially, if not entirely, but many SEAs continue to face lean times in spite of their consistently growing responsibilities under ESSA. By and large, neither budgets nor staff appear to have been restored to prerecession levels during the economic recovery. Capacity, therefore, continues to present a critical challenge as states ramp up their implementation of ESSA.[72] A report on the first year of ESSA's implementation suggests that it will be hampered by inadequate capacity in much the same way as were NCLB and RTTT. More than half of surveyed SEAs reported that their workload had increased under ESSA, and only one reported having adequate capacity to meet all requirements.[73]

If some of the struggles of the past are to be avoided, state leaders must be intentional about investing in SEA capacity. While resources alone cannot be viewed as a guarantee of policy success, SEAs cannot generate and implement robust plans for systemic reform if they are consistently starved while their responsibilities grow. Finding ways to increase the stability of funding streams may be a critical dimension of this endeavor, as predictable funding streams tend to allow for more consistent, long-term development of capacity, expertise in particular.[74] Reducing the churn among state chiefs may also be important for building capacity under ESSA; in February 2017 only fifteen had led their agencies for even two years.[75]

At the same time, this is not to suggest that there is a single path forward. As Jennifer O'Day explains, "over-relying on top-down mandates or threats has thwarted both the individual and organizational learning needed for fundamental transformation. Mandates lead to compliance (or sometimes resistance), while threats usually diminish the risk-taking needed to solve persistent and systemic problems."[76] ESSA leaves states to more independently drive reform, opening avenues for learning and adaptation, particularly with regards to the open-ended aspects of state accountability plans.

Finally, ESSA maintains pressure to work with external partners; "stakeholder" appears in the law thirteen times. By contrast, it appeared just once in the text of NCLB, and only three times in the text of the Improving America's Schools Act.[77] Given the distrust and frustration that has characterized so much of education reform in the last several years, engaging stakeholders in a more-than-perfunctory manner will be a critical component of creating opportunities for successful implementation. SEAs around the country will have to work deliberately to rebuild trust, solidify state coalitions, acknowledge and address conflicts, and ensure that avenues of communication are open—allowing information to flow out from, and back to, agency leaders and staff.

9

Sound and Fury

*Education and Civil Rights in the Bush
and Obama Administrations*

Joshua Dunn

When trying to shape decentralized public policy, the federal government has two primary tools: "bribery and blackmail."[1] Both were
on full display with the civil rights framing of education policy during the
Bush and Obama administrations. George W. Bush, of course, indicated
that his education agenda would be race-conscious when, during the 2000
presidential campaign, he promised that if elected he would attack "the soft
bigotry of low expectations." Calling the lower test scores of Latino and African American students "discrimination," he said that no child should be
"segregated by low expectations."[2] This civil rights focus helps explain the
significant bipartisan support for No Child Left Behind (NCLB) in Congress. Civil rights groups largely gave their blessing to NCLB because of
disaggregation of student achievement data, which made federal funding
contingent on states breaking student performance out by race and other
categories. When NCLB proved to be unworkable, the Department of Education used its waiver provisions to extract more reforms out of states seeking
relief. During the Obama administration, civil rights activity increased even
more. The Office for Civil Rights (OCR) issued a flurry of "Dear Colleague
Letters" (DCLs) on school discipline, school finance, and transgender students, offering novel interpretations of civil rights laws to justify aggressive
expansion of OCR's authority.[3] Schools were threatened with a loss of federal funds unless they submitted to these new requirements.

These aggressive gesticulations of the federal government accomplished little, however, and in some instances made the very problems it claimed to be addressing more intractable. There is, for instance, little evidence that this unprecedented outburst of federal "civil rights" activity did much to change voters' attitudes. Today, the public shows little concern about closing the achievement gap, and on some issues—such as school discipline—public opinion is decidedly against federal policy. One recent study found that while 64 percent of Americans view closing wealth-based achievement gaps as essential or as a high priority, only 36 and 31 percent consider closing black-white or white-Hispanic achievement gaps, respectively, as similarly important.[4] Another study of California school districts found that school board members are evaluated based on the performance of white students and that school board members face little pressure from constituents to close racial achievement gaps.[5] On school discipline, *Education Next* found in 2015 and 2016 that 71 and 72 percent of Americans, respectively, opposed "federal policies that prevent schools from expelling or suspending black and Hispanic students at higher rates than other students." Minority opinion for such policies was at best tepid. Only 39 percent of Hispanics supported such policies in 2015 and 2016, while support among African Americans dropped from 65 percent to 48 percent.[6]

After discussing the policy landscape prior to Bush and Obama, this chapter will review the "civil rights" framing of federal education policy during their administrations. This analysis leads to three conclusions about the federal government, civil rights, and education: schools are still coping organizations, federalism matters, and legally questionable actions such as conditional waivers and DCLs are unsuited for resolving complex and contentious policy disputes.

THE PRE-NCLB LANDSCAPE

When the Elementary and Secondary Education Act (ESEA) first passed in 1965, it contained little to promote greater accountability or improvement; nor was there any appetite in the Office of Education for supervising the states. Instead, most of the Title I funds—the bulk of spending under ESEA—went to initiatives such as speech therapy and parent training. With the release of *A Nation at Risk* in 1983, the conversation, if not the federal role, changed. The report raised the alarm about the performance of American schoolchildren compared to students in other countries and, to a lesser extent, the performance of minority students relative to their peers. At the state level, the report led to a flurry of standards-based reforms in the 1980s. Changes in national policy would not come until ESEA's 1994 reauthorization. In theory, President Clinton's Goals 2000 legislation required states to implement standards-based accountability systems in order to receive Title I funds. In practice, the law had few enforcement mechanisms, so it was widely disregarded.

With NCLB, everything changed. While pre-NCLB federal education policy was largely reward and little sanction, NCLB was largely sanction and little reward. As well, the sanctions were tied to the explicitly race-conscious construction of the law. States not only had to make Adequate Yearly Progress (AYP) and have all students magically achieve proficiency in reading and math by 2014, but also had to disaggregate data based on race, disability, economic disadvantage, and limited English proficiency. One democratic staffer called this disaggregation "the heart of what NCLB is all about."[7] In order to qualify for AYP, a school had to show that each of these subgroups met AYP benchmarks. If it failed to do so, NCLB's cascading set of sanctions would kick in, compelling schools, in theory, to improve outcomes and close the achievement gap. This led the chairman of the Civil Rights Commission, William Taylor, to praise NCLB as "an important civil rights tool." "Closing the achievement gap," he said, "is a major civil rights issue. It's the way to get at discrimination in a new century."[8]

The Office for Civil Rights

Before NCLB, the Department of Education's primary responsibility was to give money away, while the ostensible purpose of its Office for Civil Rights was to take it away. Section 601 in Title VI of the Civil Rights Act of 1964 allowed the Department of Health, Education, and Welfare (HEW) to withhold federal funds from unlawfully segregated school districts.[9] But Title VI contained no guidelines for determining when a school district was segregated. Therefore, when creating its first guidelines in 1965, HEW created a judicial partnership by linking some of them with judicially determined standards for desegregation. Perhaps foreshadowing the agency's legally questionable use of DCLs, OCR's 1965 guidelines were published not in the Federal Register but in the *Saturday Review of Literature*. The secretary of HEW, Anthony Celebrezze, refused to endorse HEW's guidelines, so Commissioner of Education Francis Keppel turned to the *Saturday Review* instead.

Regardless of where it published the guidelines, OCR's partnership with the federal courts led to profound and rapid changes in southern schools— but not by cutting off federal funds. That worked better as a threat than as an actual punishment since it would harm all students, both black and white. Instead, OCR asked the courts to impose sanctions on recalcitrant school officials. This turned into OCR's primary enforcement strategy. It would write the rules and then outsource enforcement to the judges. With desegregation, that arrangement worked well. Disregarding the guidelines could lead to a contempt-of-court citation and a stint in jail, a punishment that compelled formerly convinced segregationists to reconsider their principles.[10]

After 1970, OCR settled into a pattern of responding to complaints. While OCR itself occasionally came under judicial supervision, its core function did not change over the next four decades. Its job was to investigate complaints and enforce the law. Neither Republican nor Democratic administrations did much to significantly increase its role. Occasionally, it would offer new guidelines, such as 1997's DCL on sexual harassment, which went beyond existing law.[11] But those guidelines were immediately blunted by two Supreme Court decisions. In addition, OCR issued a clarifying DCL in 2003 during the Bush administration as a reminder that guidelines issued by OCR could not supersede the First Amendment.[12] The general sense was that OCR's most important days were well in the past, an impression supported by its continually dwindling staff, which shrank from 1,099 in 1981 to 696 in 2001. By 2016 it had fallen to 563.

NCLB AND CIVIL RIGHTS

The relationship between NCLB and civil rights is best seen in the litigation, specifically its absence under the act. NCLB generated little litigation for two primary reasons. First, it lacked a *private right of action*, a provision allowing individuals to challenge the administration of the law in court. Second, it gave aid to institutions, not individuals. Statutes conferring benefits directly on individuals are much better vehicles for litigation.

Put crudely, NCLB was a civil rights law without any rights. Since NCLB contained no real legally enforceable remedies, its "rights" were arguably a dead letter. The absence of significant litigation under NCLB testifies to this fact. Martha Derthick concluded, "As an instrument on which to rest lawsuits, it has been almost entirely useless."[13] This was, according to Christopher Edley, the great defect of NCLB. "As of now," he lamented, "parents and the public cannot get in the courthouse door to argue that officials are failing to live up to their statutory obligations. If the state fails to enforce environmental regulations against a polluter, members of the public can not only go to the ballot box, they can also go to court. That is true in countless areas, and it ought to be true in education."[14]

The primary "remedy" under NCLB for children in schools failing to make AYP two years in a row was to transfer to a better school in the district. Data plus choice was supposed to drive improvement. As President Bush explained, "parents, armed with options and choice, can assure that their children get the best, most effective education possible."[15] But few students and parents availed themselves of this option because they lacked the data, initiative, or better options, or because school districts made it difficult to exit.

When plaintiffs did sue they were hamstrung by the lack of a private right of action in the law. For example, in New Jersey, the Seton Hall University School of Law's Center for Social Justice sued the state, claiming that it neglected to notify students in failing schools of their right to transfer and to get supplemental tutoring. Both the district court and Third Circuit ruled that since the law contained no private right of action, the suit had to be dismissed. "Congress," the Third Circuit concluded, "did not intend to give individuals a right to enforce the notice and supplemental educational services provisions of the Act."[16]

The lack of a private right of action also appeared to dissuade some advocacy groups from suing at all. The Alliance for School Choice, led by Clint Bolick, filed complaints with the Los Angeles and Compton school districts, claiming that they were not adequately enforcing the choice provisions of NCLB. In their press release, they noted that because NCLB did not contain a private right of action, they first had to file complaints with the school districts. They later threatened to sue but never followed through.[17] Thus, because it lacked a clean administrative or judicial lever to compel compliance, the choice option of NCLB remained largely useless.

Even if NCLB had contained a private right of action, it is doubtful that litigation would have achieved NCLB's goals. Federal judges seem to have lost the appetite for lengthy restructuring and oversight of public institutions. As well, there are reasons to doubt their capacity to implement effective reforms. Judges are limited by the adversarial nature of the judicial process, their dependence on partisan experts, and their tendency to generate harmful unintended consequences. Any judicial oversight would have also been short-lived. NCLB dispensed significant pain on school officials and teachers. Opening them up to more litigation would have only generated more pain and greater pushback. Had NCLB opened the floodgates to litigation, it almost certainly would not have taken until 2014 for it to be revised and reauthorized.

Some of the litigation that did occur under NCLB should make us grateful that the law largely stayed out of court. Particularly pernicious was litigation under the ill-conceived "highly qualified teacher" provision of the law, which stipulated that all teachers of core subjects must be highly qualified, and that those who were not could not be disproportionately concentrated in poor and minority school districts. NCLB defined "highly qualified" as having a bachelor of arts, subject matter competence, and certification or licensure by the state, but left the latter to the states. Among the numerous problems with this provision was that it cut against the overall logic of NCLB. Ostensibly, NCLB was going to shift the focus to outputs, not inputs. As long as students were demonstrating progress, the federal government should not worry about how states and school districts were doing it. This provision, however, dictated how states were to provide education.

The California Case: *Renee v. Duncan*

A case from California, *Renee v. Duncan*, would expose the absence of an enforcement mechanism for the highly qualified teacher provision. The dispute arose over the Department of Education's (ED) decision to allow teachers seeking alternative certifications to count as highly qualified under No Child Left Behind. Shortly after NCLB's enactment, ED issued regulations allowing states to count members of programs such as Teach for America (TFA) as highly qualified. Many states, such as California, rely on TFA and similar organizations to supplement staff in poorer school districts. In response to ED's decision, California issued regulations stating that teachers seeking alternative certification could be considered fully certified under NCLB if they were demonstrating satisfactory progress.

ED's regulation, however, offended the California interest group Public Advocates. According to Public Advocates, ED's regulation violated NCLB and allowed California to place less qualified teachers—which they defined as those seeking alternative certification—in poorer school districts. In 2007, Public Advocates, on behalf of Californians for Justice, the California chapter of ACORN (Association of Community Organizations for Reform Now), and individual parents of children in Title I schools, filed suit, saying that the regulation created an impermissible loophole in the law. The lawsuit argued that to be certifiable, enrollees must have completed their alternative route. California had ten thousand teachers who were seeking alternative certification and thus fell short of Public Advocates' desired standard.

In 2008, a federal district court ruled against Public Advocates, claiming that the regulation did not obviously violate the intent of Congress.[18] A Ninth Circuit panel, in a 2–1 decision, initially agreed with the trial court and ordered the case to be remanded and dismissed for lack of standing.[19] The panel held that the case failed a test of redressability since they could not tell California how to define certification. In essence, there was no remedy available to the court. But the panel reversed its decision and granted Public Advocates' request for a rehearing after one member changed his mind.

After rehearing the case, the panel reversed its own initial decision on standing and the trial court's ruling on ED's regulation. The court, in a 2–1 opinion, admitted that it lacked the power to dictate to California how to define certification. But, strangely, it thought that there was still means for the court to force California and ED to change their policy. Primarily, the court believed that Secretary of Education Arne Duncan could withhold federal education funds from California until it changed its policy.

Unfortunately, the court ignored the fact that one cannot simply issue a ruling and create highly qualified teachers. Even if one grants the dubious assertion that fully certified teachers are better, it would be impossible for California to simply reassign teachers to ensure that schools serving poor and minority students did not have a lower percentage of fully certified teachers than other schools. TFA was in such demand in low-income school districts because these districts had difficulty filling teaching positions. The court, in short, had the power to strike down ED's regulation but lacked the power to actually change anything that mattered. In the end, Congress resolved the issue and averted any chance of judicially imposed educational chaos by writing ED's regulations into law in a continuing budget resolution in December 2010.

Connecticut: Strange Bedfellows

NCLB's civil rights framing also created unusual alliances when states challenged its requirements in court. One prominent example came out of Connecticut. Since 1984, the state had tested students in the fourth, sixth, and eighth grades. But NCLB mandated testing every year for grades 3 through 8, which required Connecticut to add three years of testing. Connecticut's secretary of education complained that more testing would not tell the state "anything new" and the money and time could be better used. This prompted then–Secretary of Education Margaret Spellings to chastise Connecticut and other critics of NCLB for being "un-American." NCLB, she said, was designed to close the achievement gap between white and black students, so anyone disagreeing with its requirements was practicing the "soft bigotry of low expectations."[20]

In 2005, during this unedifying war of words, the state attorney general, Richard Blumenthal, sued in federal court. He claimed that NCLB was an unfunded mandate in violation of federal law and challenged ED's denial of three requests for waivers, which would have given the state greater flexibility in implementing the law's requirements. Connecticut lost both claims. The lawsuit was also challenged by the state NAACP, which successfully intervened in the case in defense of ED and Secretary Spellings. Its attorney explained: "If we view No Child Left Behind in terms of civil rights, then we are concerned about a state begging to be excused from participating or complying with an act intended to help disadvantaged people."[21]

The case finally ended in 2011 when the Supreme Court denied its petition for certiorari. Interestingly, this denial came before the Supreme Court's decision in *NFIB v. Sebelius*, which held that losing federal funds for not complying with the Affordable Care Act's Medicaid expansion unconstitutionally coerced the states.[22] The same reasoning could very well have been applied against NCLB.

NCLB Waivers

In 2005, Margaret Spellings announced that she would allow waivers but only from states that were adhering to the "bright line principles" of NCLB. This allowed her to protect one of her boss's significant domestic achievements but also retain the mantle of reform. NCLB clearly allowed the secretary of education "to waive any statutory or regulatory requirement for a state educational agency, local educational agency, Indian tribe, or school through a local educational agency" as long as it set measurable goals and explained how a waiver would improve instruction and achievement. In some ways, ED's waivers under both the Bush and Obama administrations were necessary attempts to prevent a poorly constructed law from completely capsizing into disaster. But eventually the waivers metastasized into compelling action desired by the department but not required by law. Under Obama, waivers became legislation by other means.

In 2011, Arne Duncan began issuing waivers on a broader scale and scope than anything done by Spellings. In all, forty-three states and the District of Columbia received waivers. To obtain relief from NCLB's requirements, states had to: 1) adopt "college- and career-ready expectations for all students in ... at least reading/language arts and mathematics," 2) "develop and implement a system of differentiated recognition, accountability, and support for all [schools]," 3) adopt "teacher and principal evaluation and support systems" that "meaningfully differentiate performance" into at least three levels based on "student growth" data and other factors," 4) use that data to "evaluate teachers and principals on a regular basis" and "inform personnel decisions," and 5) "remove duplicative and burdensome reporting requirements that have little or no impact on student outcomes."[23] The effect of these conditions was to replace the legislative framework of NCLB with something entirely different. Additionally, for the first time, the federal government began dictating the curricular content and methods of teacher evaluation to states.

These waivers raised several constitutional problems. As Derek Black pointed out, when states initially agreed to NCLB, there was no notice that the federal government would impose new conditions as a prerequisite for receiving a waiver. "Thus," Black argues, "the waiver conditions likely violate the constitutional requirement of clearly stated conditions on federal spending."[24]

But speculation about possible constitutional violations is not even necessary. Not only were the waiver conditions not explicitly allowed under NCLB, some were explicitly forbidden. To make certain that the limits of the law were clear, NCLB stated: "Nothing in this subchapter shall be construed to authorize an officer or employee of the Federal Government to mandate, direct, or control a State, local educational agency, or school's specific instructional content, academic achievement standards and assessments, curriculum, or program of instruction, as a condition of eligibility to receive funds under this chapter." Hence, the college- and career-ready curriculum requirements were obviously forbidden, particularly because Duncan was demanding a specific curriculum—Common Core, or some close facsimile of it. The Obama administration's own actions also implicitly conceded that NCLB did not give ED this kind of authority. Secretary Duncan and President Obama twice asked Congress to give them the authority to compel states to adopt the reforms required by this waiver process. When Congress did not do so, Secretary Duncan said that congressional "dysfunction" "compelled" him to create his waiver system.[25]

Washington and Oklahoma: A Tale of Two States

The troubling nature of waivers under Duncan is evident in the experiences of Washington and Oklahoma. Washington was initially granted a two-year waiver in 2012. In 2013, however, the Department of Education told the state superintendent of public instruction that for the state waiver to be extended, the state must pass legislation tying teacher evaluation to student progress on achievement. In 2014, the state legislature appeared ready to do so, but after heavy lobbying from state teacher unions, Democratic senators withdrew their support for the bill. In response, ED rescinded the state's waiver. Arne Duncan wrote to the state superintendent that "should Washington obtain the requisite authority to resolve its condition, I would be pleased to reconsider Washington's request to implement ESEA flexibility at any time."[26]

While Oklahoma's story had a happier ending, it was no less remarkable. Oklahoma adopted the Common Core State Standards in 2010. Facing considerable backlash, the state legislature decided to eliminate Common Core in 2014 and revert to its old standards while the state department of education created new ones. In response, ED withdrew the state's NCLB waiver, saying that "Oklahoma can no longer demonstrate that the state's standards are college- and career-ready, and has not given any timetable by when the state will be able to provide the appropriate evidence to ED."[27] The state then filed an appeal arguing that its old standards were a suitable substitute for Common Core. A few months later, ED reinstated the waiver. While defenders of Common Core argued that this showed that ED was not mandating a particular curriculum, the more plausible explanation is that Common Core had become politically toxic and imposing it on the states would no longer be viable.

THE OFFICE FOR CIVIL RIGHTS

NCLB created the opportunity for aggressive OCR action during the Obama administration in two ways. First, by including such wildly implausible requirements, it created the conditions for the department to issue a slew of arbitrary and unlawful waivers and "federalize" education policy. This was the ground for the agency to offer strained readings of federal law in DCLs.

Thus, aggressive, unilateral, legally dubious action became standard operating procedure for the department as a result of NCLB. After launching its regime by waiver, the agency was emboldened to expand its policy-making adventures. Second, NCLB created the perception that remedying unequal outcomes was within the authority and ability of the federal government. In short, aggressive, poorly constructed federal education policy led to more aggressive, poorly constructed policy.

DCLs ostensibly just clarify existing law and, thus, are not created by formal rulemaking procedures. However, ED uses them to circumvent the rulemaking process and create entirely new regulations. Even though they are supposed to just be "guidance," ED treats DCLs as if they were lawfully created regulations and demands that states and school districts treat them as such. Three DCLs best characterized OCR's aggressiveness in K–12 education during the Obama administration's second term: school discipline, school finance, and transgender students.

School Discipline

OCR, with the Justice Department, published its school discipline DCL in January 2014. The guidelines contained the standard boilerplate about helping students "learn and thrive" and supporting "positive behavior and character development." But the core of the DCL was its application of *disparate impact* to school discipline. According to the guidelines, schools still "violate federal law when they evenhandedly implement facially neutral policies" that were adopted with no intent to discriminate but that "nonetheless have an unjustified effect of discriminating against students on the basis of race." In short, if students in one racial group are punished more than their percentage of the student population, a school could be subject to a federal investigation. In that investigation, OCR would ask if a discipline policy had an "adverse" (disproportionate) impact on a particular race, if the policy is necessary to meet important educational goals, and if other effective policies could be substituted without the adverse effect. Unfortunately, the guidelines were short on what could count as an important educational goal and what policies might be suitable alternatives. If evenhandedly designed and implemented policies could fall afoul of these standards, then any policy could.

Critics of the DCL contended that it rested on a shaky or nonexistent legal foundation and created perverse incentives that would compromise the education of the very students it claimed to protect. The DCL all but created a quota system for school suspensions even though Title VI, which it rested on, forbids the use of quotas. The DCL also encouraged schools to tolerate disruptive and dangerous behavior to avoid punishing too many students of one race. This incentive is strongest in largely minority, urban school districts, where disruptive student behavior is a more significant problem. Therefore, the guidance makes minority students the primary victims of the DCL's good intentions. Socioeconomic variables such as childhood stress, poverty, and family structure are some of the best predictors of student behavioral problems. But these are not evenly distributed by race, so to satisfy OCR, schools would have to engage in racially discriminatory discipline. Most schools would simply not punish students for disruptive or dangerous behavior if they belonged to statistically overpunished minority groups. But this creates silent victims who bear the cost of risk avoidance by school officials. Students who want to learn have their educations sabotaged by troublemakers. Unfortunately, OCR also ignored research showing that African American children suffer when disruptive students are not punished and that reducing out-of-school suspensions increases the racial achievement gap. The same research shows that the threat of suspension "deters students from ever committing an infraction."[28] Hence, policies such as those encouraged by OCR necessarily increase misbehavior by students.

OCR's own attempts to justify this DCL lent support to these criticisms. In December 2016, it published "Achieving Simple Justice," highlighting its achievements during the Obama presidency.[29] On school discipline, it favorably noted a resolution with the Lodi Unified School District in California. OCR had opened an investigation against the school district after a black student received a harsher punishment than a white student for fighting. But OCR's own investigation revealed that the black student had assaulted the white student and the white student had not fought back. Despite that, OCR found the district guilty of a "disparate impact violation" in its overall system of school discipline.

School Finance

In October 2014, OCR issued an even more extraordinary DCL on school finance. This DCL announced that any racially identifiable disparity in educational resources could trigger an investigation by the agency. The letter stated that OCR was writing to "call your attention to disparities that persist in access to educational resources, and to help you address those disparities and comply with the legal obligation to provide students with equal access to these resources without regard to race, color, or national origin."

This one also rested on disparate impact analysis. School districts and states "violate Title VI if they adopt facially neutral policies that are not intended to discriminate . . . but do have an unjustified, adverse disparate impact on students based on race, color, or national origin." Thus, schools must "demonstrate that the policy or practice is necessary to meet an important educational goal," and that "comparably effective alternative policy or practice that would meet the school district's stated educational goal with less of a discriminatory effect."

This DCL was also beset with practical and legal problems. As Shep Melnick explained, "this subjective test grants almost complete control to federal regulators to decide what constitutes an 'important educational goal' and a 'comparably effective alternative.' In effect, OCR has invented a test that no school district or state department of education can pass, and then given itself authority to determine the appropriate remedy."[30] OCR also disavowed the idea that equal spending should be the standard for determining unequal resources. A finding of unequal resources oddly might not be based on unequal resources. But if money is not the measure of resources and opportunity, then what is? Here OCR wandered deep into the swamps of supervising and managing schools. It would consider a variety of factors affecting educational outcomes, including, among many others: paint, carpets, lockers, heating and air conditioning, laboratory facilities, performing arts spaces, library resources, audio-visual equipment, availability of laptops and tablets, access to Wi-Fi hotspots, graphing calculators, digital simulations, extracurricular activities, and effective teaching and leadership. What OCR did not explain is how one federal agency of five to six hundred employees was supposed to provide this kind of "holistic" evaluation of school resources at potentially all the nation's schools.

OCR's letter also lacked any recognizable legal foundation. *San Antonio v. Rodriguez* (1973) and *Washington v. Davis* (1976), the two most important cases for determining the legality of the memo, were not even mentioned and for good reason.[31] In *Rodriguez*, the Supreme Court held that there is no constitutional right to education, so disparities in funding are not unconstitutional. In *Davis*, the court ruled that policies adopted without a discriminatory purpose but that have a discriminatory effect are not unconstitutional. In addition, there was no precedent for this kind of intervention under Title VI. The real source of OCR's alleged authority was a 2001 DCL from Bill Clinton's secretary of education, Richard Riley, that emphasized the importance of equal resources.[32] But this midnight memo from the last month of the Clinton administration provided no mandates for school districts to follow. Just as troubling was the fact that the Supreme Court had explicitly rejected OCR's disparate impact analysis in *Alexander v. Sandoval* (2001).[33] In that case, the court said that Title VI "prohibits only intentional discrimination" and declined to enforce disparate impact regulations created by the Department of Justice.

Sandoval, it should be noted, had degraded OCR's longstanding enforcement mechanism of allowing plaintiffs to sue for noncompliance of OCR's rules, which led OCR to develop other enforcement mechanisms. The key, as Melnick explained, is for OCR to "harass and colonize." As courts have been less supportive of OCR's more aggressive behavior, its strategy has been to "bludgeon schools into submission" with costly and embarrassing investigations. Hence, the process is the punishment that drives compliance. Through its edicts, OCR has been able to seed school districts and colleges with administrators dedicated to carrying out its policies. To comply with Title IX, schools have been compelled to create or expand compliance offices that work closely with the agency and have staff sympathetic to its agenda. In fact, in its infamous 2011 DCL on sexual harassment, OCR told school districts and colleges that failure to hire a Title IX coordinator was prima facie evidence of noncompliance, which naturally would open an institution to OCR investigation.

Transgender Students

The third in OCR's trilogy of memos was its May 2016 DCL on transgender students. While the guidance addressed athletics, single-sex classes, housing, and overnight accommodations, the most controversial part of the memo held that under Title IX, any institution receiving federal funds must allow students to use restrooms and locker rooms "consistent with their gender identity."

Once again, the DCL was plagued with oversights and legal infirmities. One of the most penetrating critiques of the letter came from Harvard Law School professor Jeannie Suk Gersen. She pointed out that Title IX prevented sex discrimination, and it was not at all clear that discrimination based on gender identification was the same thing as sex discrimination. Certainly, when the law was passed no one thought that it included gender identification. More fundamentally, the DCL rendered Title IX hopelessly contradictory. OCR, Suk noted, had long interpreted Title IX to prevent a hostile educational environment. But would not forcing biological females to use the same locker room as a biological male who identifies as female create a hostile environment? "The discomfort that some people, some sexual-assault survivors, in particular, feel at the idea of being in rest rooms with people with male sex organs," she pointed out, "is not easy to brush aside as bigotry." OCR was rendering Title IX incoherent and setting schools up to "be sued whichever route they choose."

Such problems, she argued, were inevitable considering the lawless nature of the DCL. "Unlike the Education Department's many regulations," she said, "the Dear Colleague letter is not law, because it wasn't enacted through legal procedures, involving public input, that federal agencies must follow when making law." Issuing edicts through letters "rather than lawful processes" prevented OCR from confronting the future consequences of its rules.[34] The normal rulemaking process would have those affected by the rules, namely school districts, raise such concerns.

In response to the DCL, Texas, along with twelve other states, sued, claiming that the DCL both misread Title IX and should have been promulgated through the ordinary rulemaking process. Another ten states, led by Nebraska, also filed a separate lawsuit. In August 2016, a federal judge granted a preliminary injunction in the Texas case forbidding the administration from enforcing the DCL while the case was ongoing.

At the same time, another case, *Gloucester County School Board v. G.G.*, filed by Gavin Grimm, a transgender student in Virginia, was already working its way to the Supreme Court. Grimm had sued the Gloucester County School Board for a policy limiting bathroom use to a student's biological gender. Grimm claimed that the policy violated Title IX. After the district court denied his request for a preliminary injunction, a Fourth Circuit panel reversed the district court and declared the school board's policy a violation of Title IX. Pointing to a 2015 opinion letter from OCR preceding the DCL that said, "a school generally must treat transgender students consistent with their gender identity," the court ruled that Title IX required allowing Grimm to use the boys bathroom.[35] Gloucester County asked the Supreme Court to put the Fourth Circuit decision on hold until it could file its petition. The Supreme Court agreed and then, in October 2016, granted the district's request for certiorari. Grimm's case would then include all of the issues contested in the state challenges.

Donald Trump's election ended up undermining the legal basis for these cases. In February 2017, the Trump administration rescinded the opinion letter relied on by the Fourth Circuit and OCR's DCL, saying that they were imposed "without due regard for the primary role of the states and local school districts in establishing educational policy."[36] In response, the Supreme Court remanded the case back to the district court to be decided in light of the Trump administration's action.

LESSONS LEARNED

The unprecedented federal action of Bush and Obama points to several cautionary conclusions.

Lesson 1: Simply Labeling Something a Civil Right Will Not Overcome the Difficulties of Managing and Reforming Coping Organizations

James Q. Wilson defined *coping organizations* as ones in which managers have difficulty monitoring employees or measuring outcomes: schools and the police are the quintessential examples.[37] It is not much of an exaggeration to say that almost all education reforms, including those of the Bush and Obama administrations, are attempts to overcome these difficulties. For example, the focus on accountability tries to create clean measures of outcomes, and demanding statistically equal rates of punishment serves as a proxy for not being able to observe school officials enforcing school discipline policies. Framing policy as a civil rights initiative lends it a moral urgency that is supposed to help cut through this fog. Rights, after all, demand protection. But for a right to be enforceable, there must be a clear remedy. Simply labeling something a civil right does not magically create a remedy, nor does it ensure that others regard it as a right. As well, labeling something a civil right makes it difficult to retreat from ineffective reforms because rights and remedies are tightly linked. If a remedy has been declared essential for its protection, it becomes nearly as sacrosanct as the right. This connection helps explain ED's intransigence when states asked for relief from NCLB's requirements, and cautions against labeling reforms as civil rights initiatives in the first place.

Lesson 2: Federalism Still Matters; Ignore It at Your Peril

Desegregation was the exception that proved the rule that education is largely a province of state and local governments. Attempts to force reform on them without adequate buy-in are doomed to failure. As a chastened

Lamar Alexander put it, dictating reform from Washington "actually creates a backlash, making higher standards more difficult to hold onto and teacher evaluation systems more difficult to create because of all the anger . . . It's just not the way you make permanent improvements in 100,000 public schools. The community has to own the change. The teachers in the school have to own the evaluation system and believe it's fair or it'll never work."[38] NCLB, and later Common Core, spurred a backlash against testing. If such accountability reforms are in fact crucial for guaranteeing a quality education for children, then both could very well have set back the progress of reform.

Lesson 3: Unilateral Federal Action Is a Poor Substitute for Legislation and Ordinary Rulemaking

When Secretary Duncan resorted to waivers, he did an end run on the legislative process. It is easy to see why. Passing laws is difficult work, and you might not get everything that you want. In fact, you are almost guaranteed not to. But the legislative process is there for a reason. It forces you to build a broad political base for action. This process also exposes the political limitations of your agenda. The political backlash to the conditions ED attached to waivers would have been easier to foresee if they had been vetted via the legislative process.

Similarly, DCLs allow OCR to engage in uninhibited policy freelancing. But avoiding legislation or ordinary rulemaking is not costless. The freedom of OCR to do what is right in its own eyes means its actions will generate significant unintended consequences. With school discipline, giving teachers, school districts, and state boards of education the opportunity to express their concerns would almost certainly have led to more modest ambitions. Now, evidence is accumulating that teachers believe that their classrooms are less safe as a result of their district's succumbing to OCR's mandate. Teacher unions around the country have surveyed their members about these reforms, and their responses indicate significant frustration.[39]

Or consider OCR's memo on transgender students. By framing it as a civil rights issue, OCR necessarily limited discussion and dialogue on a contentious area desperately needing it. Quite obviously, OCR put the concerns and statutory rights of some students at odds with the dictates of the memo. Thus, instead of building a political coalition that would bring different groups together to discuss what might be a reasonable compromise, it legalized the issue.

CONCLUSION

Overall, the past sixteen years should encourage greater modesty about what the federal government can achieve in education. The federal government can dictate only what schools *should* do. Since it does not actually run schools, it cannot ensure that its commands are implemented effectively. This distance also means that the federal government lacks the practical understanding of how schools operate, which is necessary to do much dictating in the first place. Declaring certain issues to be matters of civil rights does not overcome this basic fact about the division of labor in our system. Setting broad policy goals and a modest range of incentives is certainly within the federal government's competence and authority. When it reaches beyond those boundaries, it generates more problems than it solves.

Unsurprisingly, federal withdrawal to more sustainable limits has begun. While some of this is due to Donald Trump's election, it actually began under President Obama. The Every Student Succeeds Act (ESSA), the long-overdue reauthorization of ESEA in 2015, was a bipartisan rollback of many of NCLB's requirements on the states. In addition, critiques of OCR's promiscuous use of DCLs have been leveled from both the left and the right, along with lawsuits challenging the authority of the agency to create policy outside of normal rulemaking procedures. Of course, Trump's election meant that the federal role would be even more limited. During the campaign, he said he would like to close the Department of Education and return control of education back to states and school districts. Shuttering ED is (to say the least) unlikely, but he has done much already to make good on limiting federal authority. ED has granted even more flexibility for states under ESSA and has withdrawn the DCLs on sexual misconduct and transgender students. It would be unsurprising for the school finance and school discipline DCLs to be withdrawn as well. Thus, the next few years will certainly be ones of federal retrenchment. The question is just how far it will go. Trump will try to go further than others might have, but the past sixteen years seem to have exhausted the appetite of both the left and right for aggressive federal interventions in education policy.

Conclusion

Frederick M. Hess and Michael Q. McShane

W hen all is said and done, what *did* we learn about improving K–12 education during the Bush-Obama years? After all, for close to two decades, America witnessed a remarkable experiment in school reform. Washington took the lead and reformers pursued a raft of ambitious efforts across the land. A handful of states and districts became iconic: New Orleans. New York City. Washington, DC. Chicago. Denver. Newark. Equally familiar were the names that headlined the era's most prominent reforms: Margaret Spellings. Michelle Rhee. Joel Klein. Arne Duncan. Bill Gates.

For all the different agendas and personalities, though, we were struck in crafting this volume at just how comfortable the contributors were with the notion that "Bush-Obama school reform" was something of a unified whole. After all, we had initially wondered if it would instead seem clear that the Bush and Obama presidencies reflected two very different approaches to school reform—as they did on a range of domestic and foreign policies. Yet, for good or ill, the consensus among the contributors seems to be that the No Child Left Behind era set the table for Obama's efforts, and that the Obama years largely built on what Bush had done.

Looking back, after close to two decades of unprecedented federal leadership and ambitious activity, it's hard to make the case that American education has dramatically improved. On the National Assessment of Education Progress, math and reading performance is up modestly since 2003—the year that No Child Left Behind first required all states to take the test.[1] During the same period, the US ranking on international assessments hasn't changed materially. Indeed, the US average scores on PISA—the Program for International Student Assessment—for reading, math, and science have stayed mostly flat since 2000, and the nation's rank among OECD countries remains middling.[2] While the high school graduation rate is up substantially, troubling reports have raised questions about how much of that is real and how much is a product of gamesmanship.

In short, whatever their virtues, the Bush-Obama years failed to deliver on Bush's bold promise to "leave no child behind" or Obama's pledge to "end what has become a race to the bottom in our schools and instead spur a race to the top." Indeed, the preceding chapters suggest that efforts to boost teacher quality, turn around struggling schools, promote rigorous academic standards, and hold schools accountable generally fell short of their aims. At the same time, the contributors describe increased transparency, newfound attention to teacher quality and student data, growing capacity in many state education agencies, great strides in charter schooling, and improvements in the quantity and quality of education research.

All that said, as we noted back in the introduction, our intent here is not to grade Bush-Obama school reform but instead to see what might be learned from it. So, what have we learned?

The early chapters in this volume observe that, in practice, key reform strategies of the Bush-Obama years played out in ways quite different than advocates had hoped. Deven Carlson argues, persuasively, that while accountability reforms like No Child Left Behind did modestly improve student test scores, they came with unintended consequences, like narrowed curriculum, gamesmanship, and fierce antitesting backlash. Ashley Jochim suggests that those guiding the ambitious federal School Improvement Grant program never found a way to translate the menu of "turnaround" options into practice, running afoul of the street-level teachers and school leaders responsible for making turnarounds work. Tom Loveless takes a careful look at standards-based reform and makes the case that the push for states to adopt "rigorous" academic standards undermined the broad support required for success while changing classrooms in problematic ways.

Other contributors assess specific policy instruments that played an outsized role in the Bush-Obama years. Anna J. Egalite credits the federal government with supporting charter school growth through startup grants and financing support, while staying far enough removed that charter schooling never became seen as a creature of Washington. Robert Pianta and Tara Hofkens cheer the strides taken during the Bush-Obama years to develop the national infrastructure for supporting high-quality education research, but caution that the resulting hunt for "killer app" interventions that work across contexts is rife with problems.

Matthew A. Kraft highlights the irony of federal forays into teacher evaluation that sought to involve teachers and principals but ultimately favored rigid programs based on the intuitions of noneducators, while dictating timelines so stringent that efforts to meaningfully involve teachers became prohibitive. Patrick McGuinn finds that the federal government's use of incentives and inducements catalyzed important system changes, but also observes that these levers yielded hasty policy making that frequently stymied discussion and debate, ultimately undermining their support. And Joshua Dunn argues that the decision to frame education as a "civil rights" issue served to strengthen the hand of reformers, but that the absolute nature of the approach also made it more difficult to devise pragmatic or politically viable policies.

NINE TAKEAWAYS

As we perused these chapters, there emerged themes that seemed to cut across the various topics. Together, they paint a mixed picture of what transpired, and remind us just how complicated and hard to anticipate the fruits of reform can be. Here are nine such takeaways that struck us.

Major Reform Accomplishments Are Often Ancillary to the Intended Objective

In many cases, it appears that the biggest gains of the Bush-Obama era have turned out to be changes that were originally regarded as incidental or the infrastructure for more important reforms. As Matthew A. Kraft suggests, in the case of teacher quality, neither No Child Left Behind's "highly qualified teacher" provision nor Race to the Top's push on teacher evaluation came close to fulfilling the ambitions of policy makers and advocates. However, these efforts left in their wake new data systems, policy frameworks, and lines of research that have fundamentally altered how states and school systems think about teacher quality. While NCLB accountability and mandated remedies never delivered as promised, Deven Carlson shows that the testing and transparency requirements established by the law went on to reshape how America thinks and talks about school performance and educational equity. The burning question is whether these accomplishments were made possible only because ambitious federal policies forced movement, or whether more modest measures could have delivered the same benefits without the pushback and sometimes-ugly aftermath.

The Center of Gravity in Schooling Has Shifted from Districts to States

The signal development of the Bush-Obama years may have been the degree to which educational leadership migrated to Washington; since 2015, a prominent question has been how much 2015's Every Student Succeeds Act did to arrest or reverse that state of affairs. Less widely noted has been the way in which the Bush-Obama efforts shifted authority from school districts to states. No Child Left Behind required states to assume new responsibilities in terms of assessment, accountability, and reporting on teacher quality—tasks that had traditionally been the purview of local school districts. Race to the Top doubled down on this shift by encouraging governors and state education agencies to develop new strategies for data systems, school improvement, and teacher evaluation. As Sara E. Dahill-Brown ably chronicles, state education agencies are not necessarily equipped or staffed for this work. Nevertheless, the authority routinely accorded to a district superintendent in the years before the Bush presidency had migrated to the state capital by the end of President Obama's tenure. This changes the politics of education, brings new actors into the fold, and raises the stakes of new education initiatives.

It's Not Just About Technical Expertise

The dismal state of educational research has long led many reformers to nurture the hope that challenges will prove tractable once education research gets serious. That hope was ubiquitous in the 1990s and spurred the dramatic remaking of educational research that emerged in the Bush-Obama years. Buoyed by the Education Sciences Reform Act of 2002, determined federal leadership, and big investments by major foundations, the education research landscape matured during the Bush-Obama years. Yet the development of more sophisticated strategies to evaluate schools, teachers, and interventions made it clear that many of our biggest challenges—like turning around low performing schools or making instruction more rigorous—are not necessarily due to a lack of know-how, but are simply more difficult to do consistently and well than reformers imagined at the dawn of the millennium. Meanwhile, the faith that quantitative research holds the promise of definitive answers has had the notable side effect of elevating the role of economists in the world of education research. This has boosted the significance of complex econometric analyses, as well as the test scores that lend themselves to such analysis. Robert Pianta and Tara Hofkens ask us to wrestle with the questions of whether this kind of research has narrowed our field of vision, distorted our sense of what's important, and prompted us to focus more on measuring the effects of reform than on what it takes to make reforms work as intended.

For Good and Ill, the Ecosystem Matters—a Lot

The ecosystem around school reform grew dramatically in the Bush and Obama years, as a raft of new national advocacy groups proliferated, spearheading the push for charter schooling, teacher evaluation reform, and test-based accountability in the states. These efforts relied heavily on the funding provided by an influential new set of active, policy-engaged philanthropists. What would have been hard to appreciate in 2000, given the seismic shift from the rhythms of governor- and business-led reform in the 1980s and 1990s, is the ways in which these new advocates would amplify and interact with federal policy. The Bush administration and advocacy organizations used NCLB's status as a "civil rights" law as a cudgel in states like Connecticut to compel reluctant policy makers to embrace NCLB-style accountability. The Gates Foundation facilitated state Race to the Top applications by spending millions to help underwrite the education consultants that assisted favored states in devising their plans. Those RTTT plans tended to lean heavily on a small set of (foundation-supported) brand-name nonprofits, which served as the go-tos in applications when it came to areas like teacher quality, school leadership, or turnarounds. Reform efforts benefited from this, as did "mission-aligned" advocates and reformers. But this also meant, as Patrick McGuinn argues, that policies became colored by suspicions about favoritism, hidden agendas, and backroom agreements, and concerns that healthy debate was being stifled by a shoulder-to-shoulder phalanx of federal policy makers and big-money foundations.

Politically Feasible Timelines for Reform May Be at Odds with Educational Timelines for Effective Implementation

During the Bush-Obama years, politicians and advocates pushed for rapid, massive changes. When urged to slow down, they would respond with "Whose child do *you* want to leave behind?" and "A child only gets one shot at the fourth grade." After all, presidents and governors serve four-year terms; they want to make a difference and they need to see fast results if their efforts are to be politically viable. But it turns out that acting with an eye to a political time horizon may complicate efforts to do things effectively on an educational timeline. In the cases of both teacher evaluation and the Common Core, for instance, the Obama administration catalyzed widespread adoption via Race to the Top and NCLB waivers. However, because the RTTT-mandated timeline meant that multiple initiatives were pursued at once, teachers and schools were frequently being evaluated on standards and tests that were just being rolled out. While the problem soon became evident—most famously as partisan controversy engulfed the Common Core—it was hard to know what to do about it, given that states were already moving ahead with multipart reforms and had made time-specific commitments about how they would proceed. It turns out that federal carrots and sticks aren't just a spur to act—they're a spur to do certain things *at a certain speed*. And the way reform agendas and policy windows work is that, when things happen, they tend to happen in bunches.

Once a Reform Gains Political Momentum, It Can Be Hard to Alter Course or Make Necessary Adjustments

Common Core advocates initially promised that "the standards" would make a big difference, not because there was magic in the standards themselves but because they would make possible coordinated changes in testing, teacher preparation, instructional materials, and more. In other words, it was never just about getting states to adopt the standards, but getting states to adopt the standards in a manner that would facilitate those other changes. Yet, as Tom Loveless argues, advocates turned a blind eye to the way that turbocharged adoption (fueled by RTTT) helped to nationalize and politicize the effort, and introduce it into lots of states that were only lukewarm on the enterprise. As a result, the ability to do all the things that were needed to make Common Core successful were ultimately compromised. This risk was apparent from the earliest days of the Common Core and had become glaringly evident by 2012. Thus, only by abandoning much of what was intended to make Common Core successful were advocates— focused on winning the political battle in the here and now—able to "save" their project. Matthew A. Kraft and Deven Carlson make clear that similar tales can be told about the vagaries of teacher evaluation reform and NCLB-style accountability. In both cases, practical problems were apparent relatively early on, but advocates' enthusiasm and reluctance to risk losing momentum meant that these problems were more likely to be discounted than confronted.

Incentives Are Most Effective When Success Is Straightforward; They're Less Effective at Spurring Complex Change

It's clear that incentives can prompt states to act. When implementation is a fait accompli even after a law is changed or a rule repealed, such incentives can achieve their aims very effectively. On the other hand, when incentives are used to compel states to promise that they will eventually marshal the political resources to act, it's less clear those incentives will deliver as intended. So, for instance, the adoption of annualized state testing systems under NCLB or the lifting of caps on charter schooling under RTTT proved to be cases where Washington was able to very effectively use incentives to change behavior. On the other hand, when it came to teacher evaluation, incentives succeeded in getting states to initiate action, but the power of those incentives was ultimately no match for the complex dynamics of politics and school routine. Simply using "number of laws passed" by states or "number of policy changes enacted" to gauge the success or failure of federal efforts can fundamentally skew perceptions of how much change actually occurred, blind us to more complex dynamics, and encourage us to learn the wrong lessons about the use of incentives.

The Unsexy Machinery of Policy Turns Out to Matter a Lot

When it came to No Child Left Behind, states struggled to erect accountability systems. They struggled even more when it came to delivering the mandated interventions. The Bush administration's prized Reading First initiative was undone, in large part, by its reliance on an informal network of university centers that was overburdened and that wound up getting tangled in charges of favoritism. Similar concerns were raised with regard to the judging of the Obama administration's Race to the Top and Investing in Innovation programs. In each case, the need to hurriedly erect the scaffolding for a big-dollar, high-profile initiative made it hard to focus on design challenges or on insulating the machinery from political considerations. The tight deadlines and constantly evolving agenda meant that, outside of some of the research infrastructure described by Robert Pianta and Tara Hofkens, there was little scope for establishing the kind of impartial, nonpolitical, reliable machinery that could mollify future concerns about politicization or preferential treatment.

Nationalizing Education Politics Makes It Tougher to Build State-Specific Coalitions

In the 1980s and 1990s, school reform was typically championed by local coalitions. While this meant that little happened in states lacking such home-grown coalitions, it also meant that efforts in a given state usually reflected its political culture and voter preferences. This fostered policies that had durable support, which gave reformers a lot of leeway to make midcourse adjustments. The nationalization of education policies—especially when coupled with increasing political polarization—served to homogenize "reform" across the land, making it more difficult to tailor reform to the politics of a given state. In many states, this made it tougher to assemble and sustain broad, bipartisan coalitions. In California or Massachusetts, Bush's support made No Child Left Behind especially toxic; the same held true, in reverse, for Obama-backed measures in states like Texas and South Carolina. One of the intriguing points Anna J. Egalite makes about charter schooling is that the limited nature of federal support made it more possible for charter advocates in California or Texas to more readily proceed in distinctive and state-specific ways.

FOUR CRUCIAL TRADE-OFFS

What does all this mean for policy makers, practitioners, advocates, and researchers? Well, we fear that we don't have any solutions to offer. We're inclined to blame that on our training. You see, we're political scientists, and political science teaches that the world of politics and policy is full of trade-offs. Sorry about that. In that spirit, though, in place of cookie-cutter recommendations or generic advice, we'll close by highlighting four crucial trade-offs that may not have been fully appreciated back in 2000 but seem all too clear in retrospect.

Accountability Is Always More Appealing in the Abstract Than in the Here and Now

Back in the late 1990s, when high-stakes accountability was an oddity on display in only a few states, the pollsters at Public Agenda reported that parents and voters expressed near-unanimous support for the notion that schools should be held accountable for how students perform. Once No Child Left Behind became the law of the land, of course, that abstract consensus gradually started to unravel in the cold light of day. Concerns about undue emphasis on reading and math scores, excessive test preparation, and narrowed curriculum started to erode public support for NCLB. The law enjoyed elite support, favorable press coverage, and positive poll numbers in its early going; by the later years of Bush's presidency, however, "accountability" had become a loaded term and NCLB a poisoned brand. In the Obama years, there was something of a replay with teacher evaluation. Once again, an easy-to-like idea—that teachers should be accountable for student learning—turned divisive as states pushed forward. The cheerful promises and glowing press with which both efforts launched should also serve as a helpful reminder that any attempt to institute accountability will almost always prove much tougher to implement and maintain than policy makers may anticipate.

Scarcity Is a Powerful Lever, but Also a Slippery One

The Great Recession of 2008–2009 played an outsized role in shaping the educational narrative of the Bush-Obama years. It opened the door for the passage of the American Reinvestment and Recovery Act in 2009, equipping the Obama administration with $5 billion in funding for the Race to the Top and Investing in Innovation programs. At the same time, the housing crash and financial aftershocks left states cash-strapped and scrambling to fill holes in their budgets. Seeking every available dollar, state officials who knew little about education or the kinds of reforms that the Obama administration was pushing found themselves enthusiastic converts to the cause. Their commitment to the reforms was shallow, but the dollars made enthusiasts of everyone involved. While the combination of state need and new federal money amplified the visibility and impact of RTTT, the same hunger for revenue that drove states to pursue the funds meant that they weren't necessarily serious about the promised reforms. This ensured that new educational initiatives would face fierce competition for scarce funds as implementation proceeded. Times of scarcity may be a good opportunity to get states, cities, and school districts to embrace new initiatives, but they may also create challenges for follow-through and execution.

Brand Names Are an Asset, but Can Turn into a Burden in Short Order

The Bush-Obama years were dominated by a handful of big, brand-name reforms that tended to define what was meant by "school reform." No Child Left Behind. Race to the Top. The Common Core. National in scope and backed by federal officials, key state leaders, and influential foundations, these were the phrases that came to define what "reform" was, and who was a "reformer." And these brands proved to be hugely powerful. They concentrated the public's attention and gave the sometimes-amorphous cause of "school reform" a clear, easy-to-understand vision. They gave prominent advocates a convenient shorthand that they could use to summarize complicated agendas with lots of moving parts. In the early going, this proved to be a boon. Later on, though, things changed. Because these were big, national brands that were imbued with broad meaning, it was easy for them to become a magnet for all kinds of frustrations—with school operations, homework, teaching practice, polarized politics, and more—whether or not the programs themselves were expressly responsible. By becoming labels for bundles of complex changes (to standards, tests, reading programs, and so forth), brands suffered for bad experiences with their component parts. Turning these brands into national catchphrases made it easy for pushback that might have been localized to instead coalesce as a national force.

Labeling School Reform a "Civil Rights" Issue Is a Rhetorical Boon, but Also a Recipe for Rigidity

On the campaign trail in 1999 and 2000, then–Texas governor George W. Bush talked poignantly about "the soft bigotry of low expectations." His pledge to "leave no child behind" offered a commitment that he would be a champion of opportunity for all students, especially minority children and children growing up in poverty. In crafting No Child Left Behind, Bush and heavyweight Democratic senator Ted Kennedy reached ready agreement on the need to disaggregate results by race and income and to ensure that schools were accountable not just for overall performance, but particularly for how well they served low-income, black, and Latino students. That shared vision has come to frame twenty-first-century school reform. Education was increasingly described as "the civil rights issue of our time." Reformers made the measure of improvement a relentless focus on closing racial achievement gaps. Casting school reform as a civil rights issue lent the cause heft and urgency. It also, however, tended to make it harder for federal officials to accommodate practical concerns about how NCLB was working. After all, civil rights enforcement is a moral absolute. Any perceived softening on testing, accountability, or school improvement, even when necessary and useful, risked being depicted as a retreat on civil rights. This is not to say that casting education reform as a civil rights issues *causes* reformers to become more rigid or less pragmatic, but rather that it makes rigidity more appealing and compromise harder to justify. This rigidity magnified NCLB's impact in the early years, but it also ensured that the law's provisions would eventually become less tenable, and thus less sustainable.

A CLOSING THOUGHT

Education suffers from a curious malady. It is a field marked by passionate commitment, urgency, and high hopes. These are wonderful things. But they have also left many policy makers, reformers, philanthropists, and system leaders inclined to look always forward, confident that the next program or reform will be the one that delivers for kids. This assurance is an admirable quality, a healthy and wholly American optimism. But it can leave us lacking in perspective or understanding. As today's researchers have become increasingly intent on determining "what works," they've had less time to ask what we might learn from what has been tried. Indeed, we're struck at how often, in talking about this volume, we've heard versions of "we need to focus on what's ahead and not rehashing what's behind."

This reluctance to look back comes at a steep price. As a result, we tend to do a poor job of learning from the missteps and miscalculations that have gone before. Advocates imagine that they are pioneering approaches to turning around troubled schools when they may be revisiting strategies that have previously disappointed. Experience winds up being dismissed as negativity, and hard-earned lessons get lost along the way. So long as this is the case, school reformers are unlikely to see their efforts deliver the desired results. In that spirit, our hope is that this volume, if only in a small way, can help.

Notes

Introduction

1. Maria Glod, "Education Nominee Is Warmly Received in Senate," *Washington Post,* January 14, 2009, http://www.washingtonpost.com/wp-dyn/content/article/2009/01/13/AR2009011301651.html.
2. Rebecca Berg, "Jeb Bush in 2011: Federal Government Education Pressure 'Appropriate,'" *Washington Examiner,* March 30, 2015, http://www.washingtonexaminer.com/jeb-bush-in-2011-federal-government-education-pressure-appropriate/article/2562272.
3. William G. Howell, Paul E. Peterson, and Martin R. West, "The Persuadable Public," *Education Next* 9, no. 4 (Fall 2009), http://educationnext.org/persuadable-public/.

Chapter 1

1. Paul Manna, *Collision Course: Federal Education Policy Meets State and Local Realities* (Washington, DC: CQ Press, 2011).
2. Thomas Dee and Brian Jacob, "The Impact of No Child Left Behind on Student Achievement," *Journal of Policy Analysis and Management* 30, no. 3 (2011): 418–46.
3. Marcus A. Winters and Joshua M. Cowen, "Accountability and Student Proficiency in America's Largest School District," *Educational Evaluation and Policy Analysis* 34, no. 3 (2012); John Rockoff and Lesley J. Turner, "Short-Run Impacts of Accountability on School Quality," *American Economic Journal: Economic Policy* 2, no. 4 (November 2010): 119–47; David N. Figlio and Cecilia Elena Rouse, "Do Accountability and Voucher Threats Improve Low-Performing Schools?" *Journal of Public Economics* 90, no. 1–2 (2006): 239–55.
4. Eric A. Hanushek and Margaret E. Raymond, "Does School Accountability Lead to Improved Student Performance?" *Journal of Policy Analysis and Management* 24, no. 2 (2005): 297–327; Martin Carnoy and Susanna Loeb, "Does External Accountability Affect Student Outcomes? A Cross-State Analysis," *Educational Evaluation and Policy Analysis* 24, no. 4 (2002): 305–31.
5. Brian A. Jacob, "Accountability, Incentives and Behavior: The Impact of High-Stakes Testing in the Chicago Public Schools," *Journal of Public Economics* 89, no. 5–6 (2005): 761–96; Stephen P. Klein et al., "What Do Test Scores in Texas Tell Us?" *Education Policy Analysis Archives* 8, no. 49 (2000); Stephen Samuel Smith and Roslyn Arlin Mickelson, "All That Glitters Is Not Gold: School Reform in Charlotte-Mecklenburg," *Educational Evaluation and Policy Analysis* 22, no. 2 (Summer 2000): 101–27.
6. For evidence from Chicago, see Jacob, "Accountability, Incentives and Behavior"; Figlio and Rouse, "Accountability and Voucher Threats." For evidence from Florida, see Cecilia

Elena Rouse et al., "Feeling the Florida Heat? How Low-Performing Schools Respond to Voucher and Accountability Pressure," *American Economic Journal: Economic Policy* 5, no. 2 (2013): 251–81.

7. Laura S. Hamilton et al., *Standards-Based Accountability Under No Child Left Behind: Experiences of Teachers and Administrators in Three States* (Santa Monica, CA: Rand Corporation, 2007).

8. Dee and Jacob, "The Impact of No Child Left Behind"; Lisa M. Abrams, Joseph J. Pedulla, and George F. Madaus, "Views from the Classroom: Teachers' Opinions of Statewide Testing Programs," *Theory into Practice* 42, no. 1 (Winter 2003): 18–29; Helen F. Ladd and Arnaldo Zelli, "School-Based Accountability in North Carolina: The Responses of School Principals," *Educational Administration Quarterly* 38, no. 4 (2002).

9. Victor Bandeira de Mello, *Mapping State Proficiency Standards onto the NAEP Scales: Variation and Change in State Standards for Reading and Mathematics, 2005–2009 (NCES 2011458)* (Washington, DC: National Center for Education Statistics, 2011).

10. Jennifer Booher-Jennings, "Below the Bubble: 'Educational Triage' and the Texas Accountability System," *American Educational Research Journal* 42, no. 2 (Summer 2005): 231–68; Derek Neal and Diane Whitmore Schanzenbach, "Left Behind by Design: Proficiency Counts and Test-Based Accountability," *Review of Economics and Statistics* 92, no. 2 (May 2010): 263–83.

Chapter 2

1. President Lyndon B. Johnson, "Johnson's Remarks on Signing the Elementary and Secondary Education Act," Johnson City, Texas, April 11, 1965, http://www.lbjlibrary.org/lyndon-baines-johnson/timeline/johnsons-remarks-on-signing-the-elementary-and-secondary-education-act.

2. Christopher T. Cross, ed., *Putting the Pieces Together: Lessons from Comprehensive School Reform Research* (Washington, DC: National Clearinghouse for Comprehensive School Reform, 2004).

3. Kathryn M. Doherty, *Early Implementation of the Comprehensive School Reform Demonstration Program* (Washington, DC: US Department of Education, 2000).

4. Mark Berends, Susan Bodilly, and Sheila Nataraj Kirby, "Looking Back over a Decade of Whole-School Reform: The Experience of New American Schools," *Phi Delta Kappan* 84, no. 2 (2002): 168–75, http://www.jstor.org/stable/20440301.

5. Jeffrey Mirel, "Unrequited Promise," *Education Next*, Summer 2002, http://educationnext.org/unrequited-promise.

6. Cross, *Putting the Pieces Together*.

7. Rebecca Herman, *An Educators' Guide to Schoolwide Reform* (Washington, DC: American Institutes for Research, 1999).

8. Martin Orland et al., *Evaluation of the Comprehensive School Reform Program Implementation and Outcomes: Third-Year Report* (Washington, DC: US Department of Education, 2008), https://www2.ed.gov/rschstat/eval/other/csrd-outcomes/year3-report.pdf.

9. Phyllis McClure, *School Improvement Under No Child Left Behind* (Washington, DC: Center on American Progress, 2005).

10. Ibid.

11. Sasha Zucker, *Scientifically Based Research: NCLB and Assessment* (London: Pearson Education, Inc., 2004).

12. Emily Richmond, "NCLB's Legacy: As the ESSA Era Begins, Have Policymakers, Educators Learned from the Past?" *Hechinger Report,* June 12, 2016, http://hechingerreport.org/nclbs-legacy-essa-era-begins-policymakers-educators-learned-past.

13. Heinrich Mintrop and Gail L. Sunderman, "Predictable Failure of Federal Sanctions-Driven Accountability for School Improvement—And Why We May Retain It Anyway," *Educational Researcher* 38, no. 5 (2009): 353–64, http://journals.sagepub.com/doi/abs/10.3102/0013189X09339055.

14. Zoe A. Barley and Sandra Wegner, "An Examination of the Provision of Educational Services in Nine Rural Schools," *Journal of Research in Rural Education* 25, no. 5 (2010): 1–13, https://eric.ed.gov/?id=EJ887132.

15. Matthew Haag and Holly K. Hacker, "Dallas ISD Chafes at Tutor 'Racket,' But Program Required By State," *Dallas News,* April 14, 2012, https://www.dallasnews.com/news/education/2012/04/14/dallas-isd-chafes-at-tutor-racket-but-program-required-by-state.

16. William D. Hamel, *Final Management Report: Fraud in Title I–Funded Tutoring Programs* (Washington, DC: Office of Inspector General, 2013), https://www2.ed.gov/about/offices/list/oig/auditreports/fy2013/x42n0001.pdf.

17. Patricia Burch, *Supplementary Education Services Under NCLB: Emerging Evidence and Policy Issues* (Tempe, AZ: Education Policy Research Unit, 2007), http://epsl.asu.edu/epru/documents/EPSL-0705-232-EPRU.pdf; John Deke et al., *Impacts of Title I Supplemental Educational Services on Student Achievement* (Washington, DC: Institute for Education Sciences, US Department of Education, 2012), https://ies.ed.gov/ncee/pubs/20124053/pdf/20124053.pdf.

18. George Vernez et al., *State and Local Implementation of the No Child Left Behind Act: Volume VII—Title I School Choice and Supplemental Educational Services: Final Report* (Washington, DC: Office of Planning, Evaluation and Policy Development, US Department of Education, 2009), https://www2.ed.gov/rschstat/eval/choice/nclb-choice-ses-final/index.html.

19. Quoted in Richmond, "NCLB's Legacy."

20. James Taylor et al., *State and Local Implementation of the No Child Left Behind Act: Volume IX—Accountability Under NCLB: Final Report* (Washington, DC: Office of Planning, Evaluation, and Policy Development, US Department of Education, 2010), https://www2.ed.gov/rschstat/eval/disadv/nclb-accountability/nclb-accountability-final.pdf.

21. Ibid.

22. Lynn Olson, "US Urged to Rethink NCLB 'Tools,'" *Education Week,* December 5, 2006, https://www.edweek.org/ew/articles/2006/12/06/14fail.h26.html.

23. Ashley Jochim and Patrick Murphy, *The Capacity Challenge: What It Takes for State Education Agencies to Support School Improvement* (Seattle: Center on Reinventing Public Education, University of Washington, 2013).

24. This includes schools in need of improvement (fail to make AYP over two years), corrective action (fail to make AYP over four years), or restructuring (fail to make AYP after five years). See US Department of Education, *School Improvement Grants* Briefing, http://www2.ed.gov/programs/ sif/090825sigv2.ppt.

25. Martha Derthick, *Keeping the Compound Republic: Essays on American Federalism* (Washington, DC: Brookings Institution, 2001).

26. Bryan Shelly, "Rebels and Their Causes: State Resistance to No Child Left Behind," *Publius: The Journal of Federalism* 38, no. 3 (2008): 444–68, https://doi-org.offcampus.lib.washington.edu/10.1093/publius/pjn008.

27. Linda Wertheimer and Margaret Spellings, "Spellings: 'No Child Left Behind' Is a 'Toxic Brand,'" *NPR: Morning Edition*, March 17, 2010, https://www.npr.org/templates/story/story.php?storyId=124758597.

28. Editorial Projects in Education Research Center, "Issues A–Z: Adequate Yearly Progress," *Education Week*, July 18, 2011, http://www.edweek.org/ew/issues/adequate-yearly-progress/.

29. US Department of Education, *Race to the Top Program: Executive Summary* (Washington, DC: US Department of Education, 2009), https://www2.ed.gov/programs/racetothetop/executive-summary.pdf.

30. Catherine Gewertz, "Restructuring Schools Under NCLB Found to Lag," *Education Week*, December 9, 2009, https://www.edweek.org/ew/articles/2009/12/09/15restructure_ep.h29.html.

31. Arne Duncan, "Turning Around the Bottom Five Percent: Secretary Arne Duncan's Remarks at the National Alliance for Public Charter Schools Conference," June 22, 2009 (Washington, DC: US Department of Education), https://www2.ed.gov/news/speeches/2009/06/06222009.html.

32. David Brancaccio and Arne Duncan, "Interview: Arne Duncan," Public Broadcasting Service, May 1, 2009, http://www.pbs.org/now/shows/518/Arne-Duncan.html.

33. Andrew Brownstein, "SIG Aid Gives Schools Budget Relief—For Now," *Education Week*, April 15, 2012, https://www.edweek.org/ew/articles/2012/04/18/28sig-recession.h31.html.

34. William J. Bushaw and John A. McNee, "The 41st Annual Phi Delta Kappa/Gallup Poll of the Public's Attitudes Toward the Public Schools," *Phi Delta Kappa* 91, no. 1 (2009): 8–23.

35. William G. Howell, "Results of the President Obama's Race to the Top," *Education Next* 15, no. 4 (2015), http://educationnext.org/results-president-obama-race-to-the-top-reform/.

36. Thomas Dee, "School Turnarounds: Evidence from the 2009 Stimulus," Working Paper 17990 (Cambridge, MA: National Bureau of Economic Research, 2012); John Rice et al., *School Improvement Grants: Outcomes After Three Years* (San Francisco: WestEd, 2014); Gary T. Henry, J. Edward Guthrie, and LaTricia W. Townsend, *Outcomes and Impacts of North Carolina's Initiative to Turn Around the Lowest Achieving Schools* (Chapel Hill, NC: Consortium for Educational Research and Evaluation—North Carolina, 2015); David Dickey-Griffith, "Preliminary Effects of the School Improvement Grant Program on Student Achievement in Texas," *Georgetown Public Policy Review* (2013): 21–39; Lisa Dragoset et al., *School Improvement Grants: Implementation and Effectiveness* (Washington, DC: US Department of Education, Institute of Education Sciences, National Center for Education Evaluation and Regional Assistance, 2017).

37. Dragoset et al., *School Improvement Gains*.

38. John Rice et al., *Evaluation of Michigan's School Improvement Grant: Outcomes After Three Years* (San Francisco: WestEd, 2015).

39. Center on Education Policy, *State Implementation and Perceptions of Title I School Improvement Grant Under the Recovery Act: One Year Later* (Washington, DC: Center on Education Policy, 2012).

40. Alyson Klein, "What's the Payoff for $4.6 Billion in School Improvement Grants?" *Hechinger Report*, April 15, 2012, http://hechingerreport.org/whats-the-payoff-for-3-billion-in-school-improvement-grants/.

41. Jennifer A. Heissel and Helen F. Ladd, *School Turnaround in North Carolina: A Regression Discontinuity Analysis* (Washington, DC: CALDER Center, 2016), 157.

42. Dickey-Griffith, "Preliminary Effects."

43. Ibid.

44. Amy Buffenbarger, "Slow SIG Process Leaves Lower-Performing Schools Scrambling," *NEA Today*, July 27, 2010, http://neatoday.org/2010/07/27/schools-waiting-on -improvement-money-as-school-year-approaches/.

45. Alyson Klein, "Turnaround Aid Raising Hopes, Also Concerns," *Education Week*, September 23, 2009, https://www.edweek.org/ew/articles/2009/09/23/04title1-stim -2.h29.html.

46. Gewertz, "Restructuring Schools."

47. Alyson Klein, "School Turnaround Models Draw Bipartisan Concern," *Education Week*, May 21, 2010, https://www.edweek.org/ew/articles/2010/05/21/33turnaround.h29.html.

48. Christina LiCalsi et al., *Evaluation of Massachusetts Office of District and School Turnaround Assistance to Commissioner's Districts and Schools: Impact of School Redesign Grants* (Washington, DC: American Institutes for Research, 2015).

49. Frederick Hess, "The Missing Half of School Reform," *National Affairs* 33 (Fall 2013), https://www.nationalaffairs.com/publications/detail/the-missing-half-of-school-reform.

50. Jal Mehta, *The Allure of Order: High Hopes, Dashed Expectations, and the Troubled Quest to Remake American Schooling* (New York: Oxford University Press, 2013), 4.

Chapter 3

1. Paul Manna and Patrick McGuinn, eds., *Education Governance for the Twenty-First Century: Overcoming the Structural Barriers to School Reform* (Washington, DC: Brookings Institution Press, 2013).

2. For more on the history of educational politics and policy making in the United States, see Patrick J. McGuinn, *No Child Left Behind and the Transformation of Federal Education Policy, 1965–2005* (Lawrence: University Press of Kansas, 2006), and Paul Manna, *School's In: Federalism and the National Education Agenda* (Washington, DC: Georgetown University Press, 2006).

3. Phyllis McClure, "Grassroots Resistance to NCLB," *The Education Gadfly* 4, no. 11 (2004), http://www.edexcellence.net/gadfly/index.cfm?issue=140#a1723.

4. Tiffany Berry and Rebecca M. Eddy, "Editors' Notes," *New Directions for Evaluation, Special Issue: Consequences of No Child Left Behind on Educational Evaluation* 2008, no. 117 (2008): 2.

5. The Center for Education Reform, "National Charter School & Enrollment Statistics 2011–12," v, https://www.edreform.com/wp-content/uploads/2012/03/National-Charter -School-Enrollment-Statistics-2011-12.pdf.

6. Frederick Hess and Chester Finn, eds., *No Remedy Left Behind: Lessons from a Half-Decade of NCLB* (Washington, DC: AEI Press, 2007).

7. For more information on the ED review process for state accountability plans, see United States Government Accountability Office, *No Child Left Behind Act: Enhancements in the Department of Education's Review Process Could Improve State Academic Assessments* (Washington, DC: GAO, 2009), https://www.gao.gov/assets/300/295827.pdf.

8. See, for example, Bess Keller, "Michigan May Feel Full Force of Federal Law," *Education Week*, February 11, 2004.

9. Thomas Ahn and Jacob Vigdor, "The Impact of No Child Left Behind's Accountability Sanctions on School Performance" (National Bureau of Economic Research Working Paper No. 20511, September 2014).

10. Paul Manna, *Collision Course: Federal Education Policy Meets State and Local Realities* (Washington, DC: CQ Press, 2011).

11. Michael A. Gottfried et al., *Federal and State Roles and Capacity for Improving Schools* (Santa Monica, CA: Rand Corporation, 2011), viii.

12. Manna, *Collision Course.*

13. Thomas S. Dee and Brian A. Jacob, "The Impact of No Child Left Behind on Students, Teachers, and Schools," *Brookings Papers on Economic Activity* 2010, no. 2 (2010): 149–207; Heinrich Mintrop and Gail Sunderman, "Predictable Failure of Federal Sanctions–Driven Accountability of School Improvement—And Why We May Retain It Anyway," *Educational Researcher* 38, no. 5 (2009): 353–64.

14. Sara Mead, "RTTT and the Problem of Trying to Do Too Many Things at Once," *Sara Mead's Policy Notebook, Education Week*, August 30, 2010.

15. Patrick McGuinn, "Stimulating Reform: Race to the Top, Competitive Grants and the Obama Education Agenda," *Educational Policy* 26, no. 1 (2012): 136–59.

16. Andy Smarick, "AEI Education Stimulus Watch, Special Report 2," September 4, 2009, https://www.aei.org/publication/education-stimulus-watch-special-report-2/.

17. Timothy Conlan and Paul Posner, "Inflection Point? Federalism and the Obama Administration," *Publius: The Journal of Federalism* 41, no. 3 (2010): 443–44.

18. Richard Lee Colvin and Suzanne Kubach, "The Race to Reform: How Education Reform Advocates Are Leveraging Race to the Top: Policy Innovators in Education" (Policy Innovators in Education [PIE] Network white paper, April 2010), http://www.pie -network.org/uploads/media_items/the-race-to-reform-how-education-reform -advocates-are-leveraging-race-to-the-top.original.pdf.

19. AP, "9 States, DC, Receive 'Race to the Top' Education Funds," *USA Today*, August 24, 2010, http://usatoday30.usatoday.com/news/education/2010-08-24-race-to-top_N.htm.

20. Nancy Kober and Diane Stark Rentner, *More to Do, But Less Capacity to Do It: States' Progress in Implementing the Recovery Act Education Reforms* (Washington, DC: Center on Education Policy, 2011), 3, https://www.cep-dc.org/displayDocument.cfm ?DocumentID=346.

21. Steven Glazerman et al., *Passing Muster: Evaluating Teacher Evaluation Systems* (Washington, DC: Brookings Institution, 2011), http://www.brookings.edu/research/ reports/2011/04/26-evaluating-teachers.

22. There was a large increase in the number of states that required annual teacher evaluations (forty-three states), incorporated student achievement (thirty-two states), differentiated levels of performance (twenty-six states), conducted annual classroom observations (thirty-nine states) and multiple observations each year (twenty-two states), and utilized performance-based tenure decisions (nine states); see National Council on Teacher Quality, State of the States 2012: Teacher Effectiveness Policies (Washington, DC: NCTQ, 2012), https://www.nctq.org/dmsView/State_of_the_States_2012_Teacher _Effectiveness_Policies_NCTQ_Report.

23. William Howell, "Results of President Obama's Race to the Top," *Education Next* 15, no. 4 (2015): 58–66.

24. Irich Boser, *Race to the Top: What Have We Learned from the States So Far?* (Washington, DC: Center for American Progress, 2012).

25. Patrick McGuinn, *The State of Evaluation Reform: State Education Agency Capacity and the Implementation of New Teacher Evaluation Systems* (Washington, DC: Center for American Progress, 2012).

26. Cynthia Brown et al., *State Education Agencies as Agents of Change* (Washington, DC: Center for American Progress, 2011), https://cdn.americanprogress.org/wp-content/ uploads/issues/2011/07/pdf/sea.pdf.

27. Diane Stark Rentner and Nancy Kober, *After the Stimulus Money Ends: The Status of State K–12 Education Funding and Reforms* (Washington, DC: Center on Education Policy, 2012), http://cep-dc.org/displayDocument.cfm?DocumentID=395; Nancy Kober and Diane Stark Rentner, *State Education Agency Funding and Staffing in the Education Reform Era* (Washington, DC: Center on Education Policy, 2012), http://cep-dc.org/displayDocument.cfm?DocumentID=396.

28. Ashley Jochim and Patrick Murphy, *The Capacity Challenge: What It Takes for State Education Agencies to Support School Improvement* (Seattle: Center on Reinventing Public Education, 2013), http://crpe.org/publications/capacity-challenge-what-it-takes-state-education-agencies-support-school-improvement.

29. Frederick Hess, "The Real Obama Education Legacy," *National Affairs*, no. 25 (Fall 2015): 3–19.

30. Kenneth K. Wong, "Federal ESEA Waivers as Reform Leverage: Politics and Variation in State Implementation," *Publius: The Journal of Federalism* 45, no. 3 (2015): 409.

31. Elizabeth Mann, "The Long Term Impact of NCLB Waiver on ESEA Renewal," Brookings' Brown Center Chalkboard blog, December 20, 2015, http://www.brookings.edu/blogs/brown-center-chalkboard/posts/2015/12/10-no-child-left-behind-nclb-waivers-esea-renewal-mann.

32. Stephani L. Wrabel et al., "The Politics of Elementary and Secondary Education Act Waivers," *Educational Policy* 32, no. 1 (2016): 1–24.

33. Joseph Viteritti, "The Federal Role in School Reform: Obama's Race to the Top," *Notre Dame Law Review* 87, no. 5 (2012): 2087–2122.

34. Alyson Klein, "States Pitch Changes as They Seek NCLB Waiver Renewals," *Education Week*, April 14, 2015, https://www.edweek.org/ew/articles/2015/04/15/states-pitch-changes-as-they-seek-nclb.html.

35. Jeremy Ayers and Isabelle Owen, *No Child Left Behind Waivers: Promising Ideas from Second Round Applications* (Washington, DC: Center for American Progress: 2012), https://www.americanprogress.org/wp-content/uploads/issues/2012/07/pdf/nochildwaivers.pdf.

36. Wong, "Federal ESEA Waivers as Reform Leverage," 406, 411.

37. Christopher Loss and Patrick McGuinn, eds., *The Convergence of K–12 and Higher Education: Policies and Programs in a Changing Era* (Cambridge, MA: Harvard Education Press, 2016).

38. Alyson Klein, "Alexander: Federal Role on K–12 Will Be 'Very Different' Under ESSA," *Education Week*, December 17, 2015, http://blogs.edweek.org/edweek/campaign-k-12/2015/12/alexander_senate_will_hold_thr.html.

39. Anna Egalite, Lance Fusarelli, and Bonnie Fusarelli, "Will Decentralization Affect Educational Inequity? The Every Student Succeeds Act," *Educational Administration Quarterly* 53, no. 5 (2017).

40. David K. Cohen and Susan L. Moffitt, *The Ordeal of Equality: Did Federal Regulation Fix the Schools?* (Cambridge, MA: Harvard University Press, 2009).

41. Kerstin Le Floch, Andrea Boyle, and Susan Bowles Therriault, *Help Wanted: State Capacity for School Improvement* (Washington, DC: American Institutes for Research, 2008), http://www.air.org/expertise/index/?fa=viewContent&content_id=613; Kober and Rentner; *More to Do, But Less Capacity to Do It.*

42. Cohen and Moffitt, *The Ordeal of Equality*; Mintrop and Sunderman, "Predictable Failure"; Hess and Finn, *No Remedy Left Behind.*

43. United States Government Accountability Office, *Education Could Better Support Grantees and Help Them Address Capacity Challenges* (Washington, DC: GAO, 2015), https://www.gao.gov/assets/670/669571.pdf.

44. Jeb Bush and Joel Klein, "The Case for Common Educational Standards," *Wall Street Journal*, June 23, 2011, https://www.wsj.com/articles/SB10001424052702304070104576399532217616502.

45. Jeffrey Henig, "Mayors, Governors, and Presidents: The New Education Executives and the End of Education Exceptionalism," *Peabody Journal of Education* 84, no. 3 (2009): 283–99.

46. Bonnie Fusarelli and B. S. Cooper, eds., *The Rising State: How State Power Is Transforming Our Nation's Schools* (Albany: Albany State University of New York Press, 2009).

47. Council of Chief State School Officers, *States' Continued Commitment to Next-Generation Accountability Systems* (Washington, DC: CCSSO, 2015).

48. Dorothea Anagnostopoulos, Stacey Rutledge, and Valentina Bali, "State Education Agencies, Information Systems, and the Expansion of State Power in the Era of Test-Based Accountability," *Educational Policy* 27 no. 2 (2013): 217–47.

49. Lauren Camera, "States Eager to Shirk Obama Era Education Policies," *U.S. News and World Report*, December 18, 2015, https://www.usnews.com/news/articles/2015-12-18/states-eager-for-flexibility-in-new-education-law.

50. Joanne Weiss and Patrick McGuinn, "States as Change Agents Under ESSA," *Phi Delta Kappan* 97 no. 8 (2016): 28–33.

Chapter 4

1. Richard M. Ingersoll, "The Problem of Underqualified Teachers in American Secondary Schools," *Education Researcher* 28, no. 2 (1999): 22–37.

2. Christopher O. Tracy and Kate Walsh, *Necessary and Insufficient: Resisting a Full Measure of Teacher Quality* (Washington, DC: National Council on Teacher Quality, 2004).

3. US Department of Education, *Meeting the Highly Qualified Teachers Challenge: The Secretary's Annual Report on Teacher Quality* (Washington, DC: US Department of Education, Office of Postsecondary Education, Office of Policy Planning and Innovation, 2002).

4. Tracy and Walsh, *Necessary and Insufficient*.

5. US Department of Education, *Meeting the Highly Qualified Teachers Challenge*.

6. No Child Left Behind Act of 2001, 20 U.S.C. § 901(A)(23) (2002).

7. US Department of Education, *No Child Left Behind: Expanding the Promise, Guide to President Bush's FY 2006 Education Agenda* (Washington, DC: US Department of Education, Office of the Secretary, 2005).

8. No Child Left Behind Act of 2001, 20 U.S.C. § 2113(c) (2002).

9. No Child Left Behind Act of 2001, 20 U.S.C. § 1111 (h)(1)(C)(viii) (2002).

10. Lowell C. Rose and Alec M. Gallup, "The 34th Annual Phi Delta Kappan/Gallup Poll of the Public's Attitudes Toward the Public School," *Phi Delta Kappan* 84, no. 1 (2002).

11. US Department of Education, *Preparing and Credentialing the Nation's Teachers: The Secretary's Eighth Report on Teacher Quality Based on Data Provided for 2008, 2009, 2010* (Washington, DC: US Department of Education, Office of Postsecondary Education, 2011).

12. Tracy and Walsh, *Necessary and Insufficient*.

13. US Department of Education, *The Secretary's Eighth Report*.

14. Kate Walsh and Emma Snyder, *Searching the Attic: How States Are Responding to the Nation's Goal of Placing a Highly Qualified Teacher in Every Classroom* (Washington, DC: National Council on Teacher Quality, 2004).

15. Barnett Berry, *What It Means to Be a "Highly Qualified Teacher"* (Chapel Hill, NC: Southeast Center for Teacher Quality, 2002).

16. Heather G. Peske, Candace Crawford, and Brian Prick, *Missing the Mark: An Education Trust Analysis of Teacher Equity Plans* (Washington, DC: The Education Trust, 2006).

17. Dan Goldhaber, "Licensure: Exploring the Value of This Gateway to the Teacher Workforce," in *Handbook of the Economics of Education*, ed. Eric A. Hanushek, Stephen J. Machin, and Ludger Woessman (Amsterdam: Elsevier, 2011), 315–39; Dan Goldhaber, Trevor Gratz, and Roddy Theobald, "What's in a Teacher Test? Assessing the Relationship Between Teacher Licensure Test Scores and Student STEM Achievement and Course-Taking" (working paper, National Center for Analysis of Longitudinal Data in Education Research, American Institutes for Research, Washington, DC, 2016); Richard Buddin and Gema Zamarro, "Teacher Qualifications and Student Achievement in Urban Elementary Schools," *Journal of Urban Economics* 66, no. 2 (2009): 103–15.

18. Joshua D. Angrist and Jonathan Guryan, "Does Teacher Testing Raise Teacher Quality? Evidence from State Certification Requirements," *Economics of Education Review* 27, no. 5 (2008): 483–503; Dan Goldhaber, "Everyone's Doing It, but What Does Teacher Testing Tell Us About Teacher Effectiveness?" *Journal of Human Resources* 42, no. 4 (2007): 765–94.

19. Nelson C. Dometrius and Lee Sigelman, "The Cost of Quality: Teacher Testing and Racial-Ethnic Representativeness in Public Education," *Social Science Quarterly* 69, no. 1 (1988): 70–82; Michael T. Nettles et al., *Performance and Passing Rate Differences of African American and White Prospective Teachers on Praxis™ Examinations: A Joint Project of the National Education Association (NEA) and Educational Testing Service (ETS)* (Princeton, NJ: Educational Testing Service, 2011); Linda Tyler, *Toward Increasing Teacher Diversity: Targeting Support and Intervention for Teacher Licensure Candidates* (Princeton, NJ: Educational Testing Service, 2011).

20. William L. Sanders and June C. Rivers, *Cumulative and Residual Effects of Teachers on Future Student Academic Achievement* (Knoxville: University of Tennessee Value-Added Research and Assessment Center, 1996).

21. Eric A. Hanushek, John F. Kain, and Steven G. Rivkin, "Why Public Schools Lose Teachers," *Journal of Human Resources* 39, no. 2 (2004): 326–54; Jonah E. Rockoff, "The Impact of Individual Teachers on Student Achievement: Evidence from Panel Data," *American Economic Review* 94, no. 2 (2004): 247–52; Robert Gordon, Thomas J. Kane, and Douglas O. Staiger, *Identifying Effective Teachers Using Performance on the Job: The Hamilton Project Policy Brief No. 2006-01* (Washington, DC: Brookings Institution, 2006).

22. Jonah E. Rockoff et al., "Can You Recognize an Effective Teacher When You Recruit One?" *Education Finance and Policy* 6, no. 1 (2011): 43–74; Matthew M. Chingos and Paul E. Peterson, "It's Easier to Pick a Good Teacher Than to Train One: Familiar and New Results on the Correlates of Teacher Effectiveness," *Economics of Education Review* 30, no. 3 (2011): 449–65; Andrew J. Wayne and Peter Youngs, "Teacher Characteristics and Student Achievement Gains: A Review," *Review of Educational Research* 73, no. 1 (2003).

23. Dan Goldhaber and Jane Hannaway, *Creating a New Teaching Profession* (Washington, DC: Urban Institute Press, 2009).

24. Daniel Weisberg et al., *The Widget Effect* (Brooklyn, NY: The New Teacher Project, 2009).

25. Organisation for Economic Co-operation and Development (OECD), *PISA 2015 Results (Volume II): Policies and Practices for Successful Schools* (Paris, OECD Publishing, 2016), http://dx.doi.org/10.1787/9789264267510-en.

26. Mona Mourshed, Chinezi Chijioke, and Michael Barber, *How the World's Most Improved School Systems Keep Getting Better* (Washington, DC: McKinsey & Company, 2010).

27. Elaine Weiss, "Mismatches in Race to the Top Limit Educational Improvement: Lack of Time, Resources, and Tools to Address Opportunity Gaps Puts Lofty State Goals Out of Reach," Education Policy Institute, September 12, 2013, https://www.epi.org/publication/race-to-the-top-goals/.

28. Alaska, North Dakota, Vermont, and Texas were the only states to never apply to RTTT.

29. US Department of Education, "Awards—Race to the Top District (RTT-D)," last modified September 25, 2015, https://www2.ed.gov/programs/racetothetop-district/awards.html.

30. William G. Howell, "Results of President Obama's Race to the Top," *Education Next* 15, no. 4 (2015).

31. Elaine Weiss, "Mismatches in Race to the Top."

32. US Department of Education, "Duncan Says 82 Percent of America's Schools Could 'Fail' Under NCLB This Year," March 9, 2011, https://www.ed.gov/news/press-releases/duncan-says-82-percent-americas-schools-could-fail-under-nclb-year.

33. "PDK Polls of the Public's Attitudes Toward the Public Schools," http://pdkintl.org/noindex/PDKGallupPoll_Oct2014.pdf.

34. Matthew A. Kraft and Allison F. Gilmour, "Revisiting the Widget Effect: Teacher Evaluation Reforms and the Distribution of Teacher Effectiveness," *Educational Researcher* 46, no. 5 (2017): 234–49.

35. Matthew P. Steinberg and Morgaen L. Donaldson, "The New Educational Accountability: Understanding the Landscape of Teacher Evaluation in the Post-NCLB Era," *Education Finance and Policy* 11, no. 3 (2016): 340–59.

36. Matthew P. Steinberg and Lauren Sartain, "Does Better Observation Make Better Teachers?" *Education Next* 15, no. 1 (2015); Eric S. Taylor and John H. Tyler, "The Effect of Evaluation on Teacher Performance," *American Economic Review* 102, no. 7 (2012): 3628–51; Michael S. Garet et al., *The Impact of Providing Performance Feedback to Teachers and Principals, Executive Summary (NCEE 2018-4000)* (Washington, DC: National Center for Education Evaluation and Regional Assistance, Institute of Education Sciences, US Department of Education, 2017).

37. Matthew A. Kraft and Allison F. Gilmour, "Can Principals Promote Teacher Development as Evaluators? A Case Study of Principals' Views and Experiences," *Educational Administration Quarterly* 52, no. 5 (2016): 711–53.

38. Kieran M. Killeen, David H. Monk, and Margaret L. Plecki, "School District Spending on Professional Development: Insights Available from National Data (1992–1998)," *Journal of Education Finance* 28, no. 1 (2002): 25–50; Karen Hawley Miles et al., "Inside the Black Box of School District Spending on Professional Development: Lessons from Comparing Five Urban Districts," *Journal of Education Finance* 30, no. 1 (2004): 1–26; Lawrence O. Picus et al., *An Evaluation of Vermont's Education Finance System* (Los Angeles: Picus Odden & Associates, 2012).

39. Matthew A. Kraft et al., "The Effect of Teacher Evaluation Reforms on New Teacher Supply, Hiring, and Quality" (working paper, Brown University, Providence, Rhode Island, 2018).

40. Thomas S. Dee and James Wyckoff, "Incentives, Selection, and Teacher Performance: Evidence from IMPACT," *Journal of Policy Analysis and Management* 34, no. 2 (2015): 267–97; Susanna Loeb, Luke C. Miller, and James Wyckoff, "Performance Screens for School Improvement: The Case of Teacher Tenure Reform in New York City," *Educational Researcher* 44, no. 4 (2015); Lauren Sartain and Matthew P. Steinberg, "Teachers' Labor Market Responses to Performance Evaluation Reform: Experimental Evidence from Chicago Public Schools," *Journal of Human Resources* 51, no. 3 (2015): 615–55; Julie Berry Cullen, Cory Koedel, and Eric Parsons, "The Compositional Effect of Rigorous Teacher Evaluation on Workforce Quality" (working paper, National Center for Analysis of Longitudinal Data in Education Research, American Institutes for Research, Washington, DC, 2016); Katharine O. Strunk, Nathan Barrett, and Jane Arnold Lincove, *When Tenure Ends: The Short-Run Effects of the Elimination of Louisiana's Teacher Employment Protections on Teacher Exit and Retirement* (New Orleans: Education Research Alliance for New Orleans, 2017).

41. National Council on Teacher Quality, *2017 State Teacher Policy Yearbook: National Summary* (Washington, DC: National Council on Teacher Quality, 2017), https://www.nctq.org/dmsView/NCTQ_2017_State_Teacher_Policy_Yearbook.

42. Kate Walsh et al., *Running in Place: How New Teacher Evaluations Fail to Live Up to Promises* (Washington, DC: National Council on Teacher Quality, 2017), https://www.nctq.org/dmsView/Final_Evaluation_Paper; National Council on Teacher Quality, *2013 State Teacher Policy Yearbook: National Summary* (Washington, DC: National Council on Teacher Quality, 2014), https://www.nctq.org/dmsView/2013_State_Teacher_Policy_Yearbook_National_Summary_NCTQ_Report.

43. David Griffith, *Teacher Absenteeism in Charter and Traditional Public Schools* (Washington, DC: Thomas B. Fordham Foundation, 2017), https://edexcellence.net/publications/teacher-absenteeism.

44. Elaine Weiss, "Mismatches in Race to the Top."

45. Michael Lipsky, *Street-Level Bureaucracy, 30th Anniversary Edition: Dilemmas of the Individual in Public Service* (New York: Russell Sage Foundation, 2010).

46. "Public and Teachers Divided in Their Support for Merit Pay, Teacher Tenure, Race to the Top," Education Next, August 25, 2010, http://educationnext.org/public-and-teachers-divided-in-their-support-for-merit-pay-teacher-tenure-race-to-the-top/.

47. Matthew P. Steinberg and Matthew A. Kraft, "The Sensitivity of Teacher Performance Ratings to the Design of Teacher Evaluation Systems," *Educational Researcher* 46, no. 7 (2017): 378–96.

Chapter 5

1. Nancy Kober, "A Brief History of Federal Efforts to Improve Education Research," in *Leveraging Learning: The Evolving Role of Federal Policy in Education Research*, ed. Timothy Knowles et al. (Washington, DC: Aspen Institute, 2013), 3–9, http://www.aspendrl.org/portal/browse/DocumentDetail?documentId=2049&download.

2. Maris Vinovskis, *Revitalizing Federal Education Research: Improving the Regional Educational Laboratories, the R&D Centers, and the "New" OERI* (Ann Arbor, MI: University of Michigan Press, 2001).

3. Timothy Knowles et al., *Leveraging Learning: The Evolving Role of Federal Policy in Education Research* (Washington, DC: Aspen Institute, 2013), http://www.aspendrl.org/

portal/browse/DocumentDetail?documentId=2049&download; National Board for
Education Sciences, *5-Year Report, 2003 Through 2008* (NBES 2009-6011) (Washington,
DC: US Department of Education, 2008), https://ies.ed.gov/director/board/pdf
/20096011.pdf; Richard C. Atkinson and Gregg B. Jackson, eds., *Research and Education
Reform: Roles for the Office of Educational Research and Improvement* (Washington, DC:
National Academies Press, 2002), https://doi.org/10.17226/1973.

4. Public Law 96-88, sec 405 (a)(1); Education Sciences Reform Act (ESRA) (H.R. 3801
107th Congress).

5. Atkinson and Jackson, *Research and Education Reform.*

6. "Funding Opportunities: Search Funded Grants and Contracts," Institute for Education
Science, https://ies.ed.gov/funding/grantsearch/index.asp.

7. "Investing in Innovation Fund (i3)," US Department of Education, https://www2.ed.gov/
programs/innovation/awards.html.

8. Thomas J. Kane et al., *Have We Identified Effective Teachers? Validating Measures of
Effective Teaching Using Random Assignment* (Seattle: Bill & Melinda Gates Foundation,
2013), http://files.eric.ed.gov/fulltext/ED540959.pdf; Common Core State Standards
Initiative, http://www.corestandards.org/.

9. "Digest of Education Statistics," National Center for Education Statistics, http://nces.
ed.gov/programs/digest/d13/tables/dt13_208.10.asp.

10. Phillip Lovell and Julia B. Isaacs, *Families of the Recession: Unemployed Parents and Their
Children* (Washington, DC: First Focus Campaign for Children and the National
Association for the Education of Homeless Children and Youth, 2010), www.brookings.
edu/wp-content/uploads/2016/06/0114_families_recession_isaacs.pdf; "Projections of
Education Statistics to 2021," National Center for Education Statistics (NCES), http://
nces.ed.gov/programs/projections/projections2021/tables/table_01.asp; Michael
Leachman et al., *Most States Have Cut School Funding, and Some Continue Cutting*
(Washington, DC: Center on Budget and Policy Priorities, 2016), https://www.cbpp.org/
research/state-budget-and-tax/
most-states-have-cut-school-funding-and-some-continue-cutting.

11. William N. Evans, Robert M. Schwab, and Kathryn L. Wagner, "The Great Recession and
Public Education," *Education Finance and Policy* 0 (2017): 1–50, https://doi.org/10.1162/
edfp_a_00245.

12. "Table 213.10. Staff Employed in Public Elementary and Secondary School systems,"
National Center for Education Statistics: Digest of Education Statistics, http://nces.
ed.gov/programs/digest/d13/tables/dt13_213.10.asp.

13. Leachman et al., *Most States Have Cut School Funding.*

14. Phil Oliff, Chris Mai, and Michael Leachman, *New School Year Brings More Cuts in State
Funding for Schools* (Washington, DC: Center on Budget and Policy Priorities, 2012),
http://www.cbpp.org/files/9-4-12sfp.pdf.

15. "Databases, Tables, & Calculators by Subject," US Department of Labor, Bureau of Labor
Statistics, 2009, https://www.bls.gov/data/; Carmen DeNavas-Walt, Bernadette D.
Proctor, and Jessica C. Smith, *Income, Poverty, and Health Insurance Coverage in the
United States: 2012* (Washington, DC: US Department of Commerce, US Census Bureau,
2013), https://www.census.gov/prod/2013pubs/p60-245.pdf; Shana Pribesh and Douglas
B. Downey, "Why Are Residential and School Moves Associated with Poor School
Performance?" *Demography* 36, no. 4 (1999): 521–34; Jennifer Macomber, *An Overview
of Selected Data on Children in Vulnerable Families* (Washington, DC: The Urban
Institute, 2006), https://www.urban.org/sites/default/files/publication/50596/311351

-An-Overview-of-Selected-Data-on-Children-in-Vulnerable-Families.PDF; Shelley Waters Boots, Jennifer Macomber, and Anna Danziger, *Family Security: Supporting Parents' Employment and Children's Development* (Washington, DC: The Urban Institute, 2008), https://www.urban.org/sites/default/files/publication/33056/411718-Family -Security-Supporting-Parents-Employment-and-Children-s-Development.PDF.

16. "National Assessment of Educational Progress (NAEP): Scale Scores and Achievement Levels," National Center for Education Statistics, https://nces.ed.gov/nationsreportcard/ achievement.aspx.

17. "Program for International Studies in Achievement (PISA): Data Files," National Center for Education Statistics, https://nces.ed.gov/surveys/pisa/datafiles.asp; "Trends in International Mathematics and Science Study (TIMMS): Overview," National Center for Education Statistics, https://nces.ed.gov/timss/.

Chapter 6

1. David Stevenson, "Standards and Assessments in Goals 2000," in *Implementing Educational Reform: Sociological Perspectives on Educational Policy*, ed. Kathryn M. Borman et al. (Norwood, NJ: Ablex Publishing Corporation, 1996), 43–64.

2. Richard J. Coley and Margaret E. Goertz, *Educational Standards in the 50 States: 1990* (Princeton, NJ: Educational Testing Service, 1990).

3. James Andrew LaSpina, *California in a Time of Excellence* (Albany: State University of New York Press, 2009); Allan R. Odden, ed., *Education Policy Implementation* (Albany: State University of New York Press, 1991).

4. Marshall S. Smith and Jennifer O'Day, "Systemic School Reform," in *The Politics of Curriculum and Testing*, ed. Susan H. Fuhrman and Betty Malen (Philadelphia: Falmer Press, 1990), 233–67; Jennifer O'Day, Margaret E. Goertz, and Robert E. Floden, *Building Capacity for Education Reform* (Philadelphia: Consortium for Policy Research in Education, 1995).

5. Marshall S. Smith and Jennifer O'Day, *Putting the Pieces Together: Systemic School Reform* (New Brunswick, NJ: Consortium for Policy Research in Education, 1991).

6. Diane Ravitch, *National Standards in American Education: A Citizen's Guide* (Washington, DC: The Brookings Institution, 1995).

7. Robert B. Schwartz and Marian A. Robinson, "Goals 2000 and the Standards Movement," in *Brookings Papers on Education Policy: 2000*, ed. Diane Ravitch (Washington, DC: Brookings Institution Press, 2000).

8. Karen Diegmueller, "Standards for Language Arts Are Unveiled," *Education Week*, March 20, 1996, https://www.edweek.org/ew/articles/1996/03/20/26read2.h15.html.

9. Mathematically Correct has ceased operation. NYC HOLD continues at http://www .nychold.com/.

10. Patrick J. McGuinn, *No Child Left Behind and the Transformation of Federal Education Policy, 1965–2005* (Lawrence: University Press of Kansas, 2006).

11. Michael J. Petrilli, "A Few Reflections on the Common Core Wars," Thomas B. Fordham Institute Flypaper Blog, July 31, 2014, https://edexcellence.net/ articles/a-few-reflections-on-the-common-core-wars.

12. Martin Carnoy and Susanna Loeb, "Does External Accountability Affect Student Outcomes? A Cross-State Analysis," *Educational Evaluation and Policy Analysis* 24, no. 4 (2002): 305–31; Eric A. Hanushek and Margaret E. Raymond, "Does School Accountability Lead to Improved Student Performance?" *Journal of Policy Analysis and Management* 24, no. 2 (2005): 297–327.

13. An earlier Hanushek and Raymond (2003) analysis found no statistically significant difference between consequential accountability and simply publishing school report cards. The 2004 analysis rejected the equality of the two approaches at $p < .10$.

14. Thomas Dee and Brian Jacob, "Evaluating NCLB," *Education Next* (Summer 2010): 54–61.

15. Manyee Wong, Thomas D. Cook, and Peter M. Steiner, "No Child Left Behind: An Interim Evaluation of Its Effects on Learning Using Two Interrupted Time Series Each with Its Own Non-Equivalent Comparison Series" (working paper 09-11, Institute for Policy Research, Northwestern University). Note that a later version of the study, employing additional analytical models, arrived at a slightly more optimistic finding on reading: "We now have consistent but statistically weak evidence of a possible, but distinctly smaller, fourth grade reading effect." Maynee Wong, Thomas D. Cook, and Peter M. Steiner, "Adding Design Elements to Improve Time Series Design: No Child Left Behind as an Example of Causal Pattern-Matching," *Journal of Research on Educational Effectiveness* 8, no. 2 (2015): 245–79.

16. Grover J. "Russ" Whitehurst, *Don't Forget Curriculum* (Washington, DC: Brookings Institution, 2009).

17. Tom Loveless, *The 2012 Brown Center Report on American Education* (Washington, DC: Brookings Institution, 2012), 6–14.

18. The 1965 Coleman Report was probably the first national study to decompose test score variance and highlight that the variance associated with between-school factors is dwarfed by within-school factors. More recently, Chingos, Whitehurst, and Gallaher's (2013) decomposition of variance in Florida achievement data estimated 1.3 percent associated with district, 9 percent with school, 31 percent with teacher, and 38 percent with student differences (with the remainder unspecified).

19. Evidence was reported of a modest relationship between raising proficiency cut points and boosting scores in fourth grade.

20. William H. Schmidt and Richard T. Houang, "Curricular Coherence and the Common Core State Standards for Mathematics," *Educational Researcher* 41, no. 8 (November 2012): 294–308.

21. For the work generating the original theory of why A+ countries succeed, see William H. Schmidt et al., *Why Schools Matter: A Cross-National Comparison of Curriculum and Learning* (San Francisco: Jossey-Bass, 2001). For an international application of the focus and coherence rubric, see William H. Schmidt and Richard T. Houang, "Lack of Focus in the Mathematics Curriculum: Symptom or Cause," in *Lessons Learned: What International Assessments Tell Us About Math Achievement*, ed. Tom Loveless (Washington, DC: Brookings Institution, 2007), 65–84.

22. To underscore the favorable reception Common Core advocates gave to the MSU study, the main findings were released at a Washington, DC, event in May 2012 sponsored by organizations (including Achieve, Inc.) with strong ties to CCSS. Video available at https://www.achieve.org/videos/video-common-core-math-standards-implementation -can-lead-improved-student-achievement.

23. Morgan S. Polikoff, "Is Common Core Working? It May Be Too Early to Tell," *Education Next*, February 7, 2017, http://educationnext.org/ is-common-core-working-it-may-be-too-early-to-tell/.

24. Survey data on which the implementation index is based can be found in Ann Weber et al., *State Implementation of Reforms Promoted Under the Recovery Act* (Washington, DC: Institute of Education Sciences, US Department of Education, 2014), Table H.1,

"Standards and Assessment Indicators by State, 2010–2011," https://ies.ed.gov/ncee/pubs/20144011/pdf/20144011.pdf. Minnesota did not adopt CCSS math standards but did adopt the ELA standards. For a full explanation of state coding in the study, see Tom Loveless, *The 2014 Brown Center Report on American Education* (Washington, DC: Brookings Institution, 2014), 26–34.

25. Robert Rothman, "The Common Core Takes Hold," *Education Next* (Summer 2014): 16–22.

26. Omitting demographic controls typically does not affect short-term longitudinal analyses of NAEP data because the baseline score of each state serves, in a sense, as a control. State demographic statistics take a long time to change appreciably.

27. Also see: US Food and Drug Administration, "Defect Levels Handbook," https://www.fda.gov/Food/GuidanceRegulation/GuidanceDocumentsRegulatoryInformation/SanitationTransportation/ucm056174.htm.

28. Adam Edgerton and Laura Desimone, *Teacher Implementation of College and Career-Ready Standards: Challenges and Resources* (Philadelphia: The Center on Standards, Alignment, & Learning, 2017), https://www.c-sail.org/sites/default/files/Brief_Teachers_Implementation_0_0.pdf.

29. "Math in Focus: The Singapore Approach," EdReports.org, https://www.edreports.org/math/math-in-focus/index.html.

30. Andrew C. Porter, "External Standards and Good Teaching: The Pros and Cons of Telling Teachers What to Do," *Educational Evaluation and Policy Analysis* 11, no. 4 (Winter 1989): 343–56, http://journals.sagepub.com/doi/abs/10.3102/01623737011004343.

31. Common Core State Standards Initiative, "Myths vs. Facts," http://www.corestandards.org/about-the-standards/myths-vs-facts/.

32. Emmanuel Felton, "Does Common Core Really Mean Teachers Should Teach Differently?" *Hechinger Report*, December 12, 2014, http://hechingerreport.org/common-core-really-mean-teachers-teach-differently/.

33. Barry Garelick, "Somebody Please Kill Me, Dept.," Traditional Math Blog, September 24, 2017, https://traditionalmath.wordpress.com/2017/09/24/somebody-please-kill-me-dept/.

34. Charles W. Freeman Jr., Nixon's interpreter on the trip, says that Zhou construed the question as asking about the Paris uprising of students in May 1968. Freeman also says that the comment was "too delicious to invite correction." Dean Nicholas, "Zhou Enlai's Famous Saying Debunked," *History Today*, June 15, 2011, http://www.historytoday.com/blog/news-blog/dean-nicholas/zhou-enlais-famous-saying-debunked.

35. Some observers praise California's go-slow approach; others condemn it. Louis Freedberg, "New York Stumbles, California Advances on Common Core Implementation," *EdSource*, January 10, 2016, https://edsource.org/2016/new-york-stumbles-california-advances-on-common-core-implementation/92986.

Chapter 7

1. William G. Howell, *Thinking About the Presidency: The Primacy of Power* (Princeton, NJ: Princeton University Press, 2013).

2. National Alliance for Public Charter Schools, *A Growing Movement: America's Largest Charter Public School Communities and Their Impact on Student Outcomes* (Washington, DC: National Alliance for Public Charter Schools, 2016).

3. Cara Finnigan et al., *Evaluation of the Public Charter Schools Program: Final Report* (Washington, DC: US Department of Education, 2004).

4. Lyndsey Layton, "Charter Love: Feds Give $157 Million to Expand Charter Schools," *Washington Post*, September 28, 2015.

5. George W. Bush, *Decision Points* (New York: Crown Publisher, 2010), 23.

6. George W. Bush and Karen Hughes, *A Charge to Keep* (New York: William Morrow, 1999), 233–34.

7. David. J. Hoff, "Bush Impact on Schools to Outlive Term," *Education Week*, December 8, 2008.

8. Barack Obama, *Presidential Proclamation, National School Choice Week 2012*, May 7, 2012, https://obamawhitehouse.archives.gov/the-press-office/2012/05/07/presidential -proclamation-national-charter-schools-week-2012.

9. United States Department of Education, *Race to the Top Program Executive Summary* (Washington, DC: US Department of Education, 2009).

10. Gary D. Robertson, "N.C. Misses Out on First 'Race to the Top' Grants," WRAL.com, March 29, 2010, http://www.wral.com/news/state/story/7321383/.

11. William G. Howell, "Results of President Obama's Race to the Top" *Education Next* 15, no. 4 (2015): 58–66.

12. Alyson Klein, "Some States Without NCLB Waivers Say They Dodged a Bullet," *Education Week*, July 28, 2014, http://blogs.edweek.org/edweek/campaign-k-12/2014/07/some _states_without_no_child_l.html.

13. John King, testimony before the United States Senate Committee on Health, Education, Labor, and Pensions, Washington, DC, February 7, 2013, http://www.nysed.gov/ common/nysed/files/esea-testimony.pdf.

14. Lisa Dragoset et al., *School Improvement Grants: Implementation and Effectiveness* (Washington, DC: US Department of Education, 2017).

15. The North Carolina State Board of Education policy manual is available at https:// stateboard.ncpublicschools.gov/policy-manual/district-and-school-transformation/ reform-for-recurring-low-performing-schools.

16. The exact question wording used is as follows: "Many states permit the formation of charter schools, which are publicly funded but are not managed by the local school board. These schools are expected to meet promised objectives, but are exempt from many state regulations. Do you support or oppose the formation of charter schools?"

17. William G. Howell, Paul E. Peterson, and Martin R. West, "The Persuadable Public," *Education Next* 9, no. 4 (2009): 20–9.

18. Kathryn M. Doherty, Sandi Jacobs, and Martin F. Lueken, *Doing the Math on Teacher Pensions: How to Protect Teachers and Taxpayers* (Washington, DC: National Council on Teacher Quality, 2015).

19. Philip Gleason et al., *The Evaluation of Charter School Impacts* (Washington, DC: US Department of Education, 2010).

20. Will Dobbie and Roland G. Fryer Jr., "Are High-Quality Schools Enough to Increase Achievement Among the Poor? Evidence from the Harlem Children's Zone," *American Economic Journal: Applied Economics* 3, no. 3 (2011): 158–87; Atila Abdulkadiroğlu et al., "Accountability and Flexibility in Public Schools: Evidence from Boston's Charters and Pilots," *Quarterly Journal of Economics* 126, no. 2 (2011): 699–748.

21. Joshua D. Angrist et al., "Who Benefits from KIPP?" *Journal of Policy Analysis and Management* 31, no. 4 (2012): 837–60.

22. US Department of Education, "Equity and Education Reform: Secretary Arne Duncan's Remarks at the Annual Meeting of the National Association for the Advancement of Colored People (NAACP)," July 14, 2010, https://www.ed.gov/news/speeches/equity-and

-education-reform-secretary-arne-duncans-remarks-annual-meeting-national
-association-advancement-colored-people-naacp.

23. Alyson Klein, "Arne Duncan to Charter Schools: Here's Millions in Grants, Be More Responsible," *Education Week*, September 28, 2015.

24. US Department of Education, "Remarks by Secretary Arne Duncan to the National Alliance of Public Charter Schools," July 1, 2010, https://www.ed.gov/news/speeches/ remarks-secretary-arne-duncan-national-alliance-public-charter-schools.

25. Kevin Booker et al., "The Effect of Charter High Schools on Educational Attainment," *Journal of Labor Economics* 29, no. 2 (2011): 377–415; Tim R. Sass et al., "Charter High Schools' Effects on Long-Term Attainment and Earnings," *Journal of Policy Analysis and Management* 35, no. 3 (2016): 683–706.

Chapter 8

1. Michael M. Ting, "Organizational Capacity," *Journal of Law, Economics, & Organization* 27, no. 2 (2009): 245–71.

2. Jennifer O'Day et al., *Building Capacity for Education Reform* (New Brunswick, NJ: Consortium for Policy Research in Education, Carriage House at the Eagleton Institute of Politics, Rutgers University, 1995); Robert K. Christensen and Beth Gazley, "Capacity for Public Administration: Analysis of Meaning and Measurement," *Public Administration and Development* 28, no. 4 (2008): 265–79, doi:10.1002/pad.500.

3. Angela Minnici and Deanna Hill, *Educational Architects: Do State Education Agencies Have the Tools Necessary to Implement NCLB?* (Washington, DC: Center on Education Policy, 2007).

4. Arnold F. Shober, *Splintered Accountability: State Governance and Education Reform* (Albany: State University of New York Press, 2010), 15.

5. See table 2 in Thomas Dee and Brian Jacob, "The Impact of No Child Left Behind on Student Achievement" (NBER Working Paper No. 15531, 2009); Martin Carnoy and Susanna Loeb, "Does External Accountability Affect Student Outcomes? A Cross-State Analysis," *Educational Evaluation and Policy Analysis* 24, no. 4 (2002): 305–31; Eric A. Hanushek and Margaret E. Raymond, "Does School Accountability Lead to Improved Student Performance?" *Journal of Policy Analysis and Management* 24, no. 2 (2005): 297–327; Lee Jaekyung and Kenneth K. Wong, "The Impact of Accountability on Racial and Socioeconomic Equity: Considering Both School Resources and Achievement Outcomes," *American Educational Research Journal* 41, no. 4 (2004): 797–832.

6. Minnici and Hill, *Educational Architects*.

7. Shober, *Splintered Accountability*, 239.

8. Goodwin Liu, "Interstate Inequality and the Federal Role in School Finance," in *Holding NCLB Accountable: Achieving Accountability, Equity, & School Reform*, ed. Gail L. Sunderman (Thousand Oaks, CA: Corwin Press, 2008), 103–20.

9. Erik W. Robelen, "Lower Surplus Puts Squeeze on Education," *Education Week* 21, no. 2 (2001): 132, https://www.edweek.org/ew/articles/2001/09/12/02budget.h21.html.

10. Jessica L. Sandham, "States' Wallets Grow Thinner After Sept. 11," *Education Week* 21, no. 9 (2001): 1, 22, 23, https://www.edweek.org/ew/articles/2001/10/31/09crunch.h21.html; Jessica L. Sandham, "A Snapshot of the States' Fiscal Health," *Education Week* 21 no. 9 (2001): 22–23, https://www.edweek.org/ew/articles/2001/10/31/09crunchbox.h21.html.

11. Minnici and Hill, *Educational Architects*.

12. Gail L. Sunderman and Gary Orfield, "Massive Responsibilities and Limited Resources: The State Response to NCLB," in *Holding NCLB Accountable: Achieving Accountability,*

Equity, & School Reform, ed. Gail L. Sunderman (Thousand Oaks, CA: Corwin Press, 2008), 132–33.

13. Nancy Kober et al., *From the Capital to the Classroom: Year 2 of the No Child Left Behind Act* (Washington, DC: Center on Education Policy, 2004).

14. Minnici and Hill, *Educational Architects*.

15. Jennifer McMurrer, *Implementing the No Child Left Behind Teacher Requirements* (Washington, DC: Center on Education Policy, 2007).

16. Bess Keller, "'Qualified' Teachers: A Victory on Paper?" *Education Week* 24, no. 15 (2004): S8, S9, https://www.edweek.org/ew/articles/2004/12/08/15nclb-2.h24.html.

17. Dorothea Anagnostopoulos, Stacey Rutledge, and Valentina Bali, "State Education Agencies, Information Systems, and the Expansion of State Power in the Era of Test-Based Accountability," *Educational Policy* 27, no. 2 (2013): 217–47; Sunderman and Orfield, "Massive Responsibilities and Limited Resources."

18. Lynn Olson, "Testing Systems in Most States Not ESEA-Ready," *Education Week* 21, no. 16 (2002): 126–27, https://www.edweek.org/ew/articles/2002/01/09/16test.h21.html.

19. Sara Dahill-Brown and Lesley Lavery, "Implementing Federal Policy: Confronting State Capacity and Will," *Politics and Policy* 40, no. 4 (2012).

20. Sara Durant and Michael Dahlin, *The State of Proficiency: How Student Proficiency Rates Vary Across States, Subjects, and Grades Between 2002 and 2010* (Portland, OR: Kingsbury Center at Northwest Evaluation Association, 2011).

21. Karen Seashore Louis et al., "The Changing Leadership Role of State Education Agencies," in *Learning from Leadership: Investigating the Improved Student Learning, Final Report of Research Findings*, ed. Karen Seashore Louis et al. (St. Paul, MN: Center for Applied Research and Educational Improvement at the University of Minnesota, Ontario Institute for Studies in Education University Toronto, and the Wallace Foundation, 2010).

22. Daarel Burnette II, "States' Capacity a Nagging Issue as ESSA Gears Up," *Education Week* 36, no. 16 (2017): 7–9, https://www.edweek.org/ew/articles/2017/01/04/states-capacity-a-nagging-issue-as-essa.html.

23. Louis et al., "The Changing Leadership Role of State Education Agencies."

24. Andy Smarick and Juliet Squire, *The State Education Agency: At the Helm, Not the Oar* (Washington, DC: Thomas B. Fordham Institute and Bellwether Education Partners, 2014), https://edexcellence.net/publications/the-state-education-agency-at-the-helm-not-the-oar.

25. Louis et al., "The Changing Leadership Role of State Education Agencies."

26. Kober et al., *From the Capital to the Classroom*.

27. Shober, *Splintered Accountability*.

28. Kevin Carey, *Hot Air: How States Inflate Their Educational Progress Under NCLB* (Washington, DC: Education Sector, 2006).

29. Naomi Chudowsky and Vic Chudowsky, *Many States Have Taken a Backloaded Approach to No Child Left Behind Goal of All Students Scoring "Proficient"* (Washington, DC: Center on Education Policy, 2008).

30. Kevin Carey, *The Pangloss Index: How States Game the No Child Left Behind Act* (Washington, DC: Education Sector, 2007).

31. William D. Hamel, *Final Management Information Report: Fraud in Title I–Funded Tutoring Programs* (Washington, DC: Office of Inspector General, United States Department of Education, 2013).

32. Trip Gabriel, "Under Pressure, Educators Tamper with Test Scores," *New York Times*, June 10, 2010, https://www.nytimes.com/2010/06/11/education/11cheat.html.

33. US Department of Education, "The American Recovery and Reinvestment Act of 2009: Saving and Creating Jobs and Reforming Education," March 11, 2009, https://www2 .ed.gov/policy/gen/leg/recovery/implementation.html.

34. Andrew Saultz, Andrew McEachin, and Lance D. Fusarelli, "Waivering as Governance Federalism During the Obama Administration," *Educational Researcher* 45, no. 6 (2016), 358–66.

35. Tracy Gordon, *State and Local Budgets and the Great Recession* (Washington, DC: The Brookings Institution, 2012), http://www.brookings.edu/research/articles/2012/12/ state-local-budgets-gordon.

36. Kerstin Carlson Le Floch, Andrea Boyle, and Susan Bowles Therriault, *Help Wanted: State Capacity for School Improvement* (Washington, DC: American Institutes for Research, 2008); Louis et al., "The Changing Leadership Role of State Education Agencies."

37. There were a small number of exceptions. In Michigan, the Department of Education's budget increased by 75 percent between 2002 and 2012–2013, while full-time equivalent (FTE) staff increased by 25 percent over the same time period. See Ashley Jochim and Patrick Murphy, *The Capacity Challenge: What It Takes for State Education Agencies to Support School Improvement* (Seattle: Center on Reinventing Public Education at the University of Washington, 2013), http://www.crpe.org/publications/ capacity-challenge-what-it-takes-state-education-agencies-support-school-improvement.

38. Nancy Kober and Diane Stark Rentner, *State Education Agency Funding and Staffing in the Era of Education Reform* (Washington, DC: Center on Education Policy, 2012).

39. Claudio Sanchez, "Texas Schools Grapple with Big Budget Cuts," *Morning Edition*, National Public Radio, December 22, 2011; Gary Scharrer, "600 Texas School Districts Take Funding Complaints to Court," *Houston Chronicle*, October 21, 2012, https://www .chron.com/news/houston-texas/houston/article/600-Texas-school-districts-take-funding-3969765.php.

40. Farzad Mashhood, "TEA to Lay Off 178 Workers," *Austin American-Statesman*, July 12, 2011.

41. Paul Burka, "The Big Test," *Texas Monthly*, July 31, 2012, http://www.texasmonthly.com/ articles/the-big-test/; Morgan Smith, "Texas Schools Chief Stepping Down," *Texas Tribune*, May 1, 2012.

42. Diane Stark Rentner, *Year 3 of Implementing the Common Core State Standards: An Overview of States' Progress and Challenges* (Washington, DC: Center on Education Policy, 2013).

43. Andrew Ujifusa, "States' Rollout of Common Core Goes Under the Microscope," *Education Week* 33, no. 28 (2014): 19, 30, https://www.edweek.org/ew/ articles/2014/04/16/28implement.h33.html.

44. Robert Hanna, *Seeing Beyond Silos: How State Education Agencies Spend Federal Education Dollars and Why* (Washington, DC: Center for American Progress and the Broad Foundation, 2014).

45. Michele Mcneil, "Race to Top Winners Work to Balance Promises, Capacity," *Education Week* 30, no. 26 (2011), https://www.edweek.org/ew/articles/2011/03/30/26rtt-states _ep.h30.html.

46. Courtney Tanenbaum et al., *State Capacity to Support School Turnaround* (Washington, DC: Institute of Education Sciences, National Center for Education Evaluation and Regional Assistance, 2015), https://ies.ed.gov/ncee/pubs/20154012/pdf/20154012.pdf.

47. Ibid.

48. Ibid.

49. Bryan A. VanGronigen and Coby V. Meyers, "How State Education Agencies Are Administering School Turnaround Efforts: 15 Years After No Child Left Behind," *Educational Policy*, February 2017, doi:10.1177/0895904817691846.

50. Carrie Conaway, Venessa Keesler, and Nathaniel Schwartz, "What Research Do State Education Agencies Really Need? The Promise and Limitations of Longitudinal Data Systems," *Educational Evaluation and Policy Analysis* 37 no. 1S (2015): 16S–28S, doi:10.3102/0162373715576073; Betheny Gross and Ashley Jochim, eds., *Building Agency Capacity for Evidence-Based Policymaking, Vol. 5: The SEA of the Future* (San Antonio, TX: Building State Capacity & Productivity Center at Edvance Research, Inc., 2015), http://www.bscpcenter.org/resources/publications/SEAF_5_11.2015_final.pdf.

51. Patrick McGuinn, "Stimulating Reform Race to the Top, Competitive Grants and the Obama Education Agenda," *Educational Policy* 26, no. 1 (2012): 136–59.

52. Lauren Camera, "Tennessee on Dogged Path to Race to Top Finish," *Education Week* 33, no. 36 (2014): 1, 28, 30, https://www.edweek.org/ew/articles/2014/07/09/36tennessee _ep.h33.html.

53. Ashley Jochim and Lesley Lavery, "The Evolving Politics of the Common Core: Policy Implementation and Conflict Expansion," *Publius: The Journal of Federalism* 45, no. 3 (2015): 380–404.

54. Rentner, *Year 3 of Implementing the Common Core State Standards*.

55. Boris Shor and Nolan McCarty, "The Ideological Mapping of American Legislatures," *American Political Science Review* 105, no. 3 (2011): 530–51.

56. Laura McKenna, "How the GOP's Sweep in the States Will Shape America's Schools," *The Atlantic*, November 21, 2016, https://www.theatlantic.com/education/archive/2016/11/ how-the-gops-sweep-in-the-states-will-shape-americas-schools/508283/.

57. Hunter Woodall, "Kansas Supreme Court Rules New School Finance Formula Is Unconstitutional," *Kansas City Star*, October 2, 2017, http://www.kansascity.com/news/ politics-government/article176606731.html.

58. Minnici and Hill, *Educational Architects*.

59. Frederick M. Hess and Chester E. Finn, "Crash Course," *Education Next* 7, no. 4 (2007): 40–5, http://educationnext.org/crash-course/.

60. Patrick J. Murphy and Monica Ouijdani, *State Capacity for School Improvement: A First Look at Agency Resources* (Seattle: Center on Reinventing Public Education at the University of Washington, 2011), 21, https://www.crpe.org/publications/state-capacity -school-improvement-first-look-agency-resources.

61. Conaway et al., "What Research Do State Education Agencies Really Need?"; Jared E. Knowles, "Of Needles and Haystacks: Building an Accurate Statewide Dropout Early Warning System in Wisconsin," *Journal of Educational Data Mining* 7, no. 3 (2015): 18–67.

62. Heinrich Mintrop, "Low-Performing Schools' Programs and State Capacity Requirements: Meeting the NCLB Educational Goals," in *Holding NCLB Accountable: Achieving Accountability, Equity, & School Reform*, ed. Gail L. Sunderman (Thousand Oaks, CA: Corwin Press, 2008), 137–51.

63. Murphy and Ouijdani, *State Capacity for School Improvement*; Jochim and Murphy, *The Capacity Challenge*.

64. Jennifer Lin Russell et al., "Designing Inter-Organizational Networks to Implement Education Reform An Analysis of State Race to the Top Applications," *Educational Evaluation and Policy Analysis* 37, no. 1 (2015): 92–112, http://journals.sagepub.com/doi/ pdf/10.3102/0162373714527341.

65. US Department of Education, "Protecting Student Privacy," https://studentprivacy .ed.gov/.

66. Anagnostopoulos et al., "State Education Agencies, Information Systems, and the Expansion of State Power."

67. Pearson's correlation coefficient between the number of staff in this year and the square root of enrollments is .72. The correlation is substantially smaller for raw enrollment numbers, suggesting that the additional staff needed by an agency does not increase in a linear fashion as enrollments grow. Enrollment data come from US Department of Education, National Center for Education Statistics, "Common Core of Data," https:// nces.ed.gov/ccd/. Staffing data are from Cynthia G. Brown et al., *State Education Agencies as Agents of Change: What It Will Take for the States to Step Up on Education Reform* (Washington, DC: Center for American Progress, American Enterprise Institute for Public Policy Research, and the Broad Foundation, 2011).

68. Joanne Weiss and Patrick McGuinn, "The Evolving Role of the State Education Agency in the Era of ESSA and Trump: Past, Present, and Uncertain Future" (Working Paper 2017–1, Consortium for Policy Research in Education, University of Pennsylvania, Philadelphia, September 2017).

69. Smarick and Squire, *The State Education Agency.*

70. Ibid.

71. Patrick J. Murphy and Lydia Rainey, *Modernizing the State Education Agency: Different Paths Toward Performance Management* (Seattle: Center on Reinventing Public Education at the University of Washington, 2012), https://www.crpe.org/publications/ modernizing-state-education-agency-different-paths-toward-performance-managment.

72. Daarel Burnette II, "Capacity of State Ed. Departments Waning on Brink of ESSA Rollout," *Education Week* 35, no. 25 (2016): 17, 19, https://www.edweek.org/ew/articles/ 2016/03/23/capacity-of-state-ed-departments-waning-on.html.

73. Diane Stark Rentner et al., *States Reflect on Year One Implementation of ESSA: Planning for Progress* (Washington, DC: Center on Education Policy at George Washington University, 2017).

74. Wallace E. Huffman and Robert E. Evenson, "Do Formula or Competitive Grant Funds Have Greater Impacts on State Agricultural Productivity?" *American Journal of Agricultural Economics* 88, no. 4 (2006): 783–98.

75. Daarel Burnette II, "Steep Learning Curve on K–12 as State Leaders Take New Seats," *Education Week* 36, no. 21 (2017), https://www.edweek.org/ew/articles/2017/02/15/steep -learning-curve-on-k-12-as-state.html.

76. Jennifer O'Day, *Two Steps Forward, Many More to Go* (Washington, DC: American Institutes for Research, 2013), https://www.air.org/resource/three-decades-education -reform-are-we-still-nation-risk#O_Day.

77. Author calculations.

Chapter 9

1. Andrew Rudalevige, "Government in a Box: Challenges of Policy Implementation in the American System," in *Carrots, Sticks, and the Bully Pulpit: Lessons from a Half-Century of Federal Efforts to Improve America's Schools*, eds. Frederick M. Hess and Andrew P. Kelly (Cambridge, MA: Harvard Education Press, 2011): 38.

2. "Excerpts from Bush's Speech on Improving Education," *New York Times*, September 3, 1999, http://www.nytimes.com/1999/09/03/us/excerpts-from-bush-s-speech-on -improving-education.html.

3. Department of Justice, Civil Rights Division and Department of Education, Office for Civil Rights, "Dear Colleague Letter on the Nondiscriminatory Administration of School Discipline," January 8, 2014, https://www2.ed.gov/about/offices/list/ocr/letters/colleague-201401-title-vi.html; Department of Education, Office for Civil Rights, "Dear Colleague Letter on Resource Comparability," October 1, 2014, https://www2.ed.gov/about/offices/list/ocr/letters/colleague-resourcecomp-201410.pdf; Department of Education, Office for Civil Rights, "Dear Colleague Letter on Transgender Students," May 13, 2016, https://www2.ed.gov/about/offices/list/ocr/letters/colleague-201605-title-ix-transgender.pdf.

4. Jon Valent and Daniel A. Newark, "The Politics of Achievement Gaps: U.S. Public Opinion on Race-Based and Wealth-Based Differences in Test Scores," *Educational Researcher* 45, no. 6 (2016): 331.

5. Patrick Flavin and Michael T. Hartney, "Racial Inequality in Democratic Accountability: Evidence from Retrospective Voting in Local Elections," *American Journal of Political Science* 61, no. 3 (2017): 684–96.

6. Paul Peterson et al., "Ten-Year Trends in Public Opinion from the EdNext Poll," *Education Next* 17, no. 1 (2017): 23.

7. Quoted in Patrick J. McGuinn, *No Child Left Behind and the Transformation of Federal Education Policy, 1965–2005* (Lawrence: Kansas University Press, 2006), 189.

8. Michelle R. Davis, "Bush Has Own View of Promoting Civil Rights," *Education Week*, October 19, 2004, https://www.edweek.org/ew/articles/2004/10/20/08ocr.h24.html.

9. Alexander Bickel predicted that Title VI would "become the main instrument for accelerating and completing the desegregation of southern public schools." See "Forcing Desegregation Through Title VI," *New Republic*, April 9, 1966, 8–9.

10. Ibid., 109.

11. Department of Education Office for Civil Rights, "Sexual Harassment Guidance: Harassment of Students by School Employees, Other Students, or Third Parties," March 13, 1997, revised January 19, 2001, https://www2.ed.gov/about/offices/list/ocr/docs/shguide.html.

12. Department of Education Office for Civil Rights, "First Amendment: Dear Colleague," July 28, 2003, https://www2.ed.gov/about/offices/list/ocr/firstamend.html.

13. Martha Derthick, "Litigation Under No Child Left Behind," in *From Schoolhouse to Courthouse: The Judiciary's Role in American Education*, ed. Joshua Dunn and Martin West (Washington, DC: Brookings Institution Press, 2009), 228.

14. Nanette Asimov, "Education Act Changes Proposed; Panel Urges Allowing Suits Against Schools," *San Francisco Chronicle*, February 14, 2007, https://www.sfgate.com/education/article/Education-act-changes-proposed-Panel-urges-2617473.php.

15. https://georgewbush-whitehouse.archives.gov/news/reports/no-child-left-behind.html#7.

16. Newark Parents Association v. Newark Public Schools 547 F.3d 199 (2008).

17. Claudio Sanchez, "California Schools Could Lose Aid over 'No Child' Law," July 6, 2006, http://www.npr.org/templates/story/story.php?storyId=5538536.

18. Renee v. Spellings, 2008 U.S. Dist. LEXIS 49369 (2008).

19. Renee v. Duncan, 573 F.3d 903 (2009).

20. Michael Dobbs, "Conn. Stands in Defiance on Enforcing 'No Child,'" *Washington Post*, May 8, 2005, http://www.washingtonpost.com/wp-dyn/content/article/2005/05/07/AR2005050700973.html.

21. Jeff Archer, "Civil Rights Groups Back NCLB Law in Suit," *Education Week*, February 7, 2006, http://www.edweek.org/ew/articles/2006/02/08/22conn.h25.html?r=1090769464.

22. 567 U.S. 519 (2012).

23. US Department of Education, "ESEA Flexibility," June 7, 2012, https://www.ed.gov/sites/default/files/esea-flexibility.doc.
24. Derek W. Black, "Federalizing Education by Waiver?" *Vanderbilt Law Review* 68, no. 3 (2015): 659.
25. Lyndsey Layton, "Obama Prepares to Revamp 'No Child Left Behind,'" *Washington Post*, September 21, 2011, https://www.washingtonpost.com/local/education/obama-prepares-to-revamp-no-child-left-behind/2011/09/16/gIQAKUrXlK_story.html.
26. Arne Duncan, "Washington Extension Determination Letter," April 24, 2014, https://www2.ed.gov/policy/eseaflex/secretary-letters/wad6.html.
27. Allie Bidwell, "Feds Yank Oklahoma's School Waiver," *US News and World Report*, August 28, 2014, https://www.usnews.com/news/articles/2014/08/28/feds-yank-oklahomas-nclb-waiver-over-school-standards.
28. Josh Kinsler, "School Discipline: A Source or a Salve for the Racial Achievement Gap?" *International Economic Review* 54, no. 1 (2013): 382.
29. Department of Education Office for Civil Rights, "Achieving Simple Justice: Highlights of Activities, Office for Civil Rights, 2009–2016, December, 2016, https://www2.ed.gov/about/reports/annual/ocr/achieving-simple-justice.pdf.
30. R. Shep Melnick, "Civil Wrongs: Federal Equity Initiative Promotes Paperwork, Not Equality," *Education Next* 16, no. 1 (2016): 32.
31. 411 U.S. 1; 428 U.S. 229.
32. Richard W. Riley, "Dear Colleague" letter, January 19, 2001, https://www2.ed.gov/about/offices/list/ocr/letters/colleague-200101-title-vi.pdf.
33. 532 U.S. 275 (2001).
34. Jeannie Suk Gersen, "The Transgender Debate and the Looming Title IX Crisis," *New Yorker*, May 24, 2016, https://www.newyorker.com/news/news-desk/public-bathroom-regulations-could-create-a-title-ix-crisis.
35. G.G. v. Gloucester County School Board, 822 F.3d 709 (2016).
36. Sandra Battle, "Dear Colleague" letter, February 22, 2017, https://www2.ed.gov/about/offices/list/ocr/letters/colleague-201702-title-ix.docx.
37. James Q. Wilson, *Bureaucracy: What Government Agencies Do and Why They Do It* (New York: Basic Books, 1989): 168.
38. Haley Sweetland Edwards, "What the New Senate Education Chair Thinks About No Child Left Behind," *Time*, January 25, 2015, http://time.com/3681776/lamar-alexander-no-child-left-behind/.
39. Max Eden, *School Discipline Reform and Disorder: Evidence from New York City Public Schools, 2012–16* (New York: Manhattan Institute, 2017), 10–12.

Conclusion

1. The Nation's Report Card, "2015 Mathematics & Reading Assessments," https://www.nationsreportcard.gov/reading_math_2015/#?grade=4.
2. Secretary-General of the OECD, *Country Note: Key Findings from PISA 2015 for the United States* (Paris: Organisation for Economic Co-operation and Development, 2016), http://www.oecd.org/pisa/pisa-2015-United-States.pdf.

Acknowledgments

For the past few years, we have spent more than a little time reflecting on the legacy of twenty-first-century education reform. While many observers have celebrated or denounced the reforms of the Bush and Obama years, we've been more inclined to look back on the past two decades and ask: What have we learned? Having discussed this question with policy analysts, practitioners, and researchers in various settings over the past few years, we sought to turn those musings into something more useful. So, in summer 2017, we commissioned ten scholars to offer their take on what we've learned. In January 2018, we hosted a research conference at the American Enterprise Institute in Washington, DC, to hash this out. The volume you hold in your hands is the fruit of those efforts.

The chapters that compose this volume seek to answer the question: What lessons might we draw from the school reform efforts of the Bush-Obama years?

We are much obliged to all of those who have been involved and shaped our thinking on this project, but we would like to especially thank the following discussants and panelists for their insights and feedback at the AEI conference: Betsy DeVos, Nina Rees, Gerard Robinson, Roberto Rodriguez, Stefanie Sanford, Hanna Skandera, Emma Vadehra, and Joanne Weiss.

We are deeply indebted to AEI and its president, Arthur Brooks, as well as to EdChoice and its president, Robert Enlow, for their steadfast support. In addition, we are thankful that AEI was able and willing to provide the resources and financial support required for this project. We'd also like to acknowledge the terrific staff at AEI, especially Brendan Bell for his work managing and overseeing this project, and his colleagues Grant Addison, Amy Cummings, Sofia Gallo, Connor Kurtz, and RJ Martin for their vital assistance. Finally, we once again want to express our gratitude to the wonderful Harvard Education Press team, particularly executive editor Caroline Chauncey, who offered skillful and timely guidance throughout the course of this project.

About the Editors

Frederick M. Hess is the director of education policy studies at the American Enterprise Institute (AEI). An educator, political scientist, and author, he studies K–12 and higher education issues. His books include *Letters to a Young Education Reformer, The Cage-Busting Teacher, Breakthrough Leadership in the Digital Age, Cage-Busting Leadership, The Same Thing Over and Over, Education Unbound, Common Sense School Reform, Revolution at the Margins,* and *Spinning Wheels.* He has edited influential books on the Common Core, entrepreneurship in education, education philanthropy, the impact of education research, and the Every Student Succeeds Act. Hess's work has appeared in scholarly and popular outlets, such as *American Politics Quarterly, Harvard Education Review, Social Science Quarterly, Teachers College Record, National Affairs, USA Today,* the *Wall Street Journal,* and the *Washington Post.* He also authors the popular *Education Week* blog *Rick Hess Straight Up.* A former high school social studies teacher, Hess teaches or has taught at the University of Virginia, the University of Pennsylvania, Georgetown University, Rice University, Johns Hopkins University, and Harvard University.

Michael Q. McShane is the director of national research at EdChoice. His analyses and commentary have been published widely in the media, including in the *Huffington Post, National Affairs, USA Today,* and the *Washington Post.* He has also been featured in education-specific outlets such as *Teachers College Commentary, Education Week, Phi Delta Kappan,* and *Education Next.* In addition to authoring numerous white papers, McShane has had academic work published in *Education Finance and Policy* and the *Journal of School Choice.* He is the editor of *New and Better Schools,* author of *Education and Opportunity,* and coeditor of *Teacher Quality 2.0* and *Common*

Core Meets Education Reform. A former high school teacher, McShane is also an adjunct fellow in education policy studies at AEI and a research fellow in the Economic and Policy Analysis Research Center at the University of Missouri.

About the Contributors

Deven Carlson is an associate professor of political science and presidential research professor at the University of Oklahoma. He has written extensively on the operations and effects of test-based accountability policies and the politics of education. He has published this work in several high-quality scholarly outlets, including *Educational Evaluation and Policy Analysis, Journal of Urban Economics, Journal of Policy Analysis and Management, Economics of Education Review,* and *Journal of Public Administration Research and Theory.*

Sara E. Dahill-Brown is an associate professor in the politics and international affairs department at Wake Forest University. She is an alumna of Utah's public schools and a recovering Texas middle school teacher, and she has worked as a researcher and volunteer in the school systems of Wisconsin and North Carolina. Her work has appeared in the *Russell Sage Journal of the Social Sciences, Studies in Educational Evaluation,* and *Politics and Policy.*

Joshua Dunn is a professor and chair of the department of political science, as well as the director of the Center for the Study of Government and the Individual, at the University of Colorado Colorado Springs. His research has largely concentrated on education policy and the courts, and his books include *Passing on the Right: Conservative Professors in the Progressive University, Complex Justice: The Case of Missouri v. Jenkins,* and *From Schoolhouse to Courthouse: The Judiciary's Role in American Education.* Since 2006, he has written a quarterly article on law and education for *Education Next.* He has also written for the *Los Angeles Times,* the *Washington Post,* the *Wall Street Journal,* the *Weekly Standard, National Review,* and *Education Week.*

Anna J. Egalite is an assistant professor in the College of Education at North Carolina State University. Her research focuses on the evaluation of education policies and programs intended to close racial and economic achievement gaps. She has studied school choice policy, school size, the influence of family background on intergenerational economic mobility, and the diversification of the teacher labor force. Egalite's scholarly articles have appeared in outlets including the *Economics of Education Review, Educational Evaluation and Policy Analysis,* and *Early Childhood Research Quarterly.*

Tara Hofkens is a postdoctoral research associate at the Center for Advanced Study of Teaching and Learning at the University of Virginia. She was awarded the Learning Research and Development Center Fellowship in 2012.

Ashley Jochim is a senior research analyst at the Center on Reinventing Public Education (CRPE) at the University of Washington Bothell. Her research focuses on policy analysis and implementation, including work on school turnaround, state education agencies, K–12 accountability, Common Core standards, and district reform efforts. She is coauthor of *A Democratic Constitution for Public Education.* Jochim has published in scholarly outlets such as *Policy Studies Journal, Politics and Governance,* and *Political Research Quarterly.* Before joining CRPE, she was a graduate fellow at the Center for American Politics and Public Policy and a research analyst at the US Department of Health and Human Services, Office for Civil Rights.

Matthew A. Kraft is an associate professor of education and economics at Brown University. His research and teaching interests include the economics of education, education policy analysis, and applied quantitative methods for causal inference. He has published on topics including teacher labor markets, coaching and professional development, and teacher evaluation systems. Kraft's work can be found in scholarly outlets such as the *American Educational Research Journal, Journal of Policy Analysis and Management, Education Finance and Policy,* and *Economics of Education Review.* Before earning his doctorate from the Harvard Graduate School of Education, he taught middle and high school humanities in Oakland and Berkeley, California, public schools.

Tom Loveless is an education researcher and nonresident senior fellow at the Brookings Institution. From 2000 to 2017, he authored "The Brown

Center Report on American Education," an annual report analyzing important trends in education. He has published widely in scholarly journals and appeared in popular media to discuss school reform, student achievement, and other education topics. Loveless's books include *Lessons Learned: What International Assessments Tell Us About Math Achievement, The Great Curriculum Debate: How Should We Teach Reading and Math?*, and *The Tracking Wars: State Reform Meets School Policy*. From 1979 to 1988, he taught elementary school in the San Juan Unified School District in California.

Patrick McGuinn is a professor of political science and education at Drew University and a senior research specialist at the Consortium for Policy Research in Education (CPRE). He is the author or editor of three books: *The Convergence of K–12 and Higher Education: Policies and Programs in a Changing Era, Education Governance for the 21st Century: Overcoming the Structural Barriers to School Reform*, and *No Child Left Behind and the Transformation of Federal Education Policy, 1965–2005*. He has written extensively on federal education policy during the Bush and Obama administrations and in particular on their use of incentives and inducements to promote select school reform strategies.

Robert Pianta is the dean of the Curry School of Education, the Novartis US Foundation Professor of Education, and founding director of the Center for Advanced Study of Teaching and Learning at the University of Virginia. His research focuses on theory, measurement, and improvement of teacher-student interactions and their contributions to students' learning. He has authored more than 300 publications, led research grants totaling over $60 million, is an associate editor for AERA Open, and consults with federal agencies and foundations around the world. He is a fellow of the American Education Research Association and received the 2016 Distinguished Alumni Award from the University of Minnesota.

Index